Twayne's
Filmmakers Series

Frank Beaver, Editor

Hollywood's Dark Cinema

HOLLYWOOD'S DARK CINEMA: THE AMERICAN FILM NOIR

R. Barton Palmer

TWAYNE PUBLISHERS • NEW YORK
MAXWELL MACMILLAN CANADA • TORONTO
MAXWELL MACMILLAN INTERNATIONAL •
NEW YORK • OXFORD • SINGAPORE • SYDNEY

Twayne's Filmmakers Series
Hollywood's Dark Cinema: The American Film Noir
R. Barton Palmer

Twayne Publishers   Maxwell Macmillan Canada, Inc.
Macmillan Publishing Company   1200 Eglinton Avenue East
866 Third Avenue   Suite 200
New York, New York 10022   Don Mills, Ontario M3C 3N1

Macmillan Publishing Company is part of the Maxwell Communication Group of Companies.

Library of Congress Cataloging-in-Publication Data
Palmer, R. Barton, 1946–
    Hollywood's dark cinema : the American film noir / by R. Barton Palmer.
        p.   cm. — (Twayne's filmmakers series)
    Includes filmography, bibliographical references and index.
    ISBN 0-8057-9324-0. — ISBN 0-8057-9335-6 (pbk.)
    1. Film noir—United States—History and criticism.   I. Title.
    II. Series.
    PN1995.9.F54P36   1994
    791.43'655—dc20   93-33666
                                                           CIP

10 9 8 7 6 5 4 3 2 1 (hc)
10 9 8 7 6 5 4 3 2 1 (pb)

Printed in the United States of America

CONTENTS

ILLUSTRATIONS

FOREWORD

Of all the contemporary arts, the motion picture is particularly timely and diverse as a popular culture enterprise. This lively art form cleverly combines storytelling with photography to achieve what has been a quintessential twentieth-century phenomenon. Individual as well as national and cultural interests have made the medium an unusually varied one for artistic expression and analysis. Films have been exploited for commercial gain, for political purposes, for experimentation, and for self-exploration. The various responses to the motion picture have given rise to different labels for both the fun and the seriousness with which this art form has been received, ranging from "the movies" to "cinema." These labels hint at both the theoretical and sociological parameters of the film medium.

A collective art, the motion picture has nevertheless allowed individual genius to flourish in all its artistic and technical areas: directing, screenwriting, cinematography, acting, editing. The medium also encompasses many genres beyond the narrative film, including documentary, animated, and avant-garde expression. The range and diversity of motion pictures suggest rich opportunities for appreciation and for study.

The Twayne Filmmakers Series examines the full panorama of motion picture history and art. Many studies are auteur-oriented and elucidate the work of individual directors whose ideas and cinematic styles make them authors of their films. Other studies examine film movements and genres or analyze cinema from a national perspective. The series seeks to illuminate all the many aspects of film for the film student, the scholar, and the general reader.

Frank Beaver

PREFACE

During the last two decades, American scholars have been engaged with the rewarding task of rediscovering the treasures of the classic Hollywood cinema. Long despised as a mindless form of entertainment designed only to make a base appeal to a mass audience for strictly commercial purposes, studio films are now being understood as intriguing cultural and artistic artifacts that have much to tell the present generation about the tastes, desires, preoccupations, joys, and terrors shared by a viewing public during 60 years of turbulent history and rapid social change. Like other volumes in this series, this book attempts to contribute significantly to that developing understanding.

The focus here is on a type of Hollywood film that has long been designated by a French critical term: *film noir*, or "dark cinema." Although the films usually considered "dark" were originally produced and consumed during the 1940s and 1950s, film noir was revived by American directors in the 1970s and has since become once again (if in a somewhat different form) a staple of entertainment cinema. Dark cinema, we may say, has enjoyed two periods of popularity, only the first of which will be treated here in significant detail.

As the first chapter of this book will show, much has been written about film noir; the last ten years in particular have witnessed a profusion of books and articles on the subject. In fact, it is probably fair to say that of all the studio types—including such favorites as westerns and musicals—the film noir has received the most attention from critics since film study became a respectable discipline within the American academy. There are a number of cultural reasons for this attention.

The complex history of dark cinema has made its definition somewhat elusive, and yet such a definition is necessary if we are to understand the place film noir occupies in the history of Hollywood production. This book breaks new ground in offering a full discussion of the problems involved in defining film noir. As used by critics of the Hollywood cinema, the concept of film noir has altered significantly over time. Film noir was originally "discovered" in postwar

Hollywood films by French critics and only exported to America sometime later. It has been closely connected to three of the most important developments in postwar cinema culture: New Wave filmmaking in France; the American art cinema movement, often called the Hollywood Renaissance, during the late 1960s and early 1970s; and the evolution of poststudio American filmmaking through, in part, decisions to make films that are both more "artistic" and more "adult." None of the other types of American studio filmmaking has had such a profound impact on film culture here and abroad. As a result, film noir became a critical and creative concept over which there has been no inconsiderable struggle.

This history shows clearly, however, that the classic period of film noir must be understood within the institutional framework of the commercial Hollywood cinema. These films did not, could not (because of obvious restraints), constitute an "art cinema" of any kind. Those involved in making films noirs did not, could not, constitute a distinct "movement" within the studio system. Instead, the classic film noir is defined in large measure by a partial thematic and structural transformation of the studio film. Dark cinema resulted from an infusion of materials that did not conform easily to the standard content Hollywood worked with, materials that could not be readily accommodated within established narrative structures. These pessimistic tales of social failure, fatal attraction, and pervasive criminality derived from a popular literature tradition that, during this period, was becoming more acceptable to a broader group of middle-class consumers. Such stories could only with difficulty be given the sense of closure—all problems solved, a happy ending—usually required by film industry dramaturgy. And they could not be visualized adequately with standard cinematographic and staging techniques; a visual correlative of this dark content soon developed and came to constitute a distinct style. Film noir, however, never became a genre in the Hollywood of this period; it existed, instead, through a number of related genres whose most important common threads were a concern with criminality (most often presented from the criminals' viewpoint) and with social breakdown. The crime melodrama, the detective film, the thriller, and the woman's picture all made room for dark themes and characters.

To understand the classic film noir, then, we must examine the ways in which this new material was accommodated within established generic conventions. The classic Hollywood cinema was chiefly a narrative cinema, that is, a cinema in which storytelling demands took precedence over other aspects of the creative process. Thus the bulk of this book will be devoted to a detailed narrative analysis of selected noir films; through such analysis, a clear picture emerges of the characteristic differences of dark films from the ordinary studio product.

This study would have been impossible without the expert, invaluable assistance of the New York University Cinema Studies Department, especially Bob Stam, Bob Sklar, Bill Simon, William Everson, and Richard Allen, all of whom have provided a great deal of help and advice during my decade-long involvement with the problems posed by dark cinema. I thank them for their interest and time. Thanks are also due to Frank Tomasulo, my colleague at Georgia State University, for his continuing support of my research in this area. The Film Stills department of the Museum of Modern Art provided much needed help with illustrative stills. Finally, I owe a huge debt of gratitude to my wife Carla, who has sat patiently through many more films noirs than she would have chosen on her own to view. Many of the critical insights presented here had their origin in our lively dialogues around the VCR.

CHAPTER 1

Notions of Noir

HOLLYWOOD GENRES

During its classic period in the 1930s, 1940s, and 1950s, the Hollywood cinema developed a stable but flexible system of genres, including detective films, musicals, westerns, and costume epics among others.[1] These story types were defined by conventional plots, characters, and elements of setting, and they enabled the studios to plan and manage production efficiently. Standing exteriors, costumes, and other properties used in one film could be recycled in others of the same genre. Actors and actresses well suited to the portrayal of stereotypical characters could be contracted for numbers of similar projects. Directors, art designers, composers, and other creative personnel were able to work faster and more competently when often assigned to films of the same genre.

Genres also made it possible for the industry to organize and control consumption. The genre system encouraged viewers to develop the habit of "going to the movies" by offering ritualistic repetitions of familiar stories. Through genres, Hollywood regulated easily the variety of its otherwise quite standardized product. Audiences might tire of films that were too similar but might not approve of films unpredictable in form. Genres, in other words, controlled and exploited the opposed qualities of difference and sameness upon which the continuing appeal of Hollywood entertainment depended. Marketing their products by type, distributors and exhibitors could address broad elements of popular taste, thus ensuring a high success rate for a vast output. Individual films might fail to find an audience, but the genre as a whole, corresponding to the general form of their desire, pleased viewers. In addition, audiences could indicate their (dis)satisfaction with story types (if somewhat indirectly) at the box office. Such approval or rejection could reveal the fading popularity of a genre, the necessity for its renewal, or the pleasure it continued to afford.

Under the studio system, production existed solely to provide a continuing stream of films attractive and interesting enough to keep theater seats filled. The principal difficulty of production then was determining what the public wanted. With some idea of popular taste, the studios could satisfy a mass audience, hampered only by their own constraints (such as anticipated profit margins) and those imposed by society (especially standards of public morality). Genres—story patterns with a demonstrated appeal—and stars—performers with a continuing popularity not dependent on particular roles—provided films with greater assurance of success.

Given industry aims, it was inevitable that Hollywood attempted to capitalize on any cinematic element with proven acceptability. "Series" films are those that imitate, often closely, successful individual films, whether they belong to a genre or not. Series are differentiated from genres by the fact that they recycle to some degree particular characters, themes, settings, and narratives (for example, the *Rocky* and *Halloween* series). Genre films, in contrast, are characterized by more general patterns of resemblance. Both series and genres are further distinguished from "cycles," which are groups of films dealing with the same subject matter but often with little else in common— for example, the films about nuclear holocaust made in the late 1950s and early 1960s or the 1980s films treating poor rural life in the South. Series, cycles, and genres have all made it possible for the film industry to exploit identifiable elements of popular taste. Genres, however, were more important during Hollywood's classic period, roughly from the mid-1920s to the end of the 1960s. The reason was simple: besides their continued popularity, based in part on their satisfaction of audience desire for a good story, genres allowed an efficient allocation of resources over a considerable period of time.

Two points about the genre system are important to note here. First, the categorization of films according to genre was recognized by producers and spectators alike. Genres were an overt and acknowledged part of the movie business. Studios plotted their yearly output of films to an important degree by genre. Individual studios, in fact, often specialized in certain genres that reflected—even to some extent established—their corporate images: Warner Brothers was known for contemporary social problem films and crime dramas; MGM for musicals; Paramount for sophisticated comedy-dramas ("white telephone" films); Republic and Monogram for westerns. Advertising for individual films, especially titling, was designed to identify genres; however much trailers might call attention to what was "new" or "different" about a given movie, they emphasized generic elements as well. Poster art helped prospective viewers recognize genre films by utilizing conventional iconography, thereby lending a generic cast to the individual image for each movie.

The second point about the genre system is perhaps more important. The various genres were regulated varieties of an overarching or metagenre, the classic Hollywood film itself.[2] However much they constructed different fictional worlds, musicals, melodramas, and gangster films had much in common. Such sameness resulted to a great extent from the conditions of studio production, where established procedures—important elements of visual style or dramatic construction, for example—were followed in the manufacture of all films. Seldom working exclusively on projects in the same genre, directors, camera operators, and scriptwriters inevitably brought a general creative competence in moviemaking the Hollywood way to every film they made, regardless of type.

A certain sameness was also required by the conditions of exhibition. Theater schedules demanded "A" productions of about 90 minutes and "B" second features of about 75 minutes. These dramatic units were self-contained, not continued from week to week; an unambiguous conclusion had to be constructed before the end of the last reel. Industry dramaturgy required a narrative of relentless forward motion in all films to keep viewers interested in the story; an Aristotelian causality joined one scene to the next so that plot lines would be easily comprehensible to a mass, often undereducated audience.

Film content as well as form was affected by the role Hollywood performed—providing entertainment for the general public (including foreign viewers), regardless of age, religion, or political opinion. The studios had to be especially sensitive to and accommodating of viewers' sensibilities as well as their desires. The kinds of films the studios made were determined largely by a volatile dialectic: the opposition of traditional moral values to more modern, "permissive" forms of representation and storytelling.[3] Threatened by increasingly dire economic conditions in the early 1930s, theaters tried to lure back reluctant patrons with the erotic, the naughty, and the violent. With viewers eager for racy thrills, films such as *She Done Him Wrong* (1933), which features Mae West's unique brand of sexual humor and farce, did very well at the box office but ran into a good deal of trouble with local censors and more conservative religious groups. In effect, Hollywood addressed a largely divided American culture, a national audience composed of not only those who desired good, clean entertainment that reaffirmed traditional values but those who wanted nudity, bawdiness, and the treatment of "forbidden" subjects.

Eventually, in response to criticism from a number of quarters, particularly the Catholic Church, Hollywood developed the Production Code in the early 1930s, the enforcement of which ensured that all American commercial films followed more or less the same thematic prescriptions and exclusions (until 1968, when the ratings system superseded it).[4] The Production Code Administration (PCA), however, was more than an institution that enabled Hollywood to practice self-censorship; more important, the PCA afforded filmmakers a forum where issues of representation and theme could be debated, where compromises could be effected between the conflicting demands of conservative and less traditional moviegoers. In other words, the PCA, because it served the interests of the moviemaking community first and foremost, was naturally sensitive to shifts in public taste and was dedicated not only to freeing the industry from influence by pressure group protest (especially by the Catholic lay organization Legion of Decency) but also to keeping the Hollywood product popular.

The Code itself was based on Victorian principles of what constituted proper, uplifting fiction. Poetic justice was required; villainy could not, at least ultimately, be presented as attractive, triumphant, or sympathetic. Sexual liaisons and their consequences were imaged either with restraint (a lingering but somewhat chaste kiss as a metonymy for lovemaking) or in accordance with established morality (true love leads to either marriage or disaster). Hollywood writers followed the time-honored convention of ending with a marriage, actual or implied. The closing embrace became a transgeneric element of the classic Hollywood film, supplying an ending that emphasized the (re)establishment of the status quo, the elimination of the disruptions unleashed by the narrative process through a microcosmic image of social harmony. Ending with a clinch and all problems solved was a formula with near-universal appeal and effectiveness.

Hollywood's place in American society, in other words, made it necessary for the studios to manufacture and market movies that were more or less conservative, both socially and politically. This issue is complex and can only be outlined here. Filmmaking was a business like any other, involving the making of products—within the law, of course—whose content was not otherwise affected by government policy or dictate (the only exception being the period 1941–45 when Hollywood, conforming to the directions of official Washington, produced propaganda films to further the war effort).[5] The business the studios were in was entertainment. To provide the subject matter that interests and intrigues a mass public—constitutes what it desires to see—American films often, perhaps mostly, dealt with controversial, disturbing, and topical issues. But such subject matter was handled in an ultimately unthreatening manner, through wish-fulfillment solutions meant to reassure the spectator that all was right with the fictional world (s)he had just viewed. Hollywood was not in the business of instructing or exhorting. "If you want to send a message, call Western Union" was not just an industry joke; it was a precept as well. The Hollywood studios were dependent on the goodwill of the government and the public alike, not only in this country but also abroad, since foreign markets were vital to the continuing profitability of American filmmaking. As a consequence, the general rule followed by the PCA was to handle political and social materials carefully to avoid giving offense.

Because they were narratives, Hollywood films had to make sense, that is, represent a world of coherent social relations and values that spectators would approve of. Audiences, however, did not interpret these representations as messages. The films they enjoyed catered to their eagerness that what they already believed, valued, or hated should be confirmed. Hollywood stories and images thus seemed natural, inevitable, and "right" to filmgoers, at least to those who thought of themselves as morally high-minded, patriotic, and traditional. (Naturally, the ordinary studio product was judged escapist and banal in intellectual circles.) The Production Code enjoined filmmakers to present "correct standards of life" and not to ridicule the natural law "written in the hearts of all mankind" (Leff and Simmons, 288).[6] Thus the apparent neutrality of Hollywood on social and political questions ("that's entertainment") was, in fact, support for the status quo and mainstream opinion.

This book is concerned with an American film type that proves an interesting exception to some of the principles discussed above. As its French name suggests, film noir or "dark cinema" was not an ordinary Hollywood genre. Invented by French critics in the immediate postwar era, the term was largely unknown in the United States during the period when the films it describes were originally made and exhibited, from the early 1940s to the end of the 1950s. No studio, director, screenwriter, or art designer set out to make a film noir; no moviegoer chose to attend a noir film instead of a western or a musical as Saturday night entertainment. The notion of dark cinema was not an explicit element of either production or consumption during Hollywood's classic period.

Therefore we must first seek out its origin and development in critical rather than industrial practice. To offer a preliminary definition, film noir is a grouping of disparate films made according to intellectual taste and preferences, originally French. Most important, films identified as "dark cinema" offer a bleak vision of contemporary life in American cities, which are presented as populated by the amoral, the alienated, the criminally minded, and the helpless. Film noir, in brief, offers the obverse of the American dream. But whether film noir constitutes a genre, series, or cycle is problematic; the question will be discussed later in this chapter. At the moment, we can say that the unusual nature of this grouping does not preclude the sharing by noir films of significant features that can be described, discussed, and, after a fashion, accounted for. (This last issue will be dealt with in chapter 2.) It is important to remember that viewers at the time were hardly, if at all, aware that they were watching films substantially different from the ordinary Hollywood offerings they regularly consumed. Films noirs were understood and marketed as belonging to other genres—the detective film, the woman's picture, the thriller, and, most particularly, the crime melodrama or mystery. The qualities that made them dark (for French critics, at least) were largely unacknowledged by the industry and its public and seldom alluded to by American reviewers. What seemed a striking innovation to French "cinephiles" passed by nearly unremarked on in the country of its origin.

We shall consider in the next section why the French were predisposed to discover what Americans were not, and why they valued it so highly. But for what reason did Hollywood and its audience remain largely unaware of a new phenomenon on the nation's screens? This is a difficult question that can be answered only somewhat unsatisfactorily. First, films noirs were produced, marketed, and exhibited just like other Hollywood movies. They did not stem from an alternative form of production—they were not an "art cinema" of any kind—nor did the creative personnel involved constitute a group or school within Hollywood. Thus films noirs have much in common with the ordinary studio product, as we shall see in detail throughout this study. More important, the dark vision of American culture constructed in films noirs was acceptable to audiences at the time. Noir films would never have been made or attained popularity had their themes and form not corresponded to broad and insistent elements of popular taste, elements that may have made their blackness less striking, less noticeable, to postwar American viewers. Of course, it may also be true that audiences were unable to declare openly their pleasure with this new film type. French consumers of the Hollywood product were obviously in a different cultural situation and therefore positioned to see the changes in American popular culture more clearly than did its intended and satisfied consumers on the other side of the Atlantic.

DARK FILM FROM HOLLYWOOD: THE FRENCH REACTION

During the war years, the Hollywood product could not be shown on the screens of occupied France. After liberation in early 1945, a huge backlog of American films began to be exhibited in France en masse, especially in Paris at the Cinémathèque Française, which was frequented by leading figures of contemporary film culture. Enthusiastic admirers of a cinema they thought more vital and lively than their own, many French critics were struck by what they perceived as a radical change in American crime films, a loose category encompassing several established genres, including gangster, detective, and police procedural films as well as the crime melodrama. French intellectuals of the time were very enthusiastic about the American popular literary tradition, usually termed "hard-boiled" in this country. These grimly naturalistic stories about adultery, greed, murder, and paranoia were translated and published under the direction of Marcel Duhamel, an important cultural critic, who named them the *serie noire* or "dark series." It was thus hardly surprising that films with similar themes, many of which were based on serie noire novels or stories, were also thought of as noir.

Writing in 1946, Nino Frank was the first to use the term *film noir* in print, but we have no reason to believe—nor does he indicate—that he coined it.[7] Frank contends that Hollywood had succeeded in inventing a "new type of crime film," which he designates as "film noir" (9). Having just seen *The Maltese Falcon* (John Huston, 1941), *Double Indemnity* (Billy Wilder, 1944), *Laura* (Otto Preminger, 1944), and *Murder, My Sweet* (Edward Dmytryk, 1944), Frank estimates that these four films had rendered obsolete the traditional detective film, with its "thinking machine" protagonist, long explanations of the initially inexplicable crime, and one-dimensional, stereotypical characters. Preminger's film, which most closely follows the old formula, "introduces a pleasing study of decor and faces" (9) as well as a startlingly effective voice-over narration. Most important, however, *Laura* is more realistic in that it "attributes an emotional life to the detective character" (9). The other three movies subvert traditional genres by shifting attention away from the crime and the criminal to the "enigmatic psychology" of a strange gallery of characters, who, in their violent movements, evoke a greater sense of the "lived" than do ordinary Hollywood types (9). This above all distinguishes them from the quality films produced by the studios in the same period; exemplified for Frank by John Ford's *How Green Was My Valley* (1941), these films are "admirable but profoundly boring," "deprived of life, truth, depth, charm, atmosphere, and authentic dynamism" (14).

For Frank, the darkness of this new film type consists, perhaps paradoxically, in the greater sense of reality it evokes through concentrating on the morbid psychology of its underworld characters. Frank acknowledges that the noir film treats themes unexplored in the standard studio product; for example, three of the films he was writing about place ultimate blame on women for crime, manifesting a fear and hatred hitherto uncharacteristic of American movies. The result is stories that are "hard-hearted and misogynistic, like the better part of contemporary American literature" (9). But, finally, he thinks film noir is not a distorted but an accurate mirror because it offers a more exhilarating impression of lived experience and reveals by contrast the stagy inauthenticity, the clichéd emotionalism of standard Hollywood fare.

Reviewing, also in 1946, *Double Indemnity, Murder, My Sweet,* and *Lost Weekend* (Billy Wilder, 1945), Jean Pierre Chartier concluded, like

Frank, that the Americans were then also making films noirs (meaning that these films were like French productions that had been so designated); his reaction to the phenomenon, however, was neither welcoming nor appreciative.[8] Chartier understands the film noir as a radically new rather than more lifelike series of representations, a transposition to the screen of stories, characters, and themes previously off-limits in a Hollywood cinema controlled by the Production Code. He is especially puzzled by the fact that a film version of *Double Indemnity* had become possible after being discouraged by the PCA for a number of years. In any case, he does not regard this development as an advance for the American cinema: "[O]ne could hardly imagine being able to go further into pessimism and disgust for humanity" (67).

To Chartier, the focus of this new kind of film is on violations, both sexual and criminal. "She kisses him so he'll kill"—the poster blurb for Wilder's bitter tale of adultery, cold-blooded killing, and insurance fraud neatly sums up the film's connection of the forbidden and the erotic. Crime films prior to *Double Indemnity* emphasize the detective's problem-solving skill in the support of law and order and "[express] some confidence in human nature." But in the film noir, "all the characters are more or less corrupt" (67). Both *Double Indemnity* and *Murder, My Sweet,* in fact, offer women who are "particularly terrible," each film's sequences revealing unexpected and increasingly disgusting vices in them (67).

The centrality of these female characters indexed the new importance of sex as (im)moral fact and motive for action. Here censorship created an unexpected effect, in Chartier's view. Because the realistic display of sexual activity was prohibited by Hollywood, neither film could assign sexuality its true place in human relations. The result is that "all the characters seem affected by an inescapable fatality pushing them toward crime" (68). Fatality characterizes the story and its telling in both films as well. The first-person narration and the convoluted, incomprehensible plots are not "intriguing, but create an atmosphere of terror; because one doesn't understand, one feels threatened by unforeseen dangers" (69).

American film noir was differentiated by this unstable and morally reprehensible story world from French films, such as *Le Quai des brumes* (Port of shadows) (Marcel Carné, 1938), which had also been termed "noir." French films noirs, though also pessimistic, "hint at revolt, while love figures in them as the mirage of a better world"

(Chartier, 70). The characters may be desperate, "but they solicit our pity and our sympathy" (70). Although Chartier does not say so, these French films have much in common with some of the same period's highly valued French literature—for instance, the novels and plays of the existentialist writers Jean-Paul Sartre and Albert Camus, especially the latter's *The Stranger* (1942)—which offer a bleak, sometimes black vision of human relations. The American film noir creates a different fictional world. "Insatiable Messalinas, brutal or senile husbands, young men eager to kill in order to win the favors of a femme fatale, incurable drunks, these are the charming characters of the films we have discussed. . . . [T]hey are monsters, criminals, or sick people with nothing to excuse them, who act as they do solely because of a deadly, inner sense of evil" (Chartier, 70).

Unlike Frank, who values the realism he thinks stems from the morbidity and psychologism of early noir films, Chartier condemns their antihumanism and refusal to discover anything sympathetic or redeeming about the grasping, venal, and perverse characters they construct. The confusions and disorientation produced by the noir film, the ways in which the plot disquiets the spectator by its lack of clarity and its delight in the unexpected, do not, for Chartier, constitute a positive rejection of no longer acceptable cinematic conventions, which are boring because of their predictable message and "quality." Significantly, Chartier did not hope the film noir would replace Hollywood's tradition of well-made but facilely reassuring movies. In valuing films with a humanist message, he spoke for an important element in French film culture, represented most importantly by the eminent figure of Georges Sadoul, who, among others writing for the journal *Nouvelle Critique* (New Criticism), opposed the more praiseworthy evaluations of film noir found in left-wing journals, especially *Positif* (Positive).

Defending developments in the American cinema in *Positif*, Pierre Kast suggests that Sadoul and his followers object to "a film that depicts the exterior world in a repulsive and pessimistic way, without indicating the solution for conflicts, without revealing a regenerated world of the future, without being illuminated at the end by a small ray of light. . . . [Such a film] mystifies and discourages the spectator, distances him from the struggle, prevents him from transforming the world as it is."[9] Films noirs could certainly be understood as belonging to this category. Kast, however, emphasizes that these dark films are only apparently disengaged. He argues that "American directors and screenwriters make use of a proven technique in reversing, through an optimistic or edifying ending, a situation whose horror they had previously shown" (7). And yet the humanists were probably more correct than Kast about the film noir. This new studio type did construct a world of moral outrage and despair unrecuperable, at least for many viewers, by any formulaic happy ending. For a significant segment of French film culture, noir film was a shocking and disappointing development, a symptom of decline in both American society and its film industry.

Frank's positive reaction to dark cinema, in contrast, exemplified the opinions about film art of many of the younger members of this critical generation, some of whom were the filmmakers responsible for what has come to be known as the French New Wave.[10] The most notable of this group were François Truffaut and Jean-Luc Godard, two directors profoundly influenced by both film noir and serie noire narrative; gaining international reputations, Truffaut and Godard did much to associate noir themes and effects with the art cinema and with filmic modernism. Crucial here is that both Frank and Chartier link a changed social atmosphere—the seedy world of immoral characters intriguingly pursuing immorality—to transformations of film form, such as more emphasis on lived experience, the use of first-person narration, and convoluted narratives to disorient the spectator. Both critics thus see noir film as violating both the content and rhetoric of the Hollywood cinema, as constituting what could be viewed as an "alternative," even avant-garde film type—but only if a somewhat blind eye were turned to the conditions of production and reception, the same for films noirs as for other studio efforts.

Such a high-culture understanding and evaluation of noir film was developed by some left-wing critics, especially a number of those writing for *Positif,* who saw in dark cinema an exciting challenge to the normal social conservatism of the American entertainment movie. Opposed to Hollywood as a provider, in general, of uncritical fluff that reinforced the capitalist status quo, these leftist intellectuals naturally valued what they saw as noir film's revolutionary debunking of mainstream assumptions about right and wrong, proper and improper. For them, dark cinema was modernist and avant-garde in rhetoric and theme. (Interestingly, this debate between *Nouvelle Critique* and *Positif* was a minor restaging of the struggle over modernism and realism between German and Soviet Marxists during the previous decade, with Sadoul occupying, roughly speaking, the position defended by George Lukàcs, and the *Positif* critics that of the Frankfurtians, particularly Theodor Adorno and Walter Benjamin.)

Roger Tailleur's essay on *Ride the Pink Horse* (Robert Montgomery, 1947), written a number of years after the film's initial release, exemplifies the high-culture valuation of film noir practiced by the *Positif* circle. Here is a text, Tailleur suggests, that

> surprises, deceives, embarrasses, disturbs. The spectator isn't seduced by the quiet functioning of a well-oiled machine, convinced by the rigorous logic of its thematic development, or impressed by the fact of a masterpiece. *Ride the Pink Horse* first confirms, then jostles the spectator's expectations; he sees many things represented, but doesn't know very well what they are. . . . [H]ere it's necessary for the viewer to keep his eye open and bring his intelligence consciously into play. . . . The film becomes that table Cocteau speaks of in his preface to *Blood of a Poet,* the table constructed by the author/cabinet maker which we, our eyes wide open, must try to make speak a message. The message so perceived differs according to the viewer's predisposition. . . . This film is neither clear nor easy, but rather obscure and difficult. It is surrounded by a halo of imprecision and mystery, just like its title, by an ambiguous symbolism film titles rarely share in, *The Grand Illusion, The Big Sleep,* [titles] about which everyone forms his own opinion.[11]

I have quoted Tailleur at length because his evaluation of this studio product is so startlingly different from those of American critics at the time. The *New Republic* reviewer found *Ride the Pink Horse* "a mosaic of clichés" that, though Montgomery "juggles them a little wearily," do finally amount to "expertly manufactured entertainment."[12] The *New Yorker* was predictably dismissive, estimating the film's concern to be not the meaning of modern existence but "some obscure doings among gangsters in a Southwestern town populated largely by Mexicans who speak standard Hollywood broken English."[13] *Newsweek* was positive about the film, but not in the terms suggested by Tailleur: "[T]he one factor which makes it an above-average movie is its originality." Although "the basic situation is not new," the film avoids "several chances to be trite" and "builds up to a good climax."[14]

Like many of his generation, Tailleur, in contrast, was predisposed to see in dark and murky tales such as these a statement of the ambiguities and mysteries of the human condition. Here were films that could be reverently compared with the works of Cocteau or Renoir. These hallowed names are significant because they point to two com-

plexly related areas of cinematic value—realism and avant-gardism—
that would be later invoked, in different ways and at different times,
by critics working with the concept of film noir. Such opinions about
a Hollywood film would have seemed patently absurd to American
reviewers, who were accustomed to think of the movies as entertainment to be evaluated strictly by criteria reserved for the analysis of
popular culture. Hollywood at its best provided "quality": well-acted,
plausible stories dealing with significant themes. The studios were not
supposed to confront their customers with ambiguity and mystery or
to challenge them to rethink long-held opinions about the meaning of
life. Such confrontation was the province of other, more traditional
arts with which filmmaking was considered to have little fertile
contact.

Given these predilections, American reviewers in the 1940s cannot
be faulted too much for not seeing important differences in noir films.
Even a very perceptive observer of the artistic scene like Manny Farber missed the advent of noir, especially in the immediate postwar era
when dark cinema became an insistent presence on the nation's
screens. Only rarely did Farber sense a difference in films we now
consider noir, as in his review of *When Strangers Marry* (William
Castle, 1944), a film subsequently retitled *Betrayed*.[15] Calling attention
to the limited budget ($50,000) of this "B" programmer (a short in-
tended for the bottom half of a double bill), Farber says it is "about
as human a movie as I have seen this year." What he meant was that
a realistic rather than contrived atmosphere predominates in the film.
As he says, "[I]t realizes its hostile environment without using a gin-
gerbread house, dark warehouses, or somebody's staircase, and tor-
ments its people without starving them or threatening to shoot their
kinfolk" (746).

For Farber, the film avoids the unconvincing hyperbole of ordinary
Hollywood dramatic construction, which emphasizes "hunts, clues,
or detection." That Robert Mitchum appears "surprisingly dull, sup-
pressed, and frozen" and Kim Hunter is "as close to small-town innocence as Hollywood gets" allows *When Strangers Marry* to express
"a real sense of alienation" (746). Farber, in brief, senses in this film a
greater impression of lived experience than was typical of Hollywood's output; his view resembles that of Frank, who sees in early
noir films a greater "truth of character" (14). Importantly, however,
Farber does not appraise the film's opposition to the Hollywood
tradition of quality as a revitalizing trend. Instead he values it for ful-

filling Hollywood's implicit goal of making involving, authentic ("human") realist films. But if *When Strangers Marry* successfully avoids the false representations of most Hollywood products, it resembles for Farber a number of recent productions—including *Double Indemnity, Laura,* and *Phantom Lady* (Robert Siodmak, 1944), all of which today are considered noir—in utilizing certain "unsuccessful embellishments that are mainly snatched from German Expressionism." And yet, Farber concludes, it is the "least arty" (746) and hence the best of these. Farber's opinions are in some ways typical of 1940s critics, who, if they did not expect "art" from Hollywood, certainly disliked any pretensions commercial film might manifest and appreciated films that were less conventional as well as not too obviously contrived or melodramatic. Many noir films were seen as more realistic than the ordinary Hollywood product, a feature often praised by American reviewers. Such evaluation was one reason for the eventual blending of noir themes with realist techniques, especially location shooting and documentary stylization. The connections between noir and realism are complex and will be examined further throughout this book.

Unlike American reviewers, French cinephiles were less inclined to dismiss American commercial films because of their studio origins; in fact, they were disposed to value highly the movies they enjoyed so much. The concept of film noir permitted French enthusiasts to view the Hollywood cinema, if only in part, as an art cinema worthy of critical attention and appreciation. Dark cinema, they thought, rejected the facile optimism, the boring correctness of the usual American product. Noir films could even be seen as politically tendentious, as falsifying the American dream by concocting nightmare versions of contemporary social reality. Film noir, in other words, could be accommodated to the emerging European art cinema and valued in much the same way; it was the European art film, in fact, that received as much if not more attention than American films in French journals.

What came to be known, somewhat later, as the *politique des auteurs* or auteur theory (its usual English rendering), provided a similar perspective on Hollywood productions for French film culture.[16] Certain directors were thought to have resisted the conventionalism of the studio system through the force of their personality and obsessions. These directors could be regarded and valued as authors (*auteurs*) because their films reflected their own ideas, embodied their own style, and refused to conform and be strictly commercial, at least ideologically and aesthetically. This critical and evaluative approach, pioneered and supported by the influential journal *Cahiers du Cinéma* (Cinema Journal), dominated the French understanding of Hollywood for more than a decade, from the early 1950s until political events and cultural change made auteurism problematic in 1968.

Interestingly, the French enthusiasms for film noir and auteur theory are complexly connected. The *Cahiers* view of authorship was formed to some degree by a rejection of leftist approaches to the cinema, especially the critical line taken by *Positif*, which tended to ignore the contributions of individuals to production in favor of a more sociological approach to film meaning. The politique des auteurs was criticized by the leading light of the *Cahiers* circle, André Bazin, because it made directors and not moments in history primarily responsible for the message or significance of films. With this emphasis on the creative control exerted by certain directors, auteurism to some degree opposed the realist aesthetic espoused by Bazin and others at *Cahiers* (and at *Positif* as well). This aesthetic stressed the passivity and openness of the filmmaker to reality—a view that, had it prevailed, might have led the *Cahiers* group to pay more attention to film noir.

In any event, because *Cahiers* and auteur theory established the agenda for most French work on film in the middle and late 1950s, sociological and institutional questions, such as those posed by film noir, tended to be ignored—or, if not ignored, addressed in other ways. As it happens, many of the directors glorified for their individual approach to filmmaking were responsible for notable films noirs: Alfred Hitchcock, Nicholas Ray, Robert Aldrich, John Huston, Edward Dmytryk, and Samuel Fuller, all involved in noir productions, were the major figures taken up by critics at *Cahiers*. That these directors active in noir films were highly valued as authors is no coincidence, for it was precisely their noir films that caused them to be valued. In other words, the excitement evidenced by Nino Frank and others at the appearance of this new film type from Hollywood simply assumed under the regime of auteurism a different discursive form, one that substituted personality for genre. Auteurism became a way of explaining and dealing with film noir, even as that critical concept was passed over in silence. The politique des auteurs singled out those in Hollywood who established individuality by rejecting industry conventions; they were thereby distinguished from those competent but workmanlike craftsmen, termed *metteurs-en-scène* (scene stagers), who followed more closely accepted filmmaking procedures. Since noir films, with their insistent cynicism, contest the conservative politics of the ordinary American commercial movie, it is only natural that their directors—especially those otherwise considered maverick—would be seen as authors.

The evaluation of Edward Dmytryk's early career by Jacques Doniol-Valcroze is an illuminating case in point. Doniol-Valcroze was a central figure of the *Cahiers* circle, serving as the journal's first editor during the formative period of the 1950s and early 1960s. He finds in Dmytryk not simply one director among several working in film noir, but an engaged intellectual whose leftist politics made him critical of the status quo. (The proof of Dmytryk's engagement was furnished by his blacklisting and subsequent imprisonment during the Hollywood witch-hunt.) The confusing, amoral world of *Murder, My Sweet* thus results from personal rather than generic themes or ideas: "[T]his paradoxical ethic, vaguely Nietzschean, devoted in any case to the primacy of action, the modest charge of an existential philosophy very much now in fashion, is perhaps only a pretext for a virtuoso manipulation of a variety of dream-like or neo-surrealist images."[17] Politics and a personal philosophy may commit the director to filmmaking, but the final result is art, not a manifesto, stylistic flourish, not political statement. *Cahiers* auteurism is essentially a formalist approach to criticism and evaluation.

By the mid-1950s, French writing on the American cinema showed more interest in the individual careers of valued auteurs than in the film noir phenomenon. Film noir was, after all, an institutional development in which authorship and personality mattered less than shared themes and effects. Examining the oeuvres of directors like Ray and Huston, critics at the time concerned themselves with the similarities manifested by "signed" films, regardless of genre. For example, *The Maltese Falcon* was linked in such critical practice not to other contemporary noir detective films (*The Big Sleep* [Howard Hawks, 1946], *Lady in the Lake* [Robert Montgomery, 1946], *Murder, My Sweet*) but to the adventure film *The Treasure of the Sierra Madre* (1948), because Huston was responsible for both projects. In an early *Cahiers* appreciation of Huston (1952), Gilles Jacob provides a personal, authorial explanation for the pessimistic world constructed in *The Maltese Falcon,* in which a gallery of underworld characters, all more or less immoral, expend their energies in the fruitless pursuit of a famous art object. The dark world of *The Maltese Falcon,* according to Jacob, is not an institutional creation whose shaping can be traced across the careers of a number of directors. The film belongs to Huston, and those ideas that might otherwise be identified as noir are Huston's: "[T]he tragedy of greed and the poetry of failure are the two important themes of Huston's universe."[18] To an important degree, then, auteurism drew attention away from film noir, indeed, away from any consideration of film types and genres. The noir films of antiestablishment directors were explained by genius and personality, not by changes in Hollywood or in the tastes of its mass audience.

Interest in film noir, however, was sustained and furthered by the 1955 publication of three book-length studies, all of which afford this film type an important place in the continuing history of Hollywood. The most important is a remarkably comprehensive and insightful analysis, *Panorama du film noir américain* (Panorama of the American film noir), by the enthusiasts Raymond Borde and Etienne Chaumeton.[19] Borde was an occasional contributor to *Positif* and was responsible for a number of trenchant sociological analyses of such cinematic issues as the American social problem film and Italian neorealism. *Panorama* received the hearty endorsement of Marcel Duhamel, whose editorship of the serie noire had made him an influential figure in the cultural scene. Duhamel interestingly observes in the book's preface that noir films and novels "bring us close to reality and offer important testimony about our time" (Borde and Chaumeton, x); he thus shares with the *Positif* critics an interest in the connection between a cinematic phenomenon and its historical moment. *Panorama,* in fact, returns to the sociological perspectives that had produced this critical category some ten years earlier.

For Borde and Chaumeton, the American film noir is a series, that is, a "group of national films sharing certain features in common (style, atmosphere, subject . . .) which are strong enough to mark them unequivocally and give them, as time passes, an unmistakable character" (2). Series, they suggest, have different lengths; spectators decide whether they last two years or fifteen. Remarkably, considering the critical climate in which the book was written, this formulation avoids any consideration of auteurs—although, perhaps inevitably, when Borde and Chaumeton analyze individual films, they assume that directors are creators and thus responsible for the text's form and meaning. Given this view of film noir, criticism has three tasks: first, to mark out the limits of the series by writing its history, which is a succession of subtypes and individual texts; second, to formulate a definition of essential features; and third, to explain the genesis and demise of the series. *Panorama* addresses all three of these issues in substantial and groundbreaking ways.

In 1955 the French had no full library of Hollywood film; they lacked the resources for writing a complete history of film noir or accounting for its development and decline. The definition of film noir in *Panorama,* however, remains interesting and useful. Like Tailleur, Borde and Chaumeton recognize the crucial role of the spectator and the historical moment of his or her viewing in constituting the phenomenon: "[T]he film noir is dark for us, that is, for the Western and American public of the fifties. It answers to a certain emotionality which is as unique in time as it is in space" (22). This emotionality is a disposition to experience positively the feelings of anguish and insecurity these films produce; implicitly, Sadoul and company are out of critical touch with popular taste. Such emotionality is different from that offered by most Hollywood productions, whose effect is to reassure and comfort, at least ultimately.

What in the film noir disquiets and unsettles? Most important is the representation of crime in which violent death dominates: "[S]ordid or unexpected, death results always from the end of a tortuous journey" (5). In the police procedural—which often, in this period, had noir qualities—violent death may be present, but it is viewed from outside, from the point of view of the institution whose task is to detect crime and deliver evildoers to justice. In the truly noir film, crime is seen from the inside, from the perspective of the criminal or violator who must suffer the horrible consequences of breaking the law. Police procedurals, moreover, are constructed according to the principles of poetic justice required by the Production Code. The detectives are virtuous, the criminals vicious, and the story ends with the latter's apprehension or destruction.

The film noir, in contrast, contests official Hollywood morality not only by telling the story from the criminals' viewpoint (and thus naturally building sympathy for them) but also by representing the police, or "legitimate" society, as inherently corrupt, no better, morally speaking, than the criminals who oppose them. In the end, of course, virtue (however compromised) must triumph, even as the criminals are delivered to punishment. But noir narratives are disturbing on two counts: first, the spectator's sympathy is aroused, usually during the greater part of the narrative, for characters who must ultimately be thought unsympathetic; second, official Hollywood morality must thereby appear an unconvincing imposition, an "unrealistic" attempt at contradicting the connection between the desire of evil protagonists and complicit viewers. Such endings are particularly disorienting when all the characters are more or less immoral and supposedly respectable society appears corrupt, boring, and stifling. As Borde and Chaumeton put it, "[T]he one-dimensional hero, the grand primitive like Scarface, has disappeared from film noir, making room for a gallery of angelic killers, neurotic gangsters, megalomaniacal gang leaders and degenerate, disturbed underlings. . . . [The film noir hero] is moreover, rather frequently, a masochist, a man who destroys himself, the architect of his own troubles, who involves himself in perilous situations not so much out of a regard for justice or because of greed, but as a result of a morbid curiosity" (9).

Such characters would be out of place in a traditional genre such as the western, in which violence assumes the form of a fair fight between well-matched antagonists, a kind of judicial combat to decide the right. In the film noir, the shoot-out, the beating, and the cold-blooded execution replace such duels; the immorality and pointlessness of these encounters reveal a brutal world hostile to human happiness. Violence does not uphold or reestablish justice but signals its absence. Film noir discovers a seemingly inexhaustible repertoire of violent deaths to which its characters must submit. Death is always possible, often likely, and its forms are unpredictable, unexpected, and terrifying.

In this dark world of crime, violence, and annihilation, nothing is certain. As Borde and Chaumeton state, "[T]here is in this incoherent brutality something which resembles a dream, and such an atmosphere, moreover, is common to the majority of films noirs" (11). Characters appear and disappear, while the plot promises a significance, yet to be revealed, that somehow never fully is. The most striking alteration of Hollywood dramaturgy is that noir characters usually act from inchoate, unknown, or pathological motives. Such characters prevent the narrative from being organized according to Aristotelian principles of cause and effect. Any given scene may be staged more or less realistically, but because these scenes are often connected incoherently, the overall effect is that of a nightmare. Violence and moral ambiguity, as well as murky character and action, create the effect of film noir, which is nothing less than making the spectator experience what these desperate characters feel: anguish and insecurity. Film noir, Borde and Chaumeton conclude, manifests an "affective unity," which makes it unlike most genres or series because it is less dependent on conventional, repeated elements, although the films themselves are characterized to some extent by formal resemblances. We might say that the closest analogy is furnished by the horror film, which is similarly defined by a manipulation of the viewer's emotions.

ANGLO-AMERICAN IDEAS OF NOIR

British film criticism of the 1960s and early 1970s sympathetic to Hollywood reflected the interests and predilections of the *Cahiers* circle, but in very different cultural circumstances.[20] Little attention, therefore, was paid to film noir, though the term was not unknown in Britain at the time. Borde and Chaumeton's book had been read in French film circles, but, along with other work on noir, its views and enthusiasms were not taken up in any substantial way, especially by the *Cahiers* group. (*Positif* at least afforded the two authors the opportunity to editorialize briefly on their position.) Significantly, Eric Rohmer, who was also interested in Hollywood genres, published in *Cahiers* a brief and dismissive review essay treating the three film noir books from 1955. With the interesting exception of an article by Claude Chabrol on the evolution of the crime film (which makes little mention of dark cinema), the journal displayed no sustained interest in the noir phenomenon. Unlike the *Cahiers* circle, however, those writing for the influential British journal *Movie* eventually moved from a more or less purely auteurist view of the American cinema to investigations of genre. In fact, the *Movie* critics came to consider genre the element that, far from impeding imaginative or innovative filmmaking (the opinion of some within the *Cahiers* group), made possible the personal expression of directors. And yet, somewhat puzzlingly, film noir did not become a central critical concern for *Movie,* which would take up in-depth the Hollywood western.

An interesting exception to this general rule is the 1971 study of American gangster and thriller films by Colin Wilson, whose critical approach is very much that of the *Movie* group.[21] In *Underworld U.S.A.,* Wilson not only argues that genre study provides important insight into the workings of the commercial cinema; he also maintains that gangster films and thrillers are a neglected yet artistically significant aspect of Hollywood production. Film noir, Wilson suggests, is not a distinct genre or series but a transgeneric influence on films that treat crime, including the gangster and thriller genres. Departing from Borde and Chaumeton, his acknowledged critical source, Wilson goes on to state that film noir is a "mood," an emotional or tonal overlay to a generic text. In any case, Wilson is not very much interested in any sociological or thematic issues raised by the advent of dark cinema. His approach to genre is iconographic and auteurist. He provides an interesting analysis of the visual elements found in both genres (costuming, setting, typical forms of casting) and traces the careers of several notable directors, largely from the post-1945 group lionized initially by *Cahiers*. For Wilson, film noir is not sociologically but artistically interesting.

It was a critic outside the *Movie* group who produced in 1970, for the British journal *Cinema,* the first full-scale essay on film noir in English. Raymond Durgnat, like Colin Wilson, sees dark cinema as artistically rather than historically significant. In "Paint It Black," he calls attention to the role of 1940s French critics in defining the film noir, but unlike writers such as Tailleur and Jacob, he does not understand these dark productions as offering an important, politically tendentious critique of American culture: films noirs are "as often nihilistic, cynical or stoic as reformatory. . . . There are Fascist and apathetic denunciations of the bourgeois order, as well as Marxist ones."[22] Having suggested that dark cinema as a whole offers a somewhat confused and contradictory political protest, Durgnat not surprisingly abandons the careful thematic analysis practiced by Borde and Chaumeton. His approach is very formalistic: "[T]he film noir is not a genre, as the Western or gangster film is, and takes us into the realms of classification by motif and tone" (49). Durgnat likewise rejects the conception of the series that had helped Borde and Chaumeton ground their analysis in the industrial practices of Hollywood. He views film noir humanistically, much as the *Movie* critics viewed what they considered the best of Hollywood offerings, assimilating them to more traditional categories of "art." Thus, like Wilson, he sees the difference of dark cinema residing not so much in the overturning of Hollywood conventions and the development of different themes as in the subtle but apparent alteration of the social and emotional atmosphere, the tone of dominant cinema.

The concept of tone is a striking revision of Borde and Chaumeton's views of dark cinema, views that Durgnat otherwise depends on. In effect, the article advocates a very different kind of critical approach. Tone can be seen as the reflex of affect; that is, a certain emotional coloring affects spectators in certain ways. But tone can also designate connotation as opposed to denotation—not the meaning of a formal feature but attitudes toward it. This is how Durgnat uses the term. Auteurists, in fact, have often used the concept of tone to describe a director's discernible alterations of the institutional features—primarily generic conventions—that, under the American system, he was more or less obligated to work with. Tone or, more broadly, style is the reflex of personality, perhaps the most important index of an individual approach. Durgnat's use of motif and tone then reflects the critical assumptions and values evident in the author-centered criticism of the *Movie* circle. While the *Cahiers* writers had worked with the view that directors exert most of their creative control over mise-en-scène (literally, the process of staging events for the camera), the *Movie* group ascribed broader control to its privileged auteurs, thinking them responsible for a film's overall formal organization, its style. The studio system made stylistic expression possible only through the arrangement and alteration of given elements.

Durgnat's article was important to the subsequent development of film noir as a critical concept in two ways: first, he passed on the idea that films noirs manifest a bewildering variety of narrative themes instead of an underlying unity based on a particular handling of crime; second, his view that noir film is characterized by a tone rather than a rhetoric of affect enabled this body of films to be accommodated to auteurist views of Hollywood. For Borde and Chaumeton, the work of noir directors is determined by the overall functioning of the series, by the way in which the dialectic of production and consumption initiated, continued, and put limits on the popularity of a certain narrowly defined type. The concept of tone makes possible a new theory: that film noir resulted from a collective auteurism, from the similar stylistic subversions practiced by certain directors within the American system. Dark cinema could be seen, in other words, as the product of a movement. This new understanding led to a reconciliation of sociological and auteurist approaches; the first kind of analysis was simply collapsed into the second.

This is the main thrust of the first American discussion of dark cinema: Paul Schrader's "Notes on Film Noir," a widely influential article written in 1971 (and published a year later) as program notes for a series of films noirs screened at the first Los Angeles Film Exposition.[23] It is significant that Schrader's piece was written, at least in part, to afford viewers at a retrospective a way to value classic Hollywood films. During the 1950s, the European art film (enjoying a limited but significant popularity in proliferating art houses) had convinced American intellectuals that the cinema could be more than entertainment. In 1972, however, the studios were still widely considered commercial providers of uninteresting escapism. Despite the enthusiasm of some influential voices in American film culture (notably, the New York–based critic Andrew Sarris), auteurism never achieved the dominance here it attained in France. If the American cinema was to be valued (and there were those like Schrader who wanted this to happen), a tradition of art and seriousness would have to be discovered within it, one analogous to that which existed in several European national cinemas. In this context, Schrader's enthusiasm for film noir is hardly surprising; for here are native productions that, he suggests, are worthy of critical attention and acclaim.

Like Durgnat, whose influence he explicitly acknowledges, Schrader emphasizes the role of the French in identifying film noir, but he says that this group of films holds even more interest for cinephiles of the early 1970s in the United States. The reason is simple: "American movies are again taking a look at the underside of the American character" (8). Hollywood directors in the late 1960s and early 1970s fell very much under the influence of film noir—but indirectly, as mediated by the preeminent example of the French New Wave. These neo-noir productions from across the Atlantic constituted an art cinema characterized by an intriguing blend of cinematic modernism with classically dark themes, structures, and techniques. The French films were exciting enough to please a mass audience and yet sufficiently artistic to earn the praise of reviewers. With their somewhat contradictory homage to Hollywood, yet contestation of commercial cinema's entertainment values and form, New Wave productions, moreover, provided a perfect model for American filmmakers who wanted to alter yet perpetuate the system.

The directors of what is now known as the Hollywood Renaissance—including Arthur Penn, Francis Ford Coppola, Robert Altman, and Martin Scorsese—did much to create the American art cinema that flourished in the early 1970s. Their films, often popular as well as critical successes, were important elements in a vital developing film culture more concerned with seriousness than with the simple fact of authorship. And the Hollywood Renaissance directors looked to the classic American cinema, and particularly film noir, for models.

It is this cinematic and critical atmosphere that provides the background for Schrader's analysis of dark cinema. When he wrote this article, Schrader was intending to pursue a career as a writer and director, a goal he has subsequently achieved, having worked, in fact, on a number of noir revival productions, including Martin Scorsese's *Taxi Driver* in 1976 and his own *Hardcore* in 1979. As Schrader says, "[F]ilm noir is . . . interesting to critics. It offers writers a cache of excellent, little-known films . . . and gives auteur-weary critics an opportunity to apply themselves to the newer questions of classification and transdirectorial style" (8). The concept of a "transdirectorial" style is crucial to understanding how critical ideas about film noir developed in America during the 1970s. Schrader indicates that critics like himself are interested in understanding and appreciating Hollywood as more than a cinema of a few valued auteurs. And yet auteurist predipositions need not be abandoned entirely in the discovery of a transdirectorial style, for this is the practice of artists working as a group, as part of a movement. Thinking of film noir as a movement allows Schrader to value classic Hollywood filmmaking without either endorsing it uncritically as a whole (and thus undercutting the distinction between art and entertainment) or restricting its significance to the oeuvres of a few, exceptional creators. For this reason, Schrader theorizes about film noir as a style, that is, as a collective subversion of norms effected by the similar personal approaches of an elite directorial group.

The easiest norms to subvert, so the auteurist argument runs, are those belonging to mise-en-scène and cinematography, not narrative structure. The reason is simple: under the studio system, directors usually worked from a script not of their own devising, though they might well affect its ultimate form, while the final shape of the film was determined by editing, a stage of production also not normally under directorial control. In this context, Schrader's modification of Durgnat's position is slight but important. Durgnat says that film noir demands "classification by motif and tone." Schrader, however, suggests that film noir is not defined "by conventions of setting and conflict" (thereby discarding Durgnat's concept of motif) but rather by "the more subtle qualities of tone and mood" (8). He appears to have derived the second of these terms from Colin Wilson. Schrader does not differentiate these two near-synonyms, but it is clear from his article that he regards tone and mood as effects realized by the director's working with staging and visual style. We might add that "mood" is a very accurate translation of the German term *stimmung,* one of the central concepts associated with expressionist filmmaking. Schrader believes, in fact, that expressionism influenced the advent and development of film noir through the participation of ex-Weimar filmmakers, such as Fritz Lang. American critics following Schrader have often compared film noir to expressionism, but the comparison is problematic. Cinematic expressionism is very much a self-conscious group practice directly involved with other more traditional arts, especially painting; the noir phenomenon is not a movement in this sense. We shall explore other connections between American dark cinema and German expressionism in the next chapter.

Schrader argues that the tone of dark cinema was determined by four different elements: postwar disillusionment, postwar realism, German expressionism, and the hard-boiled tradition. This list consists of one historical and three artistic categories and thus indexes a central and unresolved contradiction in Schrader's analysis: the conflation of formal and contextual materials. For him, tone is a "meaning" established by stylistic elements, which he catalogs: night-for-night or day-for-night shooting; chiaroscuro lighting, with a heavy emphasis on expressive shadows; a preference for vertical and oblique lines over the horizontal; compositional tension as opposed to action sequences; a fascination with water; first-person narration; and complex chronological ordering. Schrader's treatment of theme is not nearly so detailed; in fact, it is so vague as to be nearly meaningless. According to him, the noir film manifests "a passion for the past and present, but also a fear of the future" (12). With Schrader, we are a long way from the detailed thematic analysis central to Borde and Chaumeton's definition.

Schrader's lack of interest in theme follows from his view that film noir is not defined by content: "[L]ike its protagonists, film noir is more interested in style than theme" (13). Such a view is in line with his desire to see dark cinema as an extraordinary achievement, not as the cyclical kind of phenomenon that, as Borde and Chaumeton argue, commercial Hollywood is bound to spawn. Much like the French auteurists, Schrader is eager to locate an area of American film practice that escapes institutional history for art: "[F]ilm noir attacked and interpreted its sociological conditions, and, by the close of the noir period, created a new artistic world which went beyond a simple sociological reflection, a nightmarish world of American mannerism which was by far more a creation than a reflection. . . . [B]ecause it was aware of its own identity it was able to create artistic solutions to sociological problems" (13).

Schrader's precise meaning is somewhat puzzling. How, after all, can we explain a commercial film type that attacks its ground of being or escapes the conditions of its production? But the general intent of his formulation is clear enough. Film noir is more style than story; it is self-conscious and critical rather than socially conservative; it emphasizes artistry over meaning or, more precisely, collapses meaning into artistry (that is, "artistic solutions"). Schrader offers no institutional explanation of how this could be. Instead, he falls back on notions of creativity: "Film noir seemed to bring out the best in everyone: directors, cameramen, screenwriters, actors. . . . [F]ilm noir was good for practically every director's career. . . . Film noir seems to have been a creative release for everyone involved. It gave artists a chance to work with previously forbidden themes, yet had conventions strong enough to protect the mediocre" (13). He does not recognize the role of critical taste and preference, shaped by the concerns of film culture of his time, as a factor in the identification and valuation of dark cinema. In any case, to valorize film noir Schrader must not only distinguish it from ordinary American movies (all story and sociological reflection) but also accommodate it to then-dominant notions of film art (style, self-consciousness, subversion, creativity). With Schrader, film noir begins to be theorized as a cinematic modernism, as an alternative form of production that took shape, somewhat inexplicably, within the studio system.

For better or worse, Schrader's article established the agenda for American work on film noir over the next 20 years. For example, in their widely quoted study of noir visual style, J. A. Place and L. S. Peterson conclude that "nearly every attempt to define film noir has agreed that visual style is the consistent thread that unites the very diverse films that together comprise this phenomenon."[24] The two authors seem unaware that the issue of visual style was introduced by Schrader into work on noir at a relatively late stage; Borde and Chaumeton only occasionally mention strictly visual effects and never argue that there is an essentially noir style. Similarly, in their immensely useful catalog of films noirs, *Film Noir: An Encyclopedic Reference to the American Style* (1979), Alain Silver and Elizabeth Ward state that film noir "is a self-contained reflection of American cultural preoccupations in film form. In short, it is the unique example of a wholly American film style."[25]

One of the most interesting recent books on film noir, J. P. Telotte's *Voices in the Dark* (1991), perpetuates and expands another aspect of Schrader's view: that noir films, like modernist forms in general, are thoroughly self-reflexive. Telotte argues that this body of film is to be distinguished from the ordinary Hollywood product by its exploration of narrative patterns; in this way dark cinema furnishes an alternative vision of American culture. Films noirs "deploy the darkest imagery to sketch starkly a disconcerting assessment of the human and social condition" and in the process manifest a "singular concern with or awareness of the nature of narration."[26] There have been dissenting voices, however. Extending the analysis of early French writers, especially Borde and Chaumeton, Bordwell, Staiger, and Thompson reject the assumption by critics like Schrader, Silver and Ward, and Telotte that films noirs constitute an essential area of difference within Hollywood practice: "[T]hese films blend causal unity with a new realistic and generic motivation, and the result no more subverts the classical film than crime fiction undercuts the orthodox novel" (77). In other words, films noirs are still Hollywood films, not a counter-cinema formed mysteriously from within. From Bordwell's institutional perspective, noir films are as American and commercial as any other studio product. Yet dark cinema, this book will demonstrate, did offer a different experience to its audience, one that results from a confluence of cinematic and literary developments. And it is the task of criticism to address this difference.

FILM NOIR: DEVELOPING AN APPROACH

Tracing the history of the term "film noir," we have seen that it has been understood in different ways. It has furthermore become apparent that these understandings reflect the intellectual assumptions and predilections of the film critics and enthusiasts writing about the Hollywood cinema over several decades and in distinct cultural circumstances. Surveying this theorizing, we must remember that film noir was not a production or reception category in the United States during the classic Hollyood period. The notion of noir was instead a product of an ex post facto critical desire to view the American cinema from a certain perspective. Like any body of texts, Hollywood films may be grouped and categorized in a probably infinite variety of ways;

the idea of a dark cinema is only one of them. But more important, film noir as a term not only describes a body of films but indicates what values were mobilized to identify them as a group.

We can better appreciate this idea by using a concept developed in recent popular culture theory: the idea of the "text to be read." Tony Bennett and Janet Woollacott use this concept not to designate the now quite familiar concept (pioneered in both German reception theory and American reader response criticism) that readers or viewers play an important role in constructing the texts that pleasure them.[27] Instead, thinking of texts as "to be read" calls attention to a related but often neglected fact of textual exchange: the same text is not available to all readers or viewers. In the case of the cinema, films are positioned for viewing and appreciation by cultural forces beyond either the producer's or spectator's control. These forces make texts available in certain historically determinate forms; in other words, these forms can and often do change according to time and place. Thus viewers of what appears to be the same film in two different cultures do not—cannot, in fact—see the same film.

We have seen how this fact applies to film noir. That films now thought of as dark were marketed for American viewers like all other Hollywood products made it difficult for this audience to see them as different in any substantial way. A discrete set of forces positioned the film noir for a segment of the French cinema audience. For culturally specific reasons—most important, an enthusiasm for Hollywood productions and a valuation of pessimistic, socially critical themes—many of those writing about the cinema for journals with an educated, intellectual readership in postwar France felt a desire to find an area of tendentious artistry within commercial American cinema. French critics, in short, were predisposed to value directors whose work contested the formal and ideological conventions of studio productions. There were two material results of this predilection: the formulation of film noir, and the construction of selected directors as authors. These ideas influenced how French cinephiles understood and valued American films; in other words, these ideas positioned the films themselves for certain kinds of readings.

The concept of the "text to be read" is a useful tool for film students because it helps identify the institutions (such as reviewing) and values (such as preferences for art or entertainment) that mediate the facts of production and consumption. Seeing films as "to be read" also helps avoid an essentialist approach: the notion, now discredited, that all the qualities viewers find in a film must somehow belong to it, must be of its essence, must have existed before it entered into socially determined networks of exchange. In the case of *Ride the Pink Horse*, we have seen that Roger Tailleur and American reviewers describe what are in fact completely different texts; they discover the divergent sets of features their predilections urge them to see. It is not that either the French or the American critics are more correct about the "true nature" of the movie (it has none); for cultural reasons, *Ride the Pink Horse* became two distinct "texts to be read," the difference between them established, in large measure, by the way in which the concept of film noir worked to position the movie as "art" for some of its French viewers and did not do so for most of its American ones.

As the previous section has demonstrated, film noir must be approached first through a cultural and intellectual analysis of the term. From this point of view, the different understandings of dark cinema are all equally important since they have contributed, in various ways, to attitudes toward the classic Hollywood film within contemporary film culture. Most important, perhaps, French high-culture views of dark cinema, as mediated and inflected by Paul Schrader, have brought about the subsequent development of film noir as a distinct genre in the American cinema of the 1970s and 1980s. When we are examining the history of postwar American film culture, it therefore does not matter whether the high-culture appraisal of noir constitutes an accurate description of the films concerned; this critical position had an important effect on filmmaking practice in any event. But tracing the evolution of noir as a critical concept is not our main concern here. The central purpose of this book is to provide a historical understanding of the classic period of dark cinema; we must therefore attempt to analyze these films in the context of their original production and reception. When we come to trace the growth and development of dark cinema, then the concept of film noir we choose does matter It is in the nature of descriptions that some are more accurate and revealing than others.

For the classic, studio-dominated period of dark cinema, Borde and Chaumeton's emphasis on thematic differences provides the most useful approach. These noir films belong to an entertainment cinema dominated by narrative and generic conventions; Hollywood, in short, was in the business of providing its mass public with various kinds of stories. As we should expect, noir films are different from but also similar to the ordinary studio product; qualities now identified as dark evolved in the Hollywood film of the period because of a significant change in the dynamic relationship between the studios and their public, as the first section of the next chapter will trace.

By now, it should be apparent that traditional concepts of genre, series, and cycle cannot be used to describe the classic film noir. For dark cinema did not constitute an explicit element of production and reception; nor were these films imitations or adaptations of a single popular text, thus becoming a series; finally, unlike films in a cycle, dark cinema did not treat a single theme. Borde and Chaumeton's view that films noirs are a "group of national films sharing certain features in common" is helpful in a preliminary sense. Given the realities of Hollywood production and consumption, however, we must take account of how these "features" make themselves manifest through the genre system.

What we discover is that the majority of films noirs from the period 1940–58 can be understood as genre pieces belonging mainly to the detective film, the thriller, and the crime melodrama or mystery— genres that are distinct but, as we shall see, also share much in common. Film noir affects some other genres as well; the most important of these is the woman's picture. Of these four genres, only the crime melodrama was dominated by noir themes during the 1940s and early 1950s; this genre can, in fact, be considered in large part a series originating from *Double Indemnity*. Classic film noir is a transgeneric phenomenon, manifesting itself through (but also often in opposition to) generic conventions. Thus the next four chapters will trace the dialogue between noir themes and genre through a close and detailed reading of notable individual films. As we will see, these films (like many of those produced by Hollywood) often make use of features from several genres, but each can usefully be understood as belonging principally to one. In choosing which studio productions to analyze, I have drawn not only on the filmography appended to *Panorama* but on the two excellent reference sources on classic noir film, those by Silver and Ward and by Robert Ottoson.[28] All the films I discuss are, by scholarly consensus, dark in interesting and central ways.

The concluding chapter will examine briefly the legacy of dark cinema to American filmmaking in the poststudio era, with a particular emphasis on the neo-noir films from the last three decades. Though heavily indebted to classic noir themes, particularly alienation, anomie, and dislocation, 1960s films noirs often develop an even darker and more pessimistic vision of contemporary America. At the time, the term "film noir" was not well known in this country, even among the filmmaking community. But noir-ness was becoming influential, if indirectly, through the prestigious example of French New Wave cinema. The Hollywood Renaissance of the late 1960s and early 1970s established a solid tradition of art cinema in America through, in part, a use of noir conventions. Yet during the late 1970s, 1980s, and early 1990s, film noir became a more regular element of American film production and reception—became accommodated, in fact, to the new requirements of the entertainment film in the poststudio age and gave rise, in particular, to the genre now known as the erotic thriller. These developments will also be traced through the analysis of notable individual films.

The latest, contemporary stage in the evolution of noir—which has recently surged in popularity—takes us back to the beginnings of dark cinema, when images of the dark American city, populated by the vicious, amoral, and terrified, were to some degree recuperated by happy endings that restored the social status quo. It is to these classic noir films that we now turn, beginning with the crime melodrama, for many students of Hollywood the most distinctive and strangely appealing form of the film noir. These stories of violation, betrayal, and social breakdown, so different in theme from the ordinary studio product, raise some important questions about the advent of dark cinema within the Hollywood system. Therefore, we must attempt to address these first.

CHAPTER 2

Dark Love:
The Noir Crime Melodrama

THE ORIGINS OF NOIR

Why did films we now see as dark become an element of studio production in the postwar era? This is a difficult question. To explain why any given kind of film evolves at a certain time, finds a new popularity, or passes out of fashion is never easy. Such explanations must in some way deal with popular taste, whose effects can easily be measured (at the box office) but whose shaping forces usually cannot be identified with certainty. Film noir, we might say, evolved and endured because moviegoers at the time were satisfied by its images and stories, by the world of social relations and values it conjured into existence. Examining a body of films, we can analyze how they draw upon various aspects of contemporary reality to produce meaningful representations. But it is never the case that films are simply "reflections" of their historical moment, that they mirror in some mechanical way the concerns, anxieties, dreams, and nightmares of the society that produces them. Instead, like all cultural artifacts, films, including those of the Hollywood entertainment variety, are constructions. That is, they are reshapings of social materials designed to create certain effects.

Much work on the origins of film noir has not taken the constructive or reshaping aspects of Hollywood filmmaking into account. It has often been said that various aspects of postwar American culture gave rise to the darkness and despair of the noir vision. The alienation of returning veterans, anxiety about the failure of the American dream produced by continuing economic instability, uncertainty about gender roles after the dislocations caused by the war, and a morbid fascination with abnormal psychology often are cited in Hollywood histories as causes of film noir. It is undeniable that these themes figure in many films now considered dark. It is also true that these same themes were present in postwar culture. But a larger question remains. Why did viewers at the time approve of and enjoy distressing representations of disturbing social realities? Hollywood's function was, in general, to offer uplifting, reassuring versions of American life. And dark cinema did not push from the nation's screens the other kinds of films the studios had been making since their establishment in the 1920s, films that were escapist, not confrontational. Dark film, in other words, was a minority practice. Indeed, this probably accounts to some degree for the lack of attention paid to these films by the critical establishment. Whatever the depressing conditions of American life in the late 1940s, it could be argued quite plausibly that they did not alter the continued functioning of Hollywood in its accustomed social role. Most American films of the period were not dark—quite the contrary—so how can we say that the discontents of postwar culture in some way brought on film noir? The advent of this new film type is better explained by a changed desire (if only in part) of movie audiences, not by any direct relationship between historical materials and their cinematic representations (there is none).

Why, then, did filmgoers at this time accept and, to some degree, welcome anxiety-provoking films from Hollywood, arguably the most important national institution for the production of positive social meanings? Film historians are not yet in a position to answer this question adequately. Much more work needs to be done exploring the attitudes and values that affected film consumption at this time, as they can best be determined at nearly 50 years' remove. We can, however, say more about the evolution of film noir, even if in so doing some of the issues involving changing popular taste must ultimately be deferred.

In most studies of dark cinema, the fact that many of these films are adaptations of pulp stories and similar hardcover novels is duly noted. Silver and Ward's treatment is typical. Granting that this fiction "reflects many of the stylistic and cultural preoccupations from which film noir ultimately emerged," they declare that the phenomenon is "equally, if not more significantly, a product of other mediating influ-

ences, of social, economic, technical and even aesthetic developments
that preceded its inception" (1). They are right in particular to under-
line how developments in Hollywood influenced the advent and
flourishing of film noir, especially the constitution of a visual style
(discussed in more detail later in this chapter). But it does not follow
that the influence of literature should be ignored or minimized. Although film noir is more than a simple transposition to the screen of
certain popular types of fiction, this fiction played a key role in the
development of the phenomenon, especially in establishing a popularity within mass culture for grim, disturbing stories about the underside of American culture.

As we have seen, film noir was a transgeneric type, an innovation
that affected many studio genres. Borde and Chaumeton, among
other French critics, call attention to the ways in which film noir provided new perspectives on crime, violence, and public morality that
were expressed through different but related genres. The history of
popular literature in the 1930s and 1940s offers an intriguing analogy
for this transgenericism.[1] Pulp fiction was aimed at a very different
class of readers than was mainstream literature. At the lower end of
the social scale, pulp fiction's readership was largely urban and male,
lacking middle-class "literary" interests. Like the dime novels that
preceded them, pulp magazines offered the sensational, the lurid, the
exciting. They also promoted, quite consciously, a wish fulfillment
that was energized by the breaking of laws and taboos, by the admission of the illicit and the uncanny into the everyday, by the discovery
of exciting transgression in an otherwise dull existence. Much like
the proletarian novel of the 1930s, but without that genre's political
tendentiousness, these texts conjure up a gloomy if also exciting view
of contemporary America. Their pessimism is even figured in the
difference between them and the mainstream realist tradition. Here
first-person narration (which avoids objective accounts of reality) is
common. Here also the classic detective story, which depends on the
restoration of law and order, is deconstructed, its measured complexity exaggerated to the point of incomprehensibility, its ultimate discovery of truth problematized. Here literary language is replaced by
a hard-edged style that is both closer to popular speech and yet a
refinement of urban dialects—becoming in this way a "high style"
opposed to standard written English.

More important for our purposes, this fiction manifested itself in a
number of genres closely related to the cinematic ones affected by the

noir movement: the detective, thriller, and crime melodrama types. Magazines such as the popular and famous *Black Mask* published a heterogeneous mixture of material. Even when they deal with the uncanny or the fantastic, such stories are always built up around crime and its consequences. Some feature the detective as protagonist, some the criminal, while others treat police crime-fighting procedures. Still others emphasize romantic intrigues leading to crime. These genres are obviously closely related. The structural differences they manifest consist largely in varying thematic emphases and changes in narrative focusing. As we will see, these differences are significant, but the fact remains that this range of fiction drew on the same worldview, providing reader interest by foregrounding the conflict between individual desire and the law. This fiction takes the side of those outside of or opposed to the established legal order—ordinary people caught up in unexpected intrigues, criminals trying to make it big, private detectives hassled or pursued by the police. It is hardly surprising that some writers, most notably Cornell Woolrich, often worked in all these fictional types.

Two developments that occurred within this tradition are important for an understanding of the advent and subsequent popularity of film noir. The first was that, as the 1930s progressed, the readership for such fiction began to change, becoming more middlebrow. Authors who had survived largely by writing for the pulps found publishers willing to take chances on book-length versions of their fiction. Woolrich is an interesting case in point.[2] After a brief and abortive career writing sophisticated comedy scripts for First National Pictures, he turned to the crime genres, selling his work to magazines such as *Dime Detective* and *Detective Fiction Weekly*. By the beginning of the 1940s, the market had changed, and Woolrich, like many others, broke into publishing hardcover and paperback novels. Especially important for our purposes is his "Black Series," which debuted in 1940 with *The Bride Wore Black* and ended, after three other publications, with *Rendezvous in Black* in 1948. These books were quite popular with a middlebrow reading public. Along with other Woolrich material, most works in the Black Series were filmed in America during the 1940s, though *The Bride Wore Black* was not transferred to the screen until François Truffaut did so in 1968. Significantly, Woolrich's formal change from short story to novel was in no way accompanied by a dilution of the pessimism and despair that so marks his earlier work. Most of the 1940s novels were simply expanded versions of already published stories, and some of them offer an even darker version of human relationships and possibilities.

In the 1940s the hard-boiled world became a grimmer place where omnipresent evil and oppressive fatality reduce individual action to insignificance. This theme is particularly apparent in the relentless determinism of Woolrich's novels. Even when conventionally linear, his narration proceeds from a space and vantage point that anticipate a horrible conclusion. In fact, the inability of individuals to alter their destinies becomes the central theme in works such as *The Night Has a Thousand Eyes* (John Farrow, 1948), in which unbelievably elaborate precautions involving all the ingenuity of the law cannot prevent a rich man from dying a horrible death at the "appointed hour" in his well-protected home. A romantic individualist, the hard-boiled detective can survive in his chosen milieu, the underworld, through strict adherence to a self-imposed code and through a shrewd acquiescence to the unpleasant realities, human and environmental, confronting him. Novels like Dashiell Hammett's *The Maltese Falcon* (1930) express a powerful disillusionment with contemporary culture but simultaneously validate the somewhat incongruous notion of a heroic individual, the private detective who lives by his own values and code. This fiction continued to enjoy a substantial popularity during the 1940s (as we shall see in the next chapter), but it began to be rivaled by very different kinds of books. James M. Cain's *Double Indemnity* (1936) and Woolrich's *Black Angel* (1946), for example, offer protagonists trapped by their circumstances who rebel against social rules and regimentation but are finally doomed by their own natures and the fatal forces of circumstance.

During the 1930s, as the readership for crime fiction became more middlebrow, perhaps coincidentally the fiction itself changed as writers constructed more hopeless versions of what Robert Warshow terms "the dangerous and sad city of the imagination."[3] These two changes together account for the advent of film noir and determine many of the phenomenon's essential features. The changing class attraction of pulp crime fiction themes helps us understand the subsequent acceptance of noir narratives by a broadly middle-class film audience. In fact, it would be very surprising if this were not the case, for a simple reason. As we have seen, Hollywood relied on elements of proven popularity to ensure a high success rate for the vast number of films produced each year. These elements included not only stars and genres but particular narratives that had demonstrated their appeal to the public. The studios reasoned, and most often correctly, that best-selling novels would make profitable films. Hollywood production was thus keyed to changing fashions in popular fiction. Not only were best-sellers usually snapped up by production executives eager for new material that was "presold," but the industry also monitored the fiction market for trends that could be exploited cinematically.

The middlebrow enthusiasm for the lurid excitement hitherto a feature only of pulp fiction in the 1930s also explains a phenomenon that has long puzzled American film historians. Many of the literary sources of film noir were published during the 1930s but filmed in the noir manner only during the war and postwar years. Of course, hard-boiled detective fiction did find its way to the screen in the 1930s. John Huston's version of *The Maltese Falcon* is thought by many to be one of the earliest films noirs. But the novel was twice filmed during the 1930s, once under its own title (1931) and once as *Satan Met a Lady,* a 1936 Bette Davis vehicle. What is missing in these earlier versions is Huston's full accommodation of Hammett's pessimism and social critique. Said another way, the earlier versions manifest a more complete reconciliation of Hammett's vision of greed, betrayal, and anomie to the mainstream optimism of Hollywood film.

Film noir developed only after the popularity of serie noire fiction had been firmly established. And by the late 1940s, this had happened, with the nearly inevitable transference to American screens not only of the adaptations of individual works but, more important perhaps, of storytelling patterns with demonstrated appeal. The advent of film noir is thus explained by Hollywood's somewhat paradoxical need to discover new narrative material while catering to story-consuming desires whose existence could be inferred from the popularity of certain individual films and types. Dark cinema is part of a larger shift in American popular culture. This change in taste is defined not only by the production of fictions that challenged the usually progressive ideology of American popular culture but also by the growing middlebrow acceptance of material previously enjoyed largely by male working-class consumers. Shifting attitudes are particularly apparent in the attitude of the Production Code Administration toward the adaptation of serie noire fiction. For one thing, these literary sources did not feature areas of theme or representation that the PCA had become very sensitive to during the turbulent course of its operation in the late 1930s. Cain's books, for example, offered neither explicit sexual description nor bawdy repartee. Their offensiveness was, instead, ideological, a rejection of ordinary moral codes and hallowed institutions (marriage, the law, romantic love) by the sympathetically presented main characters.

Why were screen versions of Cain's principal works permitted during the 1940s by the PCA? Why did these adaptations, faithful to the spirit if not the letter of the novels, fail to move religious groups, especially the Legion of Decency, to protest? The answer, as substantial box-office returns further demonstrate, must be that the dark vision of such fiction was no longer felt to be so offensive. Film noir and the serie noire mark a cultural moment in which nightmarish versions of contemporary American life became more appealing, became representations readers and filmgoers alike enjoyed. But the pessimistic noir narrative never became as important or acceptable as the concern of most Hollywood genres: the optimistic resolution of conflict, the construction of attractive wish fulfillment, and the bold expression of consensus values. Noir offered an alternative to but never replaced the mainstream American movie. But dark cinema was sanctioned and promoted by an institution, the Hollywood studio system, that strove constantly to remain within the mainstream of American culture.

Literary developments were crucial to the advent of film noir. The pulp fiction tradition, suddenly more respectable, provided film noir with that new perspective on crime that, to early critics such as Nino Frank and Jean Pierre Chartier, seems its essential feature. However, we should not reduce the phenomenon to its source material. Film is an imagistic as well as a storytelling art, and it is not surprising that noir developed a certain visual style. Noir style evokes an unpleasant and threatening environment, the perfect setting for crime, violence, alienation, and paranoia.[4]

Perhaps the most striking visual aspect of film noir is its alteration of ordinary Hollywood lighting schemes; this alteration provides dark images to match the dark stories these films tell. Normally, studio photography involved a three-point lighting system that made possible a full view of figures in their setting. Faces were brightly lit, and shadows were eliminated or minimized, an effect dependent on a bright or "high"-key light, the principal source of illumination. Noir lighting, in contrast, is often "low"-key, producing areas of hard (and for human faces, unflattering) light and shadow. Low-key lighting is both deglamorizing and mystifying, for it constructs areas of significant darkness that often seem threatening. Directors and cinematographers also experimented with different effects of light and shadow (termed chiaroscuro) that could be achieved by altering the position and intensity of light sources. Night-for-night (as opposed to normal day-for-night) shooting was even used to provide a very black sky contrasting starkly with whatever figures and aspects of setting were artificially lit.

The other principal area of noir style involves not photography but mise-en-scène, the arrangement of human figures in the frame. As Place and Peterson suggest, films noirs often feature "bizarre, off-angle compositions of figures placed irregularly in the frame, which create a world that is never stable or safe, that is always threatening to change drastically and unexpectedly" (30). In normal Hollywood practice, figures were positioned in balanced and harmonious poses; the lack of such balance in noir films is disorienting and often confusing to the spectator. Noir staging provided the perfect correlative to noir lighting schemes, and the two techniques were often used together to construct striking images of dislocation, danger, and mystery.

Place and Peterson recognize that the visual motifs of this style are not simple overlays that convey a meaning at odds with the film's narrative. Instead, these motifs shape a mise-en-scène that controls the conception of character and limits the possibilities of action. Noir style came into existence when Hollywood decided to tell different kinds of stories. Indeed, all the stylistic elements subsequently associated with film noir were already established if not central within the Hollywood repertoire. Noir, then, can hardly be considered in any essential way a stylistic movement, at least, not in the sense of constituting a significant innovation. More accurately, it involved the creation of a distinctive visual style to match storytelling needs. This evolution occurred in the work of cameramen and directors who were hardly members of a separate "artistic" group but who, as Hollywood craftsmen, were naturally subject to mutual influence.

Furthermore, it is important to note that the presence of noir visual motifs varies considerably from one film to another and, more important, hardly characterizes many films as a whole. In early films noirs—such as *The Postman Always Rings Twice* (Tay Garnett, 1946)—there is often very little, if any, noir stylization. This is undoubtedly because directors and cameramen had not yet formulated a "standard" stylistic treatment for such stories. In addition, the mainstream conventions of Hollywood cinematography were at this period too powerful for some to overthrow. The explanation of the Cain adaptation is even more complex. To get this film by the PCA, its producer and director attempted to give it a glamorous studio look, signaled primarily in the white costuming that the adulterous wife, played by Lana Turner, was given to wear throughout. *Postman,* in other words, offers a visual style deliberately at odds with its story. Moreover, in many films throughout the period sequences marked by noir motifs are preceded or followed by those conforming to normal practice. In some films, such contrasts are even structurally and thematically significant. For example, *Mildred Pierce* (Michael Curtiz, 1946) divides into a present frame where noir stylization predominates and a long flashback filmed almost exclusively in a conventional way. In general, however, noir films are stylistically distinct from the normal Hollywood product, constructing dark images that suit the moral ambiguity and despair of their narratives.

DOUBLE INDEMNITY

A consideration of visual style reminds us that filmmaking is both a collaborative and heterogeneous art. The film text consists of a number of interrelated levels, because it is produced by a stage-by-stage construction in which a (usually large) number of individuals participate. Working with a preexisting source, screenwriters create a script. The script is realized by a director, cameraman, and actors, not to mention others with important input, such as art designers and makeup artists. This realization involves two distinct stages: first, the design of a so-called pro-filmic event, consisting of the placement of figures in a setting; second, the photographing of that event, a complicated process that involves a range of artistic decisions, from the selection of film stock to camera placement. Afterward, the various bits of filmed reality must be assembled into a final product; this stage is customarily presided over by an editor and approved by the film's producers. Like all Hollywood movies, films noirs resulted from such a collaborative process.

Double Indemnity (1944) usefully exemplifies this complex intersection of forces and influences.[5] Based on the popular novel by James M. Cain, the script was cowritten by the director Billy Wilder, a German emigré, and Raymond Chandler, who was at the time becoming famous for writing serie noire novels of his own. John Seitz was the director of photography; he was already noted for the chiaroscuro effects he achieved in an earlier noir film, *This Gun for Hire* (Frank Tuttle, 1942), and was to become perhaps the most celebrated cinematographer associated with dark cinema. Miklos Rozsa composed a haunting theme, full of failed romanticism; like Seitz, he was to build an impressive career, in part, with his work for other noir films, including *The Killers* (Robert Siodmak, 1946) and *The Asphalt Jungle* (John Huston, 1950). *Double Indemnity* is a masterpiece of dark filmmaking because of the fruitful collaboration by a number of talented people, all of whom were very aware that they were producing something unusual and different.

An interesting aspect of this collaboration is that Cain's story appealed to the German-born Wilder; the screen version seems, at the same time, true to the American writer's grimly naturalistic view of human behavior and to Wilder's cynical attitude, not only toward the possibility of goodness but toward social rules and regulation as well. One of the most remarked features of American dark cinema is that it often seems to manifest an Old World view of the human condition, as opposed to the Horatio Algerism of Hollywood film as a whole. The European flavor of film noir is often explained by the fact that many of those who had worked in the Weimar cinema brought their talents to Hollywood as a result of their country's economic collapse and the advent of Hitler.

It is, of course, true that a number of noir films are distinctly European as a result of this cultural exchange. For example, Fritz Lang, a Weimar emigré, adapted from French novels two notable films noirs: *Scarlet Street* (1946) and *Human Desire* (1954). Jean Renoir also made films from these same two sources: *La Chienne* (1931) and *La Bête Humaine* (1938). Lang's attraction to a grimly deterministic fictional world undoubtedly derives to some degree from his work with the later stages of German expressionist cinema; like Renoir, he was drawn to materials that were realist in the sense that they did not construct an idealized image of human experience. Much the same could be said for other emigré directors who made careers in noir film; Anatole Litvak and Robert Siodmak are perhaps the best but not the only examples. As with *Double Indemnity*, however, the strongest fictional influence on noir film was American and derived ultimately from the hard-boiled tradition. Other influences, primarily from expressionism but also from European naturalism, were secondary and could manifest themselves in Hollywood because of the increasing acceptability of noir narrative.

There are obviously deep connections between European naturalism/realism and the hard-boiled tradition. Not only do the works of Zola make ideal source material for dark cinema—as Fritz Lang and others recognized—but hard-boiled novels could be made into realist films. The first screen version of Cain's *The Postman Always Rings Twice* was *Ossessione,* an unauthorized 1942 adaptation by Luchino Visconti, a leading figure in Italian neorealism. Serie noire fiction, we must not forget, enjoyed a pronounced popularity with European, especially French, intellectuals. Camus's *The Stranger,* its author confessed, was inspired by a reading of the same Cain novel. Emigré directors, writers, and technicians, however, did not simply transplant European themes and styles into the Hollywood productions they became involved with; instead, those themes and styles reinforced a preexisting popular fascination manifested, at least initially, in a thriving domestic literary tradition. In other words, film noir is not essentially a European but an American phenomenon. The noir world, however, provided a fictional and visual landscape that many craftsmen with a European background found congenial. In the case of *Double Indemnity,* the conjunction between native and Continental influences was a happy one.

Cain's novel had long been considered unfilmable because of its subject matter: an adulterous love affair between an insurance salesman and the wife of one of his clients that leads the illicit couple to murder the husband so that they can be together and collect on his accident policy. *Double Indemnity* evokes a seedy world of bored, brutal, and venal middle-class characters unredeemed (with one slight exception) by any virtue except cunning. The novel is narrated by Walter Huff, who is seduced by a beautiful woman and his desire to defraud the company he works for; the first-person narration places the reader inside the mind of a vicious, amoral criminal, makes the reader share values and experiences s/he would otherwise abhor. Obviously, this is material that must have seemed intractable to any Hollywood filmmaker. Not only did it fail to meet the poetic justice requirements of the Production Code (evil must not be presented sympathetically and virtue must triumph in the end), but it also left little opportunity for the development of sympathetic characters. Hollywood films depended on the favorable presentation of attractive people; the featured characters, it was felt, must be "good" in order to foster audience identification and involvement.

The project intrigued Billy Wilder, however, for it suited his cynical views of superficially respectable society. Wilder's earlier work in America had afforded him little opportunity to escape from conventional happy endings and one-dimensionsal, virtuous protagonists. But he had difficulty casting the male lead. A number of Paramount players, including George Raft, refused the role, fearful that playing an unsympathetic villain might ruin their careers. A reluctant Fred MacMurray was finally talked into the part; Barbara Stanwyck volunteered to play the femme fatale, perhaps sensing it was a juicy role that would advance her career (it did). Despite his expressed dislike for Cain's work, Chandler was hired to write the screenplay with Wilder. While the general outline of the novel was retained, the grim and downbeat tone of the book was discarded; Cain's taciturn, sexually obsessive lovers became more worldly and sophisticated plotters, masters of the wisecracking, tough-guy style that was a central feature of Chandler's own work. Thus their villainy was made less banal and more interesting.

Double Indemnity opens with a car careening through dark city streets and running through a stop sign. The sequence aptly images the out-of-control and illicit journey on which its driver, Walter Neff (Fred MacMurray), has irrevocably embarked. Though severely wounded, apparently by a bullet, he has come back to his office to dictate a memo to Barton Keyes (Edward G. Robinson), the company's chief claims investigator. This memo, which becomes the flashback occupying most of the film, is not a confession. Walter says he intends simply to set the record straight, to let Keyes, his friend, know what really happened in the apparently accidental death of a Mr. Dietrichson, one of the company's insured. "I killed him for money and for a woman. I didn't get the money, and I didn't get the woman." As the flashback begins, Walter reveals that this scheme was formulated after an unhappy accident. Dropping by a client's house to secure a renewal for an auto policy, Walter was struck by the coquettish beauty of Phyllis (Barbara Stanwyck), the man's wife. In his voice-over narration, Walter reveals that he pretended a continuing interest in the renewal but was much more intrigued by Phyllis, who, scantily clad (for the time), displayed herself unashamedly. His first attempt at seduction repulsed, but not decisively, he made plans to return, ostensibly to talk to Mr. Dietrichson. When he returned, Walter, to his

Seduced by the wife's unabashed display of sexual allure, *Double Indemnity*'s amoral insurance agent gets the unwitting husband's signature on an accident policy that makes his death profitable for the illicit lovers. Courtesy of Paramount/Museum of Modern Art, Film Stills Archive.

delight, was received by Phyllis alone, her husband and maid being conveniently away. She had a double proposal for him: not only her own evident sexual interest but also an accident policy for her husband, who was not to know he had been so insured. Walter understood, and correctly, that Phyllis meant to kill her husband for the money. Saying, "I'm not that crazy," he left.

But Phyllis comes to his dark apartment later that night, correctly reading his refusal as halfhearted. She and Walter become lovers as they determine to kill Mr. Dietrichson, who, Phyllis says, is a brute who beats and neglects her—an impression later confirmed by his indifferent and harsh demeanor. Walter is no innocent persuaded by a beautiful woman to throw away virtue for love. He admits in this last memo to Keyes that he had long been thinking about "ways to crook the house" and that Phyllis was simply the "shill to put down the bet." Walter realizes that the plan will have to be perfect in order to fool Keyes, who has a keen nose for fraudulent claims. Though fearful of deception and uneasy about killing a man who has done him no harm, Walter decides he and Phyllis will murder Dietrichson, will "go straight down the line" together.

Returning to the Dietrichsons' to get the husband's unwitting signature on a blank accident policy form, Walter meets Lola (Jean Heather), Phyllis's stepdaughter, and her boyfriend, Nino Zachette (Byron Barr). Once again Walter admits to a certain moral uneasiness about his plans; plotting the father's murder while the daughter is in the room bothers him. But he does not stop. The complicated plot involves Walter and Phyllis murdering Dietrichson in his car as she drives him to catch a train. Then Walter takes Dietrichson's place on the train and jumps off at a certain spot where Phyllis will meet him with the car. Next Walter drags the body over to the tracks to make it look as if Dietrichson fell off the train and broke his neck. The lovers hope to collect $50,000, or double indemnity: according to the policy, train accidents pay off at twice the usual capital sum.

These plans unfold intriguingly and suspensefully as Walter narrates the complicated scheme. As he murders Dietrichson in the seat beside her, Phyllis's face breaks into a thin smile. The rest of the plan works to perfection as even the unexpected is seemingly dealt with. When Walter makes his way to the rear of the train, he gets rid of a pesky witness by sending him on a fool's errand. Though Walter cannot see what could go wrong, he has a foreboding of disaster. The plotters, as it turns out, have neglected one important detail. Before the trip, Dietrichson had broken his leg; Walter has improvised a cast and uses crutches to look like his victim on the train. But if Dietrichson had just recently purchased accident insurance, he would have put in a claim for the broken leg. Not knowing he was insured, he of course did not do so. This weakness in the scheme proves fatal as soon as Keyes discovers it.

Initially, however, the lovers' plot appears successful. Keyes refutes the view of the insurance company president that Dietrichson committed suicide. But after discovering the anomaly of the broken leg, Keyes becomes convinced that the claim is a fraud, that Phyllis and someone else (as yet unidentified) murdered her husband. Now under constant surveillance, the lovers cannot meet, and an emotional distance develops between them. Lola comes to Walter's office and tells him of her suspicions that Phyllis murdered not only her father but her mother (Phyllis had been Mrs. Dietrichson's nurse). To keep her from coming forward with her suspicions, Walter becomes Lola's constant companion. Keyes is suspicious of Walter's involvement, but the man on the train does not recognize him and his alibi remains otherwise airtight. Walter learns from Lola that Phyllis has taken up with Nino Zachette, her boyfriend; Lola is convinced that Nino plotted with Phyllis to murder her father. Walter not only feels betrayed and suspicious of Phyllis's actions; when he subsequently learns that Keyes suspects Zachette himself, Walter sees a way to extricate himself from what seems to be a trap. Keyes will challenge Phyllis's claim, and Walter thinks that he will eventually be identified as her fellow plotter.

So Walter formulates a new plan. He makes a date with Phyllis that night, intending to kill her because he knows Zachette will arrive sometime later. The police, thanks to Keyes's work (Walter thinks), will pin the crime on Zachette, who will also be blamed for Dietrichson's murder. Before Walter arrives, Phyllis is shown hiding a gun in the living room, apparently intending to kill him. After Walter tells Phyllis his plan in the darkened house, he accuses her of murdering Mrs. Dietrichson and of intending Zachette to be framed later, to eliminate him. Tacitly acknowledging that she is the spider woman Walter thinks she is, Phyllis says: "We're both rotten." As Walter closes the blinds to hide his crime, Phyllis shoots him but does not kill him. She cannot shoot again, however, because she suddenly realizes she loves Walter. As Phyllis embraces him, Walter says, "Goodbye, baby," and shoots her dead. But something has changed in him also. Walter waits for Zachette outside the house and warns him off, advising him to go back to Lola, the girl who really loves him. At this point, the flashback ends. Keyes enters the office as Walter, fatally weakened by loss of blood, is asking him to take care of Lola and Zachette. Attempting to escape, Walter collapses before he reaches the elevator. Keyes acknowledges his affection for the dying man and Walter counters with, "I love you, too."

Like its novelistic source, *Double Indemnity* offers an innovative treatment of crime and its consequences. In the classic detective story, so popular on the screens of 1930s America, the spectator identifies with the detective, whose problem-solving abilities are never found wanting, even when the crime in question (and this is the usual case) seems incapable of solution. Classic detective fiction not only distances the spectator emotionally from the crime (which exists, as it were, only to be solved) but makes him or her hope for the eventual identification of the criminal, the social or psychological meaning of whose motives is ultimately irrelevant. As Geoffrey Hartman puts it, the perspective of detective fiction is moralistic, not moral. An essential element in its thematic structure is an attempt to suppress the troubling complexities of the violation whose solution becomes the narrative goal. In any case, the spectator's desire to know (which is catered to by any act of storytelling) is here explicitly linked to the functions of the law. The viewer gets to know the answer to the puzzle when the criminal is identified (and the law is served); or we might say, perhaps more accurately, that the viewer's ultimate pleasure in knowing the truth is dependent on the correct workings of the law as managed by the detective, its representative.

In *Double Indemnity,* and the many films that more or less imitate it, the detective story is turned inside out.[6] Ordinarily, after learning an effect (that is, the crime), the detective must discover its cause (the criminal). This story, in contrast, offers a cause (the separate desires of Walter and Phyllis to defraud and become rich, as well as their illicit desire for one another) and then constructs suspense concerning its effect, which, of course, is the crime to be committed. By reversing the narrative pattern, this story type transforms the spectator's identification as well. For now we are called upon to see the world through the eyes of the criminals involved, an effect that is especially heightened through the use of intermittent voice-over narration in Walter's flashback. Such a voice-over/flashback structure deepens our identification (and, in a sense, complicity) with the murderer; not only is he the main character in the images we see and in the dialogue we hear, but he is also present as a voice that increases our understanding of and involvement with the story.

Double Indemnity is otherwise quite successful in evoking viewer sympathy for the plotters. By 1944 a well-established convention of the Hollywood film was that attractive, charismatic characters are "good," and ugly, unpleasant ones are "bad." Fred MacMurray and Barbara Stanwyck appear attractive in the film—well groomed, nicely dressed, glamorized in the usual Hollywood fashion by flattering lighting and poses. Both actors, moreover, had previously portrayed "good" characters, and their performance histories, known if only in a barely conscious way to many in the original audience, would have predisposed viewers to look favorably upon Walter and Phyllis. Another Hollywood convention is that "good" characters of opposite sexes inevitably come to feel a strong attraction for one another. The adulterous nature of the plotters' relationship is minimized by the fact that the flashback begins with Walter seeing and being attracted by a quite beautiful and sexy but also solitary Phyllis. Conventionally, the audience is in favor of such a match, desires the attractive man and woman to fall in love and find romantic happiness. Dietrichson, in contrast, is played by a much older and less attractive actor (Tom Powers, who was frequently cast as an unsympathetic authority figure—the imperious boss, the brutal cop, the criminal henchman). Unlike Walter and Phyllis, who are shown to be worldly-wise, sophisticated, even polite, Dietrichson is presented in his two brief scenes as an unpleasant loudmouth, with no manners, who seems to care about nothing but himself. Despite Walter's momentary qualms about killing him, the elimination of Dietrichson, however brutal and cold-blooded, does not much trouble the spectator, who is by this time eager to see that the lovers get away with their scheme.

In this reversal of the classic detective story, the detective now becomes an antagonist, the enemy who would reveal the truth of the crime and thus doom to eventual destruction the characters with whom we have come to identify. In *Double Indemnity*, the official system of justice makes no appearance. Its indirect representative is Barton Keyes, the claims investigator for Walter's company who, in his obsession with discovering the truth about any fraud perpetrated on his employer, recalls the classic detective (for example, Sherlock Holmes). Keyes does not represent the law as either virtuous action or justice but rather as a not entirely sympathetic desire to know and tell the truth at any cost. The truth, of course, is here opposed to desire (the desire of the criminals and the desire of the spectator that this desire be fulfilled). It thus also seems opposed to happiness; it offers the barren pleasures of knowing instead of being.

Keyes is the living example of such sterility. We learn early in the film, after he listens to Walter talk to "his girl" (actually Phyllis) on the phone, that Keyes himself had once been engaged. But he could not marry the girl without having her investigated; naturally, he discovered that she was a no-good tramp and thus saved himself for a life single-mindedly devoted to the detection of fraud. Keyes displays an affection for Walter that, it is suggested throughout the film, borders on the homoerotic. His desire is to lure Walter away from sales and make him an investigative partner. This alternative is offered to

Walter just as he is becoming involved with Phyllis. And, though it promises a life of virtuous truth discovery and telling, the ill-paid role of investigator working with Keyes inevitably seems less appealing, perhaps even less "right" (considering the homoerotic overtones) than plotting with a beautiful woman to gain a small fortune.

Contrary to the official Hollywood formula, villainy in *Double Indemnity* is both attractive and sympathetic. Crime involves the relentless pursuit of self-interest (the American way?) at the expense of a brutal, unappealing man and a large company that can easily afford the loss. Though sex is involved, Phyllis and Walter's real motive is economic gain. Phyllis is no mesmerizing femme fatale (like the vampish Anna in *Criss Cross* [Robert Siodmak, 1949] and many other noir heroines). Her charms alone are insufficient to convince Walter to decide upon a dangerous undertaking. As Walter reveals to Keyes in his dying memo, he had long contemplated cheating the company (a thought planted in his mind by learning how others had tried). Phyllis thus offers him the perfect opportunity to carry out a secret desire.

Of course, Walter is a pawn himself in Phyllis's scheme not to part a man from his money but, literally, to turn him into money. Lola gets the bulk of Dietrichson's wealth, according to the will; only his death by train accident makes him valuable to Phyllis. Paradoxically, such a scheme needs a man who agrees to destroy the husband even as he takes his place to be destroyed in turn. Thus Walter must "play" Dietrichson on the train, must create the illusion of his death by pretending to die himself. His role is one of weakness, not strength, appropriately imaged by the use of crutches. (A dark image of a man on crutches, not identifiably Walter or Dietrichson, plays through the opening credits and provides an appropriate symbol for the film's presentation of masculine "strength.") And yet Walter is not just a victim; he is as much of a manipulator as Phyllis. Walter formulates alone the scheme to exculpate himself by murdering her and implicating Zachette, making another man take his place (just as Phyllis wished him to take her husband's place). Walter tells Phyllis of his intentions, and thus she shoots him, at least partly, in self-defense. When she says, "We're both rotten," she is speaking a truth most viewers would endorse.

The final midnight meeting of the lovers as well as subsequent events, including Walter's "confession" to Keyes and death by his side, are additions that alter the story's moral tone considerably. These alterations were effected to some degree because of Production Code requirements, which in part called for what the PCA termed "compensating moral value" whenever the story presented evil or crime in a sympathetic light. The lovers kill themselves, demonstrating the ultimately self-destructive nature of their evil. Walter and Phyllis pursue their self-interest together, and this paradox ultimately results in the simultaneous satisfaction but frustration of their desire, for each succeeds in killing the other, thereby ensuring that neither one survives. The wages of sin is death. This biblical moral neatly summarizes the film's finale, which certainly follows the Code's injunction that villainy cannot be portrayed as ultimately successful or go unpunished.

Walter and Phyllis, however, both experience separate changes of heart that, appropriately enough, do not save them but do preserve innocence (Zachette is not framed and rejoins Lola, his true love); reveal the truth (Keyes is informed as Walter makes up for his deception); and uncover the redeeming nature of love (Phyllis cannot fire the fatal shot, must surrender to an embrace she knows will cause her death). The tone of this ending is ambiguous, undoubtedly a product of the quite different sensibilities of the film's two writers (as mediated, of course, by PCA requirements). In the end, the film's Walter resembles Chandler's hard-boiled hero, Philip Marlowe, that "knight of the mean streets" who, despite his toughness and brutality, has an inextinguishable desire to save the innocent from destruction. At the same time, the conversions of Walter and, especially, Phyllis appear unconvincing, brought about by a grace of whose existence the film otherwise offers little or no evidence. Wilder's well-documented doubts about the possibility of human virtue are perhaps appropriately expressed by a just if not happy ending conforming to the Code but seemingly hollow and false. A similar effect is achieved in two of his other noir projects, *The Lost Weekend* (1945) and *The Big Carnival* (1951). In any case, the dominant impression of *Double Indemnity* is of criminals who are in some final sense unrepentant. Phyllis does not express remorse for or seek remission of her many vicious crimes; suddenly and fatally, she simply falls prey to an emotion, love. Love, too, motivates Walter's desire for Lola's happiness, and Zachette's preservation is simply a means to that end. But even at the last, having squared accounts with Keyes, he lurches toward the office door, still hoping to get away with everything.

Double Indemnity is innovative not only in its depiction of the crime from the viewpoint of the criminals, for whom an important amount of sympathy is developed; the film also domesticates crime, makes it an element of family life and its discontents. Walter and Phyllis seduce each other in her house and his apartment; she is attracted to him, she says, because he is unlike her brutal and neglectful husband. Dietrichson, in turn, is tricked into signing the accident policy application that becomes his death warrant during an evening at home with his family (whose tensions are made evident by quarrels and angry silences). Walter kills Dietrichson as he is being driven to the station by an apparently obedient wife so that he can take a trip. Pursued by Keyes, Walter and Phyllis meet at a supermarket where, interrupted by housewives shopping for dinner, they plot their next move. The illicit couple cannot escape a world defined by family responsibilities and ties, by the rhythms of stifling everyday life.

The night Keyes discovers the flaw in their plan, he goes to Walter's apartment; Phyllis arrives just as he is about to leave. A striking image shows a silent Phyllis clinging to the half-open door to hide herself as Walter says goodnight to his colleague; here she literally becomes the other, repressed side of ordinariness. Like Walter, Zachette is seduced and almost betrayed in the Dietrichson family home. It is there also that Walter and Phyllis have their final, fatal rendezvous. Except for Dietrichson's murder, which briefly puts Phyllis and Walter in public and hence at risk of detection, the narrative unrolls in domestic interiors and in Walter's insurance office, a home away from home where he can reveal his innermost secrets to the man who loves him best.

These settings ideally suit the film's themes. Adultery is a violation of the marriage bond, an illegal intrusion (as the word's etymology suggests) of an other into the physical tie that is the basis for family life. This violation is connected to a further, even more apocalyptic one: the murder of the husband, the transformation of Dietrichson into a lump sum of insurance money. The collective, intangible reality of family interconnection thereby becomes something of measurable, public value easily converted to the uses of individual desire. As the film suggests, money is the opposite of human relationships; it can even destroy an adulterous bond. Or, more accurately, it can pervert and distort that bond in the very moment of its establishment, for Walter and Phyllis see each other more as means to monetary ends than as objects of desire. Phyllis works to be part of a family she destroys from within; Walter is the rootless, greedy outsider eager to use the family to satisfy his own desire to "crook the house." Each is defined by a negation of social relationships. Their coupling turns out to be only an illusion, a cover for an unrepentant individualism that is transformed too late (if at all) into a less selfish attachment to others.

Walter and Phyllis never discover the proper physical setting for their anomie and selfishness, their irresistible desire for a self-assertion that is destructive and suicidal. They are in the family but not of it. (To murder Dietrichson, Walter joins the married couple on their way to the station, crouched low in the backseat, a figure of repressed violence and dissatisfaction.) And yet they also inhabit—as in the supermarket sequences where shopping becomes the "cover" for their plotting—that empty space defined by the deconstruction of family life. The noir crime melodramas that imitate *Double Indemnity* usually resolve rather than preserve this representational and narrative contradiction. Either the violation of domestic life is depicted from within—effected by the family itself rather than outsiders—or those who restlessly seek romantic connections they themselves destroy are shown in an environment that mirrors, even furthers their dislocation—a world of nightclubs, sleazy bars, transient motels, dance halls, and bus stations. This public sphere is charged both by a desire for the illicit (extramarital sex, alcoholic self-indulgence, the abandonment of bourgeois notions of respectability, making a "big score") and by an obsessive detachment—the thrill of wandering as a stranger, escape from family life and identity, the possibility of always moving on, never putting down roots.

THE PITFALL

In André de Toth's *The Pitfall* (1948), the drama of violation has become truly domestic; here the family is threatened, perhaps destroyed, by exterior forces and desires whose power is unleashed by a fatal mistake made by the husband and father. The film's script is by Karl Kamb, who worked from an unpublished novel of the same title by Jay Dratler, himself a screenwriter much involved in film noir. *The Pitfall* is in many ways a reworking of *Double Indemnity*'s fatal triangle, though the pessimism of Cain/Wilder is transformed, if only partially, into a more conventional moralism. John Forbes (Dick Powell) is an insurance agent and investigator living the postwar ideal of American happiness and success. The film opens with what should be a scene of

domestic bliss: a convivial breakfast Forbes shares with his attractive
wife and adoring son in their comfortable suburban home. Sue (Jane
Wyatt) was "voted the prettiest girl in the class," as Forbes reminds
her. But this husband who apparently has it all is evidently going
through a life crisis. He is worried about money—couldn't little
Tommy (Jimmy Hunt) stop growing for a while and not need more
new clothes?

More important, however, Forbes considers his routine job a poor
substitute for as yet unrealized adolescent dreams of sailing around the
world with Sue, who brings him down to earth by reminding him to
get going and earn a living to support his family. The ennui and resentment Forbes feels have even begun to poison his marriage. Sue's
innocent question about what time he is coming home elicits a self-
pitying response about the going-nowhere regularity of his daily routine ("Sometimes I feel like a wheel within a wheel within a wheel").
She complains about his perfunctory good-bye, the outer sign of sexual malaise ("I'm getting a little bored with that kiss on the cheek,
too"). But the scene ends with Forbes acquiescing to the facts of his
life; he promises to be in a better mood that evening, not suspecting
that he will keep that promise in a shocking and unforeseen fashion.

Forbes's dissatisfaction with his life is finally only superficially similar to Walter Neff's. Marriage, family responsibilities, and the inescapable dullness of an office-bound job have made him uneasy and
restless. His unrealistic dream is somehow to be special, not just another white-collar worker enjoying the ordinary rewards of respectable middle-class existence. His crisis is psychological, not moral. It
derives from a failure of energy and will power. In contrast, Walter
wants money and a woman to indulge his fantasies of power and control. Forbes has no idea what exactly he is after, only what has become
tiring to him. He is respectable in the sense that his life has been lived
openly beyond reproach. Walter's respectability, however, is a mirage,
a useful cover for a man who makes a very successful living "selling
himself." At first simply a superficial lie concealing contrary desires,
Walter's public persona becomes a deceptive surface meant to distort
and deflect an immoral reality. Such a self must be manufactured, as
in the elaborate alibi that is built to cover his murder of Dietrichson.
Walter must do one thing and be another; or, more accurately perhaps,
he must be two different people separated in place and time to survive.
Pretending to sell Dietrichson insurance, Walter actually gets him to
participate unwittingly in his own murder. Ostensibly aiding Keyes

in the investigation, he is actually its object. Most tellingly, perhaps, Walter must be in two places at once to commit the perfect crime (that is, the crime so perfect it does not seem to be a crime). He must appear to be in his apartment even as he is, in fact, on the train, "being" someone else.

Forbes, in contrast, does not want to be two people at once: the criminal and his apparently innocent alter ego. He desires an alternative existence defined by the fanciful transformation of his family life: he and Sue sailing the South Seas without a care and without any responsibility for raising a family. Forbes longs for an authenticity and selfhood that, he feels, life has denied him. Like many of the characters in more conventional social melodrama, however, he discovers that the ties that bind him cannot be loosened, even for a moment, without immense pain and suffering, both for him and for his loved ones.

Walking indifferently into his office that morning, Forbes discovers a private detective named MacDonald (played by a very threatening-looking Raymond Burr) waiting for him. MacDonald has been investigating an embezzlement case for the company, which was forced to pay out heavily on the loss and is eager to recover whatever it can. Bill Smiley (Byron Barr), the embezzler, stole the money to buy impressive presents for his beautiful girlfriend, Mona Stevens (Lizabeth Scott), whom MacDonald, as he admits, has fallen for. With this information, Forbes proceeds to Mona's apartment to discover exactly what Smiley gave her. Taunted by an angry Mona about his company-man detachment (exactly the self he is now unhappy with), Forbes makes an impulsive decision. To convince Mona he is not a heartless automaton, he invites her for a drink; she counters with an offer of an afternoon on her speedboat, one of the "presents" received from Smiley. Though he is obviously taken with her (as she gets dressed he thumbs intently through her model's portfolio of seductive photographs), the attraction of abandoning work and breaking his routine is stronger.

The boat trip, while fun, is hardly Forbes's dream odyssey to the South Seas. The speedboat must return to port (eventually to be repossessed by the company), and Forbes must go back to his wife. But an early evening spent in a dark bar lowers his defenses. Mona is no femme fatale, yet she is alluring, available, and needy—exactly the kind of forbidden fruit that would appeal to this jaded insurance man, desperate for a boost to his ego. She asks if there is anywhere he has to go; he lies and says no, unable to acknowledge his attachments.

The Pitfall's straying husband finds a beautiful woman to satisfy his dream of escaping a dull domestic routine, but he cannot evade the surveillance of the jealous detective who wants her for himself. Courtesy of United Artists/Museum of Modern Art, Film Stills Archive.

The fantasy he enjoys briefly with Mona is a freedom from responsibilities, the prospect of a kinder (because less regulated) self. Forbes's dinner with Mona ends with him creeping back silently into his shadow-crossed bedroom while his trusting wife sleeps soundly. MacDonald, however, has tailed him and tries to warn him the next day at work. The warning does not take. Determined to tell Mona himself that her boat will be repossessed, Forbes returns to her apartment that night. Vulnerable and alone, Mona is seduced by his unexpected demonstration of solicitude ("You're not at all like the man who walked in here yesterday"). They become lovers.

Once again MacDonald has followed him to Mona's apartment. He trails Forbes home, confronts him with his indiscretion, and beats Forbes senseless to underscore the point. Forbes is barely able to stumble inside, where he tells Sue he was waylaid by two men with a grudge, convincing her not to call the police. The episode is humiliating: Tommy feels a need to apologize for his father's apparent weakness as the doctor called in on the case leaves Forbes with a "prescription for boxing lessons." Forbes has left his briefcase, symbol of a continuing commitment to work and responsibility, behind in Mona's apartment. She tries to return it to his office but, discovering he is out sick, drives to his house, where she overhears Sue and the doctor talking. Humiliated, Mona leaves.

Recovered a few days later, Forbes makes a date with Mona. She confronts him with his deception and breaks off their relationship. Forbes is relieved to have gotten off easy, and another scene in the family kitchen dramatizes his psychological renewal. We never discover whether it is the fear of a dangerous involvement or the pleasure received from his "vacation" that has made him content. But sitting at the table with Tommy and making a wooden airplane, he advances to a somewhat incredulous Sue the view that most people do not know how lucky they are. A passionate kiss and embrace between husband and wife completes the image of a now-restored domestic happiness.

His luck does not hold. MacDonald relentlessly pursues Mona and, when she protests, threatens he will go to Mrs. Forbes with what he knows. Frightened for herself and Forbes, she contacts her former lover with the news. In an appropriate turnabout, Forbes waylays MacDonald and beats him senseless, threatening to kill him if there is any more interference. MacDonald, like Forbes, does not scare easily; he contacts Smiley in jail and tells him about Mona's flirtation with

Forbes. Meanwhile, Mona has determined to make her relationship with Smiley work. But when he is released, she finds him angry, distrustful, and obsessed with revenge. MacDonald gets Smiley drunk, gives him a gun, and convinces him to go after Forbes. Smiley goes to the Forbes house that night and, though warned off once, is finally shot dead by Forbes when he enters a second time, gun drawn. The police are convinced by Forbes's story that Smiley was simply a prowler. Overcome by guilt, however, Forbes confesses to Sue about his affair and its unfortunate consequences. She tells him not to cause a public scandal if he wishes to keep his family.

But while Smiley was gunning for Forbes, MacDonald was plotting to take full advantage of the situation. He goes to Mona and makes her listen to the police calls on the radio that reveal the assault on Forbes. Thinking he has in this way neatly disposed of his two rivals, MacDonald is surprised when Mona picks up his gun and shoots him. Wandering the streets all night, Forbes goes to the police to confess and is there informed about Mona's arrest (MacDonald has not died, at least not yet). Though the police do not charge him, he is chastised by the district attorney. If he had simply called them when he knew Smiley was coming, no one would have died and Mona would not be in trouble. As he leaves the building, Forbes watches silently as Mona is led off to jail. Outside, Sue picks him up in the family car and agrees to continue their marriage even though, she says, things will never be the same.

The Pitfall is a cautionary tale, full of characters who tell Forbes he has made a terrible mistake in beginning a relationship with an available and vulnerable single woman. First Mona, righteously angry at his deception, wonders why he is unhappy with what looks to her like a wonderful family life; Forbes has no good answer for her. Then Forbes's superior and close friend, shocked by the fix Forbes is in because of MacDonald's threats, chastises him severely for his stupid indiscretions. Both MacDonald and Sue accuse him at different times, but it is the police captain who most squarely puts the blame for the tragic twists and turns of his involvement with Mona on Forbes's shoulders. The moral strain pervading the film probably results from Toth's involvement with the project. Most famous for his work on westerns with a strong sense of poetic justice (*Ramrod* [1947], *Man in the Saddle* [1951]), Toth also indulged in his other noir projects an urge to examine a protagonist's flaws in the context of established social values, whose validity is never questioned but always reaffirmed.

Toth's support of the social status quo contrasts markedly with Wilder's cynicism and produces a very different kind of noir experience: a terrifying descent into destruction and death that could have been prevented by constant moral vigilance, by defusing any temporary resentment or ennui. For example, in *Guest in the House* (1944) (ostensibly directed by John Brahm but with uncredited help from Toth and Lewis Milestone), a young woman, as an act of kindness, is invited to live in the home of a successful artist. She seduces him, influences the young daughter to be manipulative and grasping, incites the servants into defiant disobedience, and is finally stopped only when her own fears are exploited by one of the family and she commits suicide. This more apocalyptic vision of what happens when familial discontents are aroused by a malevolent outsider makes the same moral point as *The Pitfall*: a household must defend itself against those who would pull it apart.

The Pitfall, we might say, both reverses and problematizes the pattern of identification found in *Double Indemnity*. In Wilder's film, the spectator's sympathies lie with those who would destroy the family, which is shown to be hardly worth saving; in fact, the narrative's most innocent and conventional character, Lola Dietrichson, is herself dissatisfied with her father's imperiousness and her stepmother's coldness, and when we first see her, she is doing her best to escape to her lover's arms. *The Pitfall*, in contrast, constructs John Forbes as both the discontented wage slave who seeks excitement and release outside the marriage bond and the outraged head of the family who does his best to preserve his happy home. Conversely, his affair with Mona is both the tonic needed to strengthen his failing commitment to wife and son and the exterior, illicit attachment that eventually brings a homicidally minded gunman to the family door. *The Pitfall* is thus more melodramatic than *Double Indemnity*: its ultimate concern, like that of *Guest in the House,* is with the continuing safety and well-being of the bourgeois family.

And yet *The Pitfall* is more noir in its realization of a world outside the family home, an alternative to domestic life that, however dangerous, still exerts a strong appeal. The initial sequences of the film develop a good deal of sympathy for the harried Forbes, whose dissatisfaction is presented, and convincingly, as generated by the benefits of bourgeois living: a family that loves and needs him but in the process stops him from surrendering to caprice and a need for adventure; a standard of living that affords comfort but demands constant work to pay the bills; a job that offers security but requires unending commitment to sameness and constancy. Forbes's life is indeed a trap because security and comfort have their price. His role as breadwinner does not afford him the freedom and release associated with the underside of middle-class life he encounters most tellingly in Mona Stevens's apartment. While his wife sends him off that morning to earn a living for the family, Mona encourages him to indulge his desire for a break, even manages to furnish a boat, if not the one of his dreams. Sue is pretty but a known quantity apparently concerned more about Forbes earning a living than indulging any dream for an escape from responsibility. Mona, a criminal's mistress, is beautiful and exotic, and she needs Forbes not to support but to protect her; her vulnerability requires him to be a man of strength but also a rule-breaker. At first unsympathetic to her situation, which he regards somewhat disdainfully, he comes to feel sorry for Mona when she associates his indifference with dutiful obedience to company regulations. He not only enjoys a ride on her boat but, hoping she can keep it, neglects to list it on his report when he returns to the office.

But the world to which Mona belongs only apparently and deceptively offers the release from routine and obligation Forbes seeks in his adolescent daydreams. The other side of middle-class respectability is actually a dangerous ground where unrestrained sexual desire leads almost inevitably to murder. Unlike many films noirs, *The Pitfall* constructs sexual violation as more male than female. Mona is beautiful but trustworthy; she does not try to seduce Forbes or use her charms on MacDonald to get what she wants. She responds to Forbes with honest and unpremeditated emotion and seems eager to cater, in a domestic way, to his needs. Perhaps, under different circumstances, she could have become his wife. The sequence where she drives to Forbes's house on a mission of mercy does not contrast Sue with Mona so much as it establishes that Forbes already has one wife and does not need another. Mona painfully realizes that the world of respectable middle-class life makes no room for her, and Toth, using point-of-view editing, makes the spectator sympathize with her rejection and pain. Unlike Sue, Mona did not meet the right man at the right time. Smiley, she says, was the first to offer marriage, but he was unable to support her without embezzling money; his expensive presents, all of which must be returned, index the futility of a coupling based on spurious luxury rather than on honesty and hard work.

The initial crime results in a chain of others. Smiley's indiscretion brings MacDonald and Forbes into Mona's life. The genuine affection she feels for Forbes then makes it impossible for her to get rid of MacDonald. Like Forbes, she desperately tries to preserve appearances and restore balance to a life gone wrong. The two are equally prisoners of virtue at different points in the story. Mona and Forbes, however, are unable to prevent further wrong and scandal. In this netherworld of duplicity and unbridled desire, nothing can stop MacDonald from continuing to pursue what he wants. Forbes gives him a thorough beating, but the fight is no judicial combat; it does not deter MacDonald from convincing another to do the dirty work of killing his rival. Mona tries to patch up her relationship with Smiley, but she cannot put right the damage done by MacDonald, who can only be stopped by another crime, one that, we are led to believe, will land Mona in prison. Forbes, in turn, tries desperately to save appearances and Smiley, but jealousy proves too powerful a motive.

Ironically, the police initially believe Forbes was simply defending his home against a prowler; yet Smiley is an avenging angel who has come not to destroy the middle-class home but to punish the husband's invasion of his own life and space. Essentially a virtuous man, Forbes cannot stand the strain caused by constant deception. His conscience makes him tell the truth, and he is lucky enough not to be charged with a crime. Being a middle-class homeowner gives him the right to kill Smiley; but Mona, lacking those same claims on respectability, is culpable for shooting MacDonald. Significantly, Sue picks Forbes up only after he has been released; this seems to be the precondition for her limited forgiveness. Forbes has extricated himself from the claims of that other world of desire and danger. Chastened, he is driven home.

For all its obvious concern with poetic justice and conventional morality, *The Pitfall* is very much a film noir according to Borde and Chaumeton's definition. Though it represents the unpleasant consequences of immoral behavior, the film hardly reassures. Forbes's behavior is condemned by a number of moral spokesmen, and yet his transgression is presented sympathetically. Even Sue seems surprised that a man who has led a completely respectable life with the exception of only a 24-hour lapse has managed to bring such troubles down upon his head. The violation of rules both marital and professional seems venial at first but leads him eventually to murder against his will. Respectable middle-class life thus generates the forces that can easily destroy it. Its repressed underside—a world inhabited by beautiful, needy, and available women and desperate, threatening men—is close at hand. Forbes enters that world simply by doing his job and forgetting himself a little. Like Walter Neff, he becomes the prisoner of his own desire and dreams, deeply wounded by his rebellion, however temporary, against conventionality and virtue.

CRISS CROSS

Like many noir melodramas, *The Pitfall* implicitly treats class politics, contrasting two environments: a suburb of single-family homes to which white-collar husbands drive their new automobiles after a hard day working in city offices; and an urban landscape of apartments inhabited by unattached women, jails, seedy detective agencies, and, inevitably, cocktail lounges. This urban landscape in *The Pitfall* has no independent existence but functions symbolically as the immoral correlative of happy family life, as the locus of an attractive but destructive otherness.

And yet gloomy images of that "dangerous and sad city of the imagination" dominate films noirs as a group, providing the usual setting for its stories of desperation, alienation, and failure. A masterful example is Robert Siodmak's *Criss Cross* (1949), which relocates *Double Indemnity*'s melodramatic narrative of adultery and betrayal in a hostile and unpleasant urban jungle: a Los Angeles both real (the exterior sequences shot in that city) and contrived (the claustrophobic studio interiors where many of the film's scenes are played out). Here the impersonal public spaces of a modern megalopolis—bus stations, roadhouses, drugstores—provide the perfect visual correlative to a narrative of deadly romantic attraction. No comfortable suburb exists in *Criss Cross* as an alternative environment of financial success, marital bliss, and social stability. Just as the main character fails to escape his fate—an inextinguishable passion for a duplicitous woman—so the grim mise-en-scène offers no refuge or protection. Even a hospital room cannot afford the crippled hero safety, cannot prevent him from being abducted and driven to his destruction.

The serie noire novel by Don Tracy (1935) is expertly adapted for the screen by Daniel Fuchs, who worked on a number of other noir projects with strongly fatalistic themes, including *Panic in the Streets* (Elia Kazan, 1950) and *Hollow Triumph* (Steve Sekely, 1948). The film opens with what proves to be an ironic visual motif: an airplane traveling shot of nighttime L.A., the camera knowingly searching for the story it will tell. Its restless and seemingly effortless gaze locates a static scene: a nightclub parking lot where a couple, Steve (Burt Lancaster) and Anna (Yvonne DeCarlo), embrace nervously in the shadows, avoiding the glaring headlights of a passing car as they anxiously discuss a plot against her husband. "You'll see, it'll be just you and me, the way it should have been from the start," she says, her beautiful and sensual face in close-up as she looks into the camera and her lover's eyes. The look he gives her is full of trust and hope. The scene shifts inside to the slickly dressed nightclub owner, Slim Dundee (Dan Duryea), who questions his wife angrily and intently as she returns to him.

Steve enters the establishment through the bar, where he meets a cop and friend, Pete Ramirez (Stephen McNally). Ramirez warns him to stay away from Dundee, who is hosting a going-away party because he plans to move to Detroit the next day. Ignoring his friend, Steve confronts Dundee, and they fight until Ramirez breaks it up, threatening to arrest Dundee, who is apparently a well-known criminal. When Ramirez leaves in frustration, the fight between Dundee and Steve is revealed as a setup designed to deceive the police. Actually, Dundee's gang and Steve are planning to rob the next day the armored car that Steve drives. But there is bad blood between Steve and Dundee, and the issue is Anna, who used to be married to Steve but now is Mrs. Dundee.

In the morning Steve starts out on his run with an older guard named Pop (Griff Barnett), whom he obviously likes. As they drive toward the rendezvous with the rest of the gang, Steve remembers Anna's words from the night before, triggering other memories of some eight months before, narrated in flashback. A streetcar drops a solitary Steve off in downtown L.A. In voice-over, he says he has traveled all over the country in an attempt to forget and has only returned now that he is "over" what happened. Certain that he will not see her, he confesses that he could not help himself, that it was "all in the cards" and could only go "one way." He goes to his mother's house, discovers no one home, and suddenly finds himself in the "Round-up," which, he says, was their old place. Ramirez comes in and takes his friend back home, where he enjoys a reunion dinner with his brother Slade (Richard Long) and mother (Edna N. Holland). But the temptation to see "her" (Anna is as yet unnamed) proves too strong to resist. He watches Slade and his girlfriend embrace, recognizes what he is missing, and returns to the nightclub. There, in the midst of a crowd of sweaty dancers doing the mambo, he sees Anna, her body moving wildly to the sensual beat. Anna spots him in the crowd, and they talk about their marriage and subsequent divorce. Unable to get along, they shared an evident sexual passion and apparently still do. When Dundee comes to sit beside her, Steve leaves angrily, rejecting Anna's plea that he give her a ring sometime.

So she has to make the first move and does, arranging a meeting at a soda fountain. They argue but decide to see each other. Steve goes with Anna for some time, despite the warnings of his mother and Pete Ramirez, who try to tell him she is no good. He does not listen. One night they are to meet at the Round-up, but when Anna does not show, Steve has to learn the bad news from the bartender: she has run off and married Slim Dundee. Four months pass, and Steve thinks he has gotten over Anna this second time. But a chance encounter in the Union Station (where she has seen off Dundee) reunites the couple. At his apartment, Steve accuses her of being a tramp, and Anna says that she abandoned Steve because Ramirez warned her off, saying she would wind up in prison if she kept seeing her ex-husband. Then she strips off her blouse to show Steve the marks of Dundee's beatings and, feeling sympathy and passion at the same time, he makes love to her.

Steve gets drunk and confronts Ramirez with what he has done; Pete says that seeing Anna can only lead to his being killed. Steve replies: "I'm going to do whatever I want to, see Anna whenever I please." Anna goes to Steve's apartment, and the lovers discuss their desperate situation: no money, no place to go, no way to escape the anger of Dundee once he knows Anna has left him. Working in the strangest of ways, destiny affords them a way out. Dundee and his gang have discovered Anna's deception and are waiting for the couple when they go downstairs. To provide an alibi for her presence, Steve tells Dundee he is eager to team up with him to rob the armored car he drives. He contacted Anna and asked her to meet him because he could not get in touch with Dundee directly. Though Dundee does not believe this improbable story, he is interested in the caper Steve

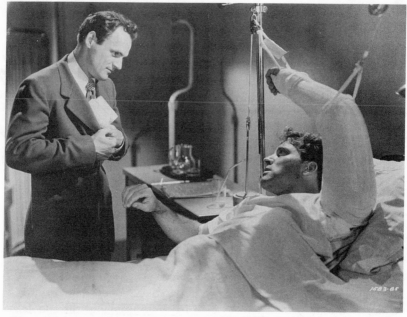

Wounded during the bungled robbery, the crippled hero of *Criss Cross* is easily deceived by the hired killer who will soon deliver him to destruction. Courtesy of Universal-International/Museum of Modern Art, Film Stills Archive.

proposes. A gang is assembled and plans are made for the hijacking, which, Steve and Anna think, will provide them with the money and opportunity to escape Dundee. At this point the flashback ends.

Steve and Pop drive into the trap planned by the gang. As they park the car to deliver the payroll to a factory, a smoke bomb goes off and the guards are attacked by the gang, who are secreted in different parts of the area. Pop is killed, and it becomes apparent that his erstwhile comrades plan the same fate for Steve. But he fights them off, saves half the money, and, though shot in the arm, retreats safely into the car. When he wakes up in the hospital, Steve discovers that everyone considers him a hero, including his loving family, who leave when Ramirez comes to visit. The sharp detective has figured out the gang's scheme and tries to get Steve to admit his guilt and finger the others, who, quite apparently, have betrayed their partner.

But Steve refuses, and when Ramirez leaves he is left all alone in the corridor, except for a man he sees waiting on a chair outside. The nurse introduces him as a father anxious about family members injured in an auto crash, but, once she leaves, he reveals himself as one of Dundee's men. Steve is bundled up into a car and driven toward the gang's hideout. In desperation, he attempts to bribe his captor with money from the holdup, still in Anna's possession, and tells him how to find their secret rendezvous. When they arrive, Anna is obviously surprised and upset to see Steve. Knowing of the gang's plans to double-cross Steve, she had double-crossed the double-crossers. Telling Steve that she only cares for her own safety and well-being, Anna attempts to abandon him to his fate. But Dundee arrives before she can exit and shoots the doomed couple dead as Anna tries desperately to find protection in Steve's embrace. Dundee, wounded also during the robbery, limps toward the door and is himself killed by police.

Like many noir productions of the late 1940s and early 1950s, *Criss Cross* is a somewhat contradictory text. As originally planned by the producer, Mark Hellinger, the film was to be a meticulously realistic staging of a complex robbery. This kind of material was officially prohibited by the Production Code, presumably to avoid having the entertainment film become a training document for would-be criminals, but it was increasingly allowed during the postwar era, as a growing number of similar productions attests, the most notable being Stanley Kubrick's *The Killing* (1957). It was the prospect of doing a gritty caper film that attracted Burt Lancaster to the project. But Hellinger died unexpectedly during preproduction, and as a result, *Criss Cross* became more of a vehicle for Robert Siodmak's thematic obsessions, although the film, with its frequent use of actual locations, does still have a realistic look. Siodmak's other noir films, notably *The Killers,* also thematize his interest in the destructiveness and irrationality inherent in a man's romantic attraction to a beautiful but immoral woman. Fatal attraction is the central element of the noir crime melodrama, but with its emotional rather than environmental view of human nature, that theme has little direct connection to the sociological perspectives of late 1940s realism. This impulse to record the collective discontents of contemporary urban life is best realized in Hellinger's *Naked City* (1948). Influenced profoundly by the films of Italian neorealism (many of which, such as *Paisan* [1947] and *Bicycle Thief* [1948], did unexpectedly good business in the United States), this American realism, perhaps inevitably, became expressed largely through the established crime genres. *Criss Cross* exemplifies how often noir films of this period are characterized by contrary intentions: on the one hand, they represent the public sphere, but on the other hand, they probe the inner world of characters trapped by illicit or irrational desire.

Siodmak's central thematic concern as a director was perhaps derived from the later stages of German expressionistic cinema, with which he had been involved at the beginning of his career. He was fascinated by the subjective self for whom the exterior world figures as merely the objective correlative of inexpressible feelings and drives. In *Criss Cross,* Siodmak uses first-person, flashback narration to create such a self. This technique does not figure in many noir films simply to personalize the narrative, as is commonly thought. Consider its effects in Wilder's tale of murder and betrayal. In *Double Indemnity,* Walter's confession objectifies all that he had spoken silently to his friend and coworker during the investigation; it contains what he could not say to Keyes when he was hoping to get away with murder and fraud. Just as the film demonstrates that what characters attempt to hide must come to light, so Walter fittingly chooses to tell his own story; in doing so, he converts thought into dialogue and is able to rejoin the world of objective, social relations. It is appropriate in this regard that he returns to his office and dictates a "memorandum" to Keyes. As he sits at his desk, Walter solves the case and saves his company from loss. Thus he regains the self he was forced to deny as part of the plot—which required him, we remember, to be someone else, to be, in fact, a dead man. Revealing himself reconnects the private to the public, the subjective to the objective. Social relations become dominant over emotion and inner speech. Through that confession the shadowy "someone else" of Keyes's speculative reconstruction of the crime becomes Walter Neff, insurance salesman and murderer.

First-person, flashback narration is used quite differently in *Criss Cross*. In *Double Indemnity*, the achronic reordering of events, in the classic manner of in medias res construction, allows the story to begin with a crisis (the fact that the main character is seriously, perhaps fatally, wounded), then build back toward it, and finally go forward to a resolution. Siodmak, however, discards the obvious advantages of in medias res construction for creating suspense. The film positions Steve's flashback at a point in the narration (just before the armored truck is robbed) when the increasingly exciting progress of events is for some time retarded. Hence suspense is lost, not created.

The onset of the flashback radically and suddenly alters the point of view of the narrative; this seems to be the effect Siodmak is after. From the opening airplane panorama of a nighttime Los Angeles to the disparate but connected events at the Round-up on the eve of the robbery and the morning preparations of Steve and his partner, the director deliberately avoids creating the impression that the unfolding drama belongs in any special way to Steve. The initial rendezvous of the guilty lovers in the parking lot does not privilege either his body or speech. Back inside the club, the camera focuses first on the manager, then on Ramirez at the bar; the angry confrontation between Steve and Dundee is not even represented. Ramirez hears a commotion and rushes to a private dining room, where he finds the two men in the obvious aftermath of a scuffle. The following sequence, in which the gang contemplates the next day's events, likewise does not privilege Steve. He is shown as part of the group and is not even in the frame as the scene begins. Unlike most classic Hollywood productions, which construct a main character from the outset, *Criss Cross* initially adopts the sociological perspective of Hellinger's brand of cinematic realism: the film's story appears collective, offering every character a significant role to play.

The flashback decisively undermines this objectivity. A seemingly neutral shot of Steve driving the truck unexpectedly becomes subjective as the camera dollies in to a close-up of his worried face; at the same time, his thoughts suddenly become "audible" on the sound track. In *Double Indemnity*, the narration and flashback are motivated by Walter's desire to tell Keyes the truth. As spectators, we readily accept Walter's role as the major source of the story because he takes over the function of narrating (from the film's unseen and impersonal initial storyteller) at such an early point. Walter, in other words, is a plausible narrator; the film's investment in his subjectivity seems a by-product of his memorandum, not an arbitrary privileging of his consciousness. As someone telling the story in which he himself is the main character, he can hardly avoid relating it from his point of view. For the spectator, this subjectivity is revealed by the complex relationship between the evoked story world (the past, where Walter is only a character) and his represented moment of dictation (a present in which he is the narrator with an ability to comment or correct). A disjunctive relationship between narration and story world establishes the duplicity of Walter's actions: his narrating self reveals that, as he is doing or saying one thing, he is actually thinking something entirely different. A further irony is that Walter now says what earlier he had only thought, thus furnishing, if only in retrospect, a public, accessible version of his experiences.

In contrast, Steve is not a plausible narrator, for he possesses no narratee; there is no one to whom he wishes to confess or reveal the mess he has gotten himself into. He has nothing to say, except to himself, and the sudden access to his thoughts that the film provides the spectator is thus somewhat shocking and disorienting. Similarly, the sudden privileging of Steve undermines the coherence that more objective forms of narration had been affording the story. At first, it seems that the complex, multilayered series of events (the opening scenes construct a confusing series of related spaces and introduce six speaking characters) will culminate in the robbery. But then the narration becomes an exploration of personal memories that, initially at least, have little to do with the film's ostensible subject.

The effect is nothing less than to deconstruct the film's realism, which is dependent on an impersonal handling of collective behavior, the gang and the seedy, morally ambiguous nightclub equally functioning as microcosms to be represented and understood. Unlike *Double Indemnity, Criss Cross* features a voice-over narration that produces a conjunction; the subjectification of image and sound reveals the deeper truth of Steve's experiences, the desperate sense in which every twist and turn seems inevitable (as it must from the temporal viewpoint of his narrating), determined by some all-controlling and malevolent chance. Steve's narration does not correct or amplify what is said in those moments he remembers; the voice-over is used almost exclusively over images unaccompanied by dialogue, images of a brooding, silent self. Because it is not part of a dialogue, moreover, this narration appears to be a "pure" realization of Steve's thoughts, a truth about his inner feelings that can be made available only in this way. The visual style in the flashback corresponds to its intense subjectivity. The framing consistently privileges Steve and makes him the dominant, often the only, figure. Moreover, Siodmak uses sustained point-of-view editing at the crucial moment when Steve, returned from his wandering across the country, enters the Round-up at night and spots Anna on the dance floor. Probably because of concerns about the Code, Anna is pictured only in a tight medium shot or close-up; her lower body is not shown. But a concentration on her sensual expression and obvious pleasure is steamily erotic and provides an unspoken yet convincing motive for Steve's obsession.

The flashback transforms the spectator's initial view that the armored car robbery is simply an objective fact, a type of criminal behavior characteristic of the menacing world evoked from a distance in the opening panorama. Steve, we learn, comes up with the plan to steal from his employers only when Dundee has trapped the guilty couple in a tryst. Unlike Walter Neff, who desires the chance at an illicit score more than Phyllis does, Steve cares more about Anna than about the crime's potential reward. The caper is in fact only a pretext to permit continued access to Anna. And yet Steve's deception of Dundee fittingly expresses his feelings for Anna and hers for him; the robbery and its aftermath allow the inner truth of their relationship to be expressed and hence resolved. Steve is willing to risk everything for Anna, and the robbery gives him a chance to act on that resolution. Anna, at the same time, looks out for her own welfare. Incapable of love, she can only betray, not only the man who wants to use her (Dundee) but the one who truly loves her (Steve).

When the flashback ends, the viewer must view the unfolding of the robbery less as a series of exterior events than as the working out of ambiguous motives, divided loyalties, and dangerous emotions. Appropriately, the sequences detailing the actual crime are stylized, deliberately unrealistic. A bird's-eye camera shows the truck moving toward its destination from a directly overhead position; at this ironic distance, what is happening seems beyond the control or understanding of the human characters involved, all of whom are in some sense trapped by the illicit relationships that bind them. The robbery itself, which begins with the explosion of an underground smoke bomb, takes place in a deadly mist where Steve is pursued by one former comrade after another until, wounded, he struggles back with his money bags into the truck. The strangely balletic movements of these fog-enshrouded figures, including gang members equipped with otherworldly gas masks, epitomize the film's concern with disguise and deception.

The closing scenes of *Criss Cross* treat these themes even more ironically. Steve thinks he can buy off Dundee's messenger with part of the money from his share, which he thinks Anna is keeping for him at their rendezvous. But the security he thereby purchases is illusory. Finding himself apparently safe with his girl and the loot, he realizes that she cares nothing for him, was in fact intending to leave that very night alone to make good her escape with the money. Considering herself beyond discovery, Anna realizes when she sees Steve stumble out of the car that her plans are ruined. Dundee, she reasons correctly, had expected Steve to bribe his messenger and in this way lead him to Anna and the money. When Dundee enters with a gun, she now asks the man she had betrayed to save her life. Dundee is himself thwarted when the police arrive and shoot him dead; they had apparently trailed him as he trailed Steve.

Steve, unlike Walter Neff, is not redeemed from his selfishness by a desire to preserve innocence. During the robbery, he becomes a hero by accident; seeking only to save himself, he winds up keeping his former gang from making off with part of the loot. Once again trying to save himself, he seals his own fate, and Anna's too, by stupidly leading Dundee to the beach house. Anna is no better. Phyllis is permitted a last-minute conversion to love. Anna, in contrast, chooses greed over her evident passion for Steve, who, unlike Walter, was not at first simply a means to a monetary end. The film's final scene is an apocalyptic one hardly typical of mainstream Hollywood production. *Criss Cross* ends with an embrace, but it is hardly romantic. Evildoers have been punished, but the largely innocent character with whom we have identified is destroyed by events beyond anyone's control. The desire of the protagonist thus goes for nothing. All he achieves is his poetically just but disquieting self-destruction.

CHAPTER 3

Discovering the Darkness:
The Noir Detective Film

The three noir films we examined in the last chapter are equally melo-dramatic in a central sense. Crime and its consequences are viewed from a middle-class perspective, that is, as phenomena not ordinarily a part of law-abiding, (petit) bourgeois existence. In such films, a frightening but alluring urban landscape functions as the locus of un-fulfilled desire, as the place where urges that cannot be satisfied within the confines of respectability can (if only perilously) be acted upon. The crime melodrama characteristically images the illicit, the illegal, and the erotic as an otherness apart from safer forms of living—in particular, a family life defined by marriage and parenthood. *Double Indemnity* is somewhat unusual in this regard. In this film, the other-ness where Walter and Phyllis play out their desperate game has no independent existence; it is, instead, a deceptive layering of the osten-sibly upright lives both plotters lead. Walter and Phyllis create and sustain their private world by the secret protocol to murder and de-fraud that defines their relationship. The deadly lovers do not seek a different mode of life; we never discover what they plan to do with the money once they get it. Rather, their sole aim is to commit the crime that is perfect because it conceals the identity and actions of the criminals involved.

The Pitfall and *Criss Cross,* by way of contrast, create worlds di-vided into areas of respectability and illicitness or criminality. In both films, crime is the social outcome of inner, moral failing. John Forbes violates his marriage vows and fails to take his work seriously; the result—though not the intention—is that two men are shot and a woman he cares for must pay for a violent crime committed, to some degree, on his behalf. Returned from his wandering, Steve is bored by the placidness of life in the family home, a life that excludes him from sexual desire; a telling sequence shows him reclining on the couch alone, looking longingly at his brother and a girlfriend kissing. As in *The Pitfall,* the violation of respectable standards and values brings him unwillingly into crime. Meeting a married woman in his mother's house, Steve is trapped by her husband and conceives the plot for the armored car robbery in order to save appearances. As a result, his close friend, a respected senior colleague tellingly named "Pop," is killed and his own life is destroyed. Interestingly, *Criss Cross* establishes an immediate connection between moral or rational behavior and crime. Pete Ramirez tells Steve that Anna is a no-good tramp he should stay away from; when Steve disregards his friend's advice and is trapped by his own recklessness, Pete becomes the policeman who correctly identifies him as the criminal. In melodrama, reason and propriety constitute the law, the force and penalties of which are not required in a universe ruled by poetic justice; Ramirez leaves Steve in the hospital to his fate, which soon overtakes and crushes him.

In all three crime melodramas, the male characters who are destroyed or punished fail to act rationally. Walter should know from his experience in the insurance business that the fraud he contemplates cannot be pulled off, and yet he disregards caution to pursue a self-destructive desire. The film's most telling image of Walter's irrationality is furnished by the closing sequence: fatally weakened by blood loss, he still attempts to escape from the police but proves unable to walk more than a few steps. Like Walter, John Forbes is tired of being good and tries to satisfy his childish impulses in spite of their impracticality. Steve is even more obviously a victim of emotion; he is so in love with Anna he will do anything to be with her, even plan a crime he does not have much will to commit. Steve dies because he cannot resist what should be resisted, cannot remain in and be satisfied by the normal, respectable world from which he comes. Walter and John share similar fates.

The type of noir film we will examine in this chapter lacks—or at least, plays down—the moralizing perspective of melodrama. In these films, most often derived directly from serie noire detective fiction, criminality is not imaged as a willful fall into a different and self-destructive form of living; nor does the noir detective either come from or discover an area of comforting middle-class life that provides an alternative to the sinister environment he customarily inhabits. The noir detective discovers darkness everywhere, finds it to be life's ruling principle, and learns that even the rich and privileged are usually no better than the poor and deprived. In the battle between good and evil, the greater strength is wielded by the latter. This fictional world is not ordered by poetic justice but by an amoral determinism. People are inherently evil and self-centered. Death comes unexpectedly to all. Chance, not intention, governs human experience. Any tracing of crime to its source is thus insignificant, a triumph not of virtue but of the detective's relentlessness and cunning. The bleak America where the private dick practices his profession holds out no real hope for a restoration of order and justice. Here crime results from the pathological pursuit of gain; it is the preeminent and inalterable fact of life, not a social or moral problem.

As many commentators have noticed, John Huston's version of *The Maltese Falcon* (1941) set the pattern for such cinematic fiction. At the film's end, the conspirators discover that the priceless jeweled statue they have been struggling over is, in fact, a worthless copy. Rather than conclude that their quest is hopeless folly, however, they resolve to track down the genuine item, disregarding their own safety and paying no mind to what others may have to suffer. Only the duplicitous woman is made to bear the legal costs of their misadventures, which include three murders. She is handed over to the police by her erstwhile lover, the detective Sam Spade (Humphrey Bogart), who gives up the woman he loves because he prefers looking out for himself. This grim world, governed by the rule of red tooth and claw, is imaged again and again in the films we are about to examine.

MURDER, MY SWEET

To some degree, *Murder, My Sweet* is an imitation of *The Maltese Falcon,* whose somewhat surprising popularity at the box office convinced Hollywood producers that American audiences were eager for this kind of story. However, the significant differences between the two reveal Edward Dmytryk's film to be more typically noir; in fact, it would be the progenitor of many similar productions during the next ten years or so. *The Maltese Falcon*'s Sam Spade is an older, somewhat more world-weary version of Dashiell Hammett's fictional hero, but the Bogart portrayal is otherwise quite faithful to the novelist's vision. Though amoral and deceitful, Spade is an intelligent manipulator who skillfully plays the different villains off one another until he manages to extricate himself successfully from their machinations at the very end. In the process, he solves the case, but this epistemological triumph is less impressive than his mental and psychological ones, which climax in his total domination of the thieves he falls among. *Murder, My Sweet*'s detective is a very different kind of character.

The film derives from Raymond Chandler's *Farewell, My Lovely* (1940); Chandler was much influenced by Hammett, but his Philip Marlowe only vaguely resembles Spade.[1] John Paxton's screenplay emphasizes these differences. Spade is a survivor whose cynicism about human nature is a handy tool that permits him to master and even, at least to some degree, control his world. He cares about no one but himself. Spade feels comfortable with his alienation, his unswerving distrust of others, his disbelief in either generosity or virtue. Marlowe, on the other hand, while cynical and world-weary, is a less able manipulator or interpreter. As played by Dick Powell, he furthermore lacks Spade's self-confidence and mastery of others. His signal virtue is relentlessness. At one point in the narrative, Marlowe has been knocked out by a blackjack, pistolwhipped in the face, choked unconscious, and shot full of narcotics. Though as of yet he understands little of what is happening to him and others, he is still eager to pursue the case. As another character tells him: "You go barging around without a very clear idea of what you're doing. Everybody bats you down, smacks you over the head, fills you full of stuff. And yet you keep hitting between tackle and end." Marlowe agrees with her assessment: "I don't know which side anybody is on. I don't even know who's playing."

Marlowe's confusion is matched by that of the spectator. Like Chandler's novel, the film's narrative seems a haphazard tangle of seemingly unrelated episodes that fall into a clear pattern of Aristotelian cause and effect only at the very end. I offer an especially detailed summary here (and of the two similar films discussed in this chapter) in order to afford the reader an accurate idea of this narrative complexity. It is in this feature of his fiction that Chandler differs most tellingly from his model: *The Maltese Falcon* develops a gallery of characters whose common goal, the acquisition of the falcon, is revealed at a fairly early stage; the complexity of the film resides in the multilayered performance with which Spade hoodwinks the crooks, constantly playing them off one another through appeals to their greed while he exploits their mutual mistrust.

The opening sequence of *Murder, My Sweet* deploys images that attest to the difficulty involved in discovering where the truth lies. The credits play through shots of a police interrogation; three shirt-sleeved men sit around a table looking intently at a blindfolded fourth. The camera surveys this grouping, then tilts, in a seemingly random fashion, to focus on the unshaded bulb overhead, a light so bright the screen becomes completely white. Dmytryk apparently plays here with the common metaphor of "shedding some light" but deconstructs its usual meaning, showing instead that the more light there is, the less one can see. The stylistic turn, like several others in the film, is clearly derived from German expressionism. Harry J. Wild's photography constructs a visual environment entirely suitable to Chandler's narrative, which, like a nightmare, evokes a reality that is hardly sociological but rather the correlative of fear and desire. As his work on such other noir projects as *Macao* (Josef von Sternberg, 1952) and *Johnny Angel* (Edwin L. Marin, 1945) demonstrates, Wild was adept at producing murky, blurred images that suggest lurking and unidentifiable dangers. The realism inherent in the novelist's story of frustrated desire, venality, and the all-destroying drive of a woman to find and maintain social respectability is modulated by Dmytryk's expressionistic mise-en-scène. Thus what seems to be an objective world is in many respects a projection óf the subjective self. The world of *Murder, My Sweet* is never naturalistic or plausible, but nightmarish—real only in the sense that it realizes terrifying thoughts and secret desires.

Consider the story that the blindfolded man, Philip Marlowe (Dick Powell), is persuaded by his interrogators to relate. His unlikely tale suits exactly someone who has been deprived, if only temporarily, of his sight and made a prisoner by his own guilty-appearing actions. Marlowe's flashback projects failure, isolation, and frustrated desire. Having just given up as a lost cause the pursuit of a wandering husband, the detective returns late at night to his shabby downtown office, where his thoughts turn to a woman. He calls her and she's busy. So he sits and drinks, hoping she'll break her date and call back. Then, as Marlowe looks out the window, a huge face appears in one of the panes, but the neon light flashes and the face, just as suddenly, disappears. Like a signal, it reappears only to vanish once more. This mirror image of his own unsatisfied needs, this insubstantial messenger

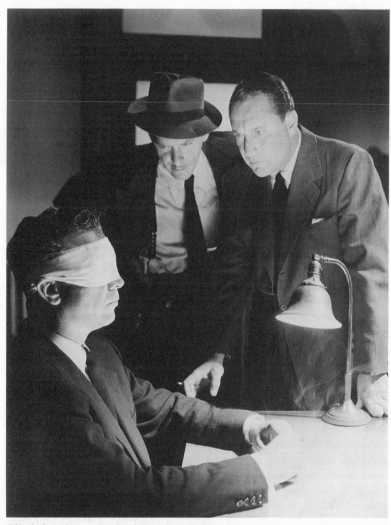

Blinded and suspected of murder by the police, *Murder, My Sweet*'s Philip Marlowe must talk fast to save himself. Courtesy of RKO/Museum of Modern Art, Film Stills Archive.

who summons him to adventure is a hoodlum named Moose Malloy (Mike Mazurki). Just released from prison, Moose wants Marlowe to locate "his Velma," or so the detective infers from the giant's almost incoherent speech. Marlowe ignores the ringing phone on his desk and exits with Moose in pursuit of a woman who obviously betrayed her lover but remains his dominating obsession. Interestingly, this quest will end with Moose's desire forever thwarted but Marlowe's unexpectedly fulfilled.

Marlowe at first takes charge of the investigation but soon proves incapable of dealing with a rapid succession of bewildering events. The pair go to the nightclub where Velma used to work, but no one there can offer any help even though Moose knocks over a few tables and threatens the bartender. Marlowe proceeds alone to interview the former owner of the club, an alcoholic woman named Jessie Florian (Esther Howard), who says she has never heard of Velma. But Marlowe finds a signed photograph of Velma in her room and, as he leaves, sees Jessie, obviously quite upset, calling someone on the phone. Apparently on to something, Marlowe is at this point side-tracked by another offer of work. An overdressed and effeminate man named Marriott (Douglas Walton) hires him to be his bodyguard while delivering money to thieves in exchange for some stolen jewelry. Marlowe accompanies Marriott to the rendezvous, is knocked unconscious by a blackjack, and awakens to find Marriott dead, his skull crushed by repeated blows from the same weapon. Given two assignments, Marlowe has so far failed at both.

The detective, however, is more than a victim; found alone with Marriott's corpse, he becomes the prime suspect in the man's murder. But Marlowe persuades the police that he had nothing to do with the crime. They tell him that Marriott worked for Jules Amthor (Otto Kruger), an underworld figure with high-society connections. But he does not act on the tip. Instead, returning to his office, the detective is confronted by a woman claiming to be a reporter who wants more information on the Marriott case. As Marlowe quickly discovers, however, she is Ann Grayle (Ann Shirley), the stepdaughter of the woman whose jewels Marriott was apparently sent to retrieve. A quick trip with Ann to the Grayle mansion (Marlowe: "It wasn't as large as Buckingham Palace") introduces the detective to the old and feeble Mr. Grayle (Miles Mander), a collector of fine jade, and his much younger, somewhat vulgarly flirtatious wife. Helen Grayle (Claire Trevor) makes sure that Marlowe gets a good look at her impressive legs. Alone with her, Marlowe receives yet another offer of work: she wants him to get back the missing jewels. But when she comes to his apartment the next night and invites him out to a local nightclub, he soon finds himself abandoned. Ann Grayle, however, mysteriously arrives to offer him $1,000 to halt the investigation. Then she too disappears when Moose Malloy comes in and hustles Marlowe off to a meeting with an unnamed man who Moose thinks will help him find Velma. Event follows event with the associational logic of the unconscious while Marlowe, like a dreamer held captive to his own secret desires, is carried along with the flow, always reacting, never acting. Unlike Spade, he never takes charge of the situations in which he discovers himself.

Instead, Marlowe himself becomes the object of yet another inquiry whose meaning escapes him. The man Moose wants him to see turns out to be Jules Amthor, the polished and, like Marriott, somewhat effeminate gangster who had appeared at the Grayles' just as Marlowe was leaving. Amthor tries to get information from Marlowe about the jewels but, failing this, allows Moose to choke the detective for not finding Velma. Amthor is disgusted by Marlowe's suggestion that he and Marriott had been working a scheme to seduce and rob rich, lonely women. And he tells Marlowe that the detective is "a dirty stupid man in a dirty stupid world"—a description that would suit equally well all the male characters in the story's rogues' gallery, including Amthor himself. When Marlowe recovers from Moose's throttling, he strikes Amthor, who strikes him back with a pistol across the face, knocking the detective unconscious.

At this point, as in the earlier scene where he was blackjacked, Marlowe's thoughts and feelings are expressed by subjective images—the shot of him knocked down dissolves into swirling shapes, while other shots offer surreal vistas, including that of an anxious Marlowe pursued by Moose's disembodied head, trying to make his way through a series of closed doors. It is as if these violent encounters, even as they separate Marlowe from the slippery and perilous world of consciousness, offer him a distilled version of its nightmarishness. The strange dreaming that a blow to Marlowe's head produces conjures up an allegory of his experience. The dream is waking reality, and waking reality is the dream. The continuity between the two states is especially marked in the next sequence. Marlowe comes to in a cell where a malevolent orderly shoots him full of drugs. The air, he thinks, is thick with a strange mist or haze, just as it had seemed to be when he was asleep. (This effect is created by a spotty filminess superimposed on the image.) Marlowe, however, fights the haziness, overpowers his guard as well as the resident "physician," and finally escapes into the street, where the seemingly ever-present Moose forces a taxi driver to give him a ride to safety.

Recovered, Marlowe begins to take action to solve the mystery that is threatening him in so many deadly ways. He goes to Ann's apartment, expecting a delegation of police at his own. But the cops, mysteriously, locate him there anyway, and he is forced to tell them some of what he has discovered. They allow him to remain free, and he goes immediately with Ann back to the Grayle house to discover what he can about the necklace. They arrive in time to prevent Mr. Grayle from shooting himself in the head; the old man is ashamed that the police have been questioning him, and he suspects that his wife has been involved in crime. Grayle begs Marlowe to stop the investiga-

In *Murder, My Sweet* the private eye is tempted but never deceived by the apparently helpless beauty of the femme fatale. Courtesy of RKO/Museum of Modern Art, Film Stills Archive.

tion, but when he and Ann leave the old man, Marlowe persuades her to go with him to the beach house, where they suppose Mrs. Grayle may be found. Ann is reluctant to go on. She says: "You take some sort of horrible satisfaction in seeing people torn apart," an indictment more properly leveled, perhaps, at the spectator enjoying this film.

At the beach house, Marlowe and Ann acknowledge that they are attracted to one another, but then Mrs. Grayle arrives and leads Ann to think that she and the detective are romantically involved. Ann leaves Marlowe alone with her stepmother, who proceeds to tell him that she is being blackmailed by Amthor because of her past. She begs Marlowe to kill her tormentor, and he leaves, inexplicably, to embark upon another mission. At Amthor's house, Marlowe finds the man already dead—with a broken neck, suggesting that Moose had questioned him a bit too roughly. Puzzled, he returns to his office and runs into Moose, who tells him that the woman in the detective's picture of Velma (taken from Jessie Florian) is, in fact, not her.

Finally he solves the puzzle. Marlowe returns to the beach house, correctly concluding that Mrs. Grayle is Velma. Once there, Marlowe figures out that Velma had made up the story about the stolen jewels (they are not really missing) in order to get him alone so that he could be killed. Jessie Florian had warned Velma that a detective hired by Moose was looking for her. Because Marriott and Amthor were indeed blackmailing her (Velma had been Moose's partner in a crime that he took the rap for but could still hold against her), they were eager to prevent Moose from uncovering Velma's identity and thereby ruining their livelihood. So Velma intended to kill both Marriott and Marlowe but was able at that time to eliminate only one of the men who threatened her safety. With Marriott and Amthor dead, only Marlowe stands in her way. She draws a gun, intending to kill the nosy detective, who, though he has solved the case, proves unable to take charge of it.

But Ann and Mr. Grayle arrive in time to stop her. He fools his wife into thinking that he is on her side and takes the gun. But then he shoots Velma, disgusted by the evil, twisted thing she has revealed herself to be. Waiting outside, Moose hears the shots, sees his Velma dead, and tries to kill Grayle, who puts two bullets into Moose but not before taking one himself. Marlowe grabs for the gun to prevent Moose from being shot but is blinded by the muzzle flash and does not witness the final outcome.

This unlikely tale secures Marlowe's release. The police are joined by Ann, who does not signal her presence to Marlowe. He asks repeatedly about the fate of the "kid," meaning her. A detective, followed silently by Ann, leads him to a waiting taxi. Marlowe proves his good faith by returning the jade necklace given him by Velma. Ann persuades the detective to leave and sits beside Marlowe, whose sense of smell reveals the true identity of his fellow passenger. He asks for a kiss, and the couple embrace as he removes his gun from its holster and drops it on the seat beside him. Marlowe, now very much the gentleman, obeys unasked Velma's earlier expressed view that he shouldn't kiss with a gun in his pocket.

The disavowal of male power that makes possible this happy ending is true to the spirit of Chandler's novel, if not to its letter. In the book, Marlowe does not get the girl, but the detective is concerned with rescuing and preserving innocents, especially women, not only in this novel but in the others of the series that feature him as main character. Marlowe's world-weariness has its romantic, genteel side. His perseverance, unlike Spade's, is not fueled by the simple joy of mastering weaker, more venal others. Because he detests the pervasive corruption of his world, he does not quit. *Murder, My Sweet* rewards the detective for such virtue; the various adventures he passes through are thus so many tests that seem designed at the end to qualify him for the bounty he receives. The final test, of course, is Ann, her presence unknown, hearing what Marlowe really thinks about her so that she may judge accurately the genuineness of his lovemaking. Like a hero from a chivalric romance, Marlowe negotiates this trial of his truthfulness and wins the hand of the fairy princess.

Of course, this ending is also Hollywood's way of saving appearances by presenting "compensating moral value." The formula was a simple one. If the story was weighted toward the sympathetic presentation of evil (such as the depiction of a world nearly devoid of goodness or conscience), then the film would be certificated by the PCA only if it offered something in the way of an offsetting goodness. Transforming the novel's morally ambiguous Ann into a good woman and coupling her with Marlowe, who himself comes to stand for truth and against self-interest, constitutes such a moral balancing act.

At the same time, however, the film as a whole still strongly makes Chandler's original and despairing point that American culture, from top to bottom, is sick with anomie, mindless pursuit of self-interest, and obsessive psychopathology. Marriott and Amthor are superficially respectable parasites who live well by blackmailing a woman with a shady past. (Chandler's homophobia, undoubtedly shared by most of the film's original viewers, gives the villainy of these two characters a sexual dimension.) Grayle is a narrow-minded, weak, and pathetic old man interested only in his possessions; for him, the jade he collects and the trampy young wife whose affections he has purchased are equivalent objects. All brawn and no brains, Moose is willing to do anything, even murder anyone, to get back the woman with whom he is romantically obsessed. As in *The Maltese Falcon,* these despicable characters relate to one another only through greed and selfish desire; it is entirely fitting that they kill each other off until only Marlowe and Ann are left alive. But what world outside the fallen city where the story is set would these two virtuous characters be able to live in? What will Marlowe do now that he has given up the investigation of vice? The ending saves the pure in heart, but for what? The nightmare ends, and yet the film offers nothing to take its place.

In *The Maltese Falcon*, the criminals are motivated by greed, by the desire for the object that proves worthless once attained. (The novel and hence the film have an easily readable Marxist subtext, which critiques the acquisitiveness of capitalist society.) In *Murder, My Sweet*, however, the chain of crime can be traced to quite a different source: the desire of an evil woman to attain, through means nefarious and cruel, a position of social eminence. Because she is beautiful and appealing (Claire Trevor's performance exudes a sluttish sensuality), Velma can make Moose do her bidding, including suffer alone the punishment for joint crime.

That same beauty and appeal enable Velma to transform herself by marrying Grayle. And yet, having become a woman of wealth, Velma cannot settle completely into her new social station. Indiscretion brings Marriott and Amthor into her life, and as a result, she faces exposure unless she pays blackmail. Even more serious, perhaps, is the threat posed by Moose, who seeks the fulfillment of Velma's promise and is too obsessed to realize that this manipulative woman wants nothing further to do with him. Velma is at the center of all the crime, deceit, and suffering in the story. She is hardly the victim she initially makes herself out to be, but a clever manipulator who aims to deflect all threats to her bogus identity as a respectable woman. Through a poetically just reversal, Velma is destroyed by the very man who gave her social legitimacy. Velma, however, is first stopped by the man who can resist her charms and unravel her plots, by the detective not fooled by the spider woman's lies, charm, and sensuality. Marlowe puts a name to her evil, and Grayle punishes it.

Together they end the menace offered by the upwardly mobile woman who uses her beauty to attain position and wealth and remains coldly aloof from the passion she excites in men. On the level of the film's engagement with chivalric romance, the evil stepmother is destroyed so that the imprisoned princess may marry her handsome rescuer. The film's misogyny, in other words, makes the femme fatale not only a selfish criminal but a barrier to the good woman's happiness. Hammett offers a Hobbesian nightmare of unrestrained greed; Chandler and Dmytryk blame all evil on an Eve, a whore who does not know her proper place and wants to pose as an honest woman, disrupting family relationships and breaking the circuit of normal desire.

D.O.A.

When *Murder, My Sweet* was in the early stages of production, it was decided that the novel's original title, *Farewell, My Lovely,* could not be used since it offered no firm indication of the film's genre. This marketing problem was exacerbated when the lead role went to Dick Powell, previously most often cast as a song-and-dance man in films such as *42nd Street* (Lloyd Bacon, 1933) and *The Gold Diggers of 1935* (Busby Berkeley, 1935). The producer's choice of a substitute was apt. Like many noir titles, *Murder, My Sweet* accurately reflects the obsession of dark cinema with the connection between romance and crime, love and death. Desire leads to crime, and crime leads to what Chandler, in perhaps his most famous Marlowe novel, terms "the big sleep," the not always unwelcome prospect of annihilation that haunts all his stories.

In the crime melodrama, death figures as the rightful punishment for those who fail to be rational and moral. But in the noir detective film, death is the final truth of the human condition, the limitation placed on desire and action, the reality we all flee from but must finally face. Chance, which obeys no moral law, determines who will die and when; no one (but the detective, of course) escapes this iron rule.

Perhaps the bleakest and most ironic treatment of this theme in dark cinema is Rudolph Maté's *D.O.A.* (1950), a film that makes it clear why film noir appealed to French intellectuals, who were much influenced by the existentialist ethic then fashionable on the Continent. In the classic detective story, the detective remains, by convention, invulnerable, a character protected from the evident dangers of the world whose mysteries he seeks to solve. Interpreter of the signs and traces of the crime, he remains beyond the reach of the criminal, who always proves powerless to prevent his detection through force or violence. As we have seen in *Murder, My Sweet*, hard-boiled detective fiction transforms the rules that govern the detective's action. No longer presented with a case to be solved, the hard-boiled detective like Philip Marlowe becomes inextricably involved in an unfolding complexity of evil and deception. He is always jeopardized by his discoveries and must often act decisively to save himself, using not only mental but physical powers. No longer simply a thinking machine skilled in the solution of enigmas, the hard-boiled detective is a complete protagonist, a hero with whose trials we identify fully (an effect heightened by the frequent use of first-person narration). The investigation is his adventure, and its outcome testifies to his virtue.

Like a number of other films in the noir canon, *D.O.A.* develops the detective character further in this direction by making him more fully a part of the noir netherworld. If *Murder, My Sweet* is a nightmare, then Philip Marlowe is the dreamer who awakes intact from the worst he can imagine. Throughout the narrative, in fact, the detective's escapes and endurance are equally implausible but required by the fact that, as in a dream, the dreamer's fictional reflex—the self that is a character in the vision—cannot be destroyed. *D.O.A.*, in contrast, offers a reality in which the worst can and does happen; the film's hero comes to the end of his adventure, learns the truth about his life, and dies. Like Marlowe, he negotiates successfully the various tests that constitute his passage through a world of illicit desire and hidden violence; unlike Marlowe, he cannot "live happily ever after," for his exercise of ingenuity, strength, and resolution can gain him nothing. He is a dead man when he begins. As he says: "I'm not alive. I can stand here and talk, but I'm not alive."

The film's opening credits play against a sequence dominated by a stark contrast that structures the film. The camera tracks a man (Edmond O'Brien) walking with determination through the realistically photographed streets of Los Angeles until he arrives at the police building. He enters and goes straight to the homicide department, where he announces that a murder has been committed. The police lieutenant asks him who was killed. The man answers, "I was." The assembled detectives are hardly shocked by this revelation since their San Francisco colleagues have warned them to be on the watch for a certain Frank Bigelow. The man admits he is Bigelow and then sits down to tell his story.

The forceful realism of images and dialogue is counterpointed by the richly romantic scoring of Dimitri Tiomkin. Music is especially important in this film since it often cues the spectator to the interior, emotional reality of the characters. As often in the studio film, the music serves as the objective correlative of Bigelow's feelings and establishes a disjunction between the everyday banality of life in the big city and the poignant tragedy of this man's experience. In this sequence and others throughout the film, the "benign indifference" (to borrow a phrase from Camus) of real locations photographed in a documentary fashion contrasts with the subjective life of the hero, who becomes passionately occupied with the meaning of his existence in a world he had previously taken for granted. If Dmytryk's film, with its obvious debt to expressionism, conjures up an exterior reality that is the projection of the hero's desires and fears, then Maté's does quite the opposite. Here the solidity and givenness of real space provide the only possible, but at the same time quite inappropriate setting for a tragic drama of solitary, frustrated desire. D.O.A. shows that the world is not what we would wish it to be.

The flashback begins (D.O.A. eschews voice-over) with Bigelow, some two days earlier, finishing up business in an office where his coworker, Paula Gibson (Pamela Britton), is desperately in love with him. This opening offers an intensely eroticized series of images: Bigelow at his desk and on the phone; an attractive female client sprawled over the papers by his elbow; Paula and the woman exchanging deadly glances and making barely polite conversation about topics other than the real one on their minds.

Initially, the narrative is melodramatic, concerned only, as the mise-en-scène suggests, with male and female roles. Paula is Frank's girlfriend of long standing; she had hoped they would be married by now. But Frank is shying away from commitment, ostensibly because of a bad experience in his past, but more obviously because he cannot yet agree to monogamy. Living in Banning, a small California town, where he enjoys a steady companion, Frank is evidently bored and has therefore arranged a solitary "pleasure trip" to San Francisco, a trip he has "neglected" to tell Paula about until the last minute. Paula does not want him to go, correctly fearing that Frank intends to spend his time with other women. Finally, however, she agrees to send him off with her blessing, hoping, as she tells him, that this adventure will help him make up his mind about her one way or the other.

The San Francisco in which Frank arrives for his vacation answers to his desire for a world without strings and commitments but full of desirable women who find him irresistible. Checking in at the hotel, he is struck dumb by the number of unescorted, attractive, and obviously friendly members of the opposite sex. He leers unabashedly, while his unmistakable sexual desire is mockingly echoed by a wolf whistle that blows brashly on the sound track. Walking toward his room, Frank literally has to pick his way through a crowd of beauties who seem as eager for uninvolving involvement as he. Inside his room, he leaves the door open so that he can observe the somewhat wild party across the hall. An overanxious female guest careens into his room by mistake, but Frank is soon asked to join the party, where he is drooled over by an overdressed and drunken saleswoman who proclaims her desire to have fun before resuming her role as a housewife.

This group soon finds the perfect setting for its revels: a waterfront jazz joint appropriately named "Jive" where a black quintet plays wild bebop to entertain an audience of hipsters and tourists. (The sequence in the nightclub draws on all Maté's skills in designing mise-en-scène; wild gyrating figures enjoy what amounts to a musical orgy. Ernest Laszlo's photography is equally skilled; the images, including some striking ultra-close-ups of the musicians' faces, have an otherworldly quality emphasized by the rapid montage sequence into which they are organized.) Tired of the overamorous drunk he came with, Bigelow drifts toward the bar, shadowed by an unknown figure, a tall, thin man so muffled in hat, coat, and scarf that his face remains invisible. At the bar, Bigelow picks up a pretty woman who communicates in no uncertain terms her sexual interest. Absorbed in conversation with her, he does not notice the tall man switching drinks with him. But he does discover that something is amiss when, after draining his glass, he tastes the wrong liquor. Assuming the bartender has made a mistake, Bigelow thinks nothing more about it and leaves the club with the phone number where his attractive new friend can be contacted later that evening.

Bigelow's behavior at the club exemplifies his divided state of mind. Put off by the too obvious and somewhat vulgar attentions of the woman he came with, he looks for another companion and finds someone with a bit more class and poise who resembles Paula. We discover, however, that when he returns to his room, his desire for this woman is just as easily dismissed. On his wardrobe is a vase of flowers sent by Paula, along with a note in which she confesses she will always love him. Bigelow looks fondly at the flowers and reads the note with a smile; he takes out the paper with the phone number written on it, compares it to Paula's note, then tears it to shreds, which he dumps in the wastebasket. The decision Paula had hoped he would make in her favor has been made. Bigelow undresses and goes to bed—alone.

Bigelow's story has hardly begun before it appears to have arrived at a happy ending. The opening frame, however, tells us that this happiness must be an illusion, that there must be "something more." The screenplay by Russell Rouse and Clarence Green is, in fact, deliberately deceptive, suggesting as it does initially that Bigelow's story has everything to do with the understanding and policing of desire. The film appears to offer a narrative about a man who must be content with the limitations imposed by true feelings (influenced by conventional morality) on his sexual urges. The true subject of the narrative, however, has yet to emerge, though the mysterious appearance and actions of the muffled figure correctly hint at the workings of an arbitrary, capricious malevolence. Rouse and Green were inspired by the late expressionist film *Der Mann, Der Seinen Mörder Sucht* (The Man Looking for His Own Murderer) (Robert Siodmak, 1931). In fact, *D.O.A.* reflects much of the existential anxiety and terror that figure as central themes in its model. (Having started his career as a cameraman in the Weimar cinema, working first under the renowned Karl Freund, Maté was very drawn to such narrative, which depends on interesting photographic effects as well as on nonstop action.)

The real problem life poses, the film suggests, is not that the best outlet for the satisfaction of desire must be found, but rather that an unreasoning annihilation may crush dreams and hopes at any moment. Obviously, the central fact of death makes irrelevant any question of desire. It does not matter whether Bigelow loves Paula if he is about to die, as the protagonist now discovers he must. Waking up, Bigelow feels strangely ill. At a doctor's office, he is first told that his health is perfect, but then a blood test prompts a different diagnosis: he is suffering from luminous poisoning, a condition that, beyond cure at this point, will kill him in the space of a day or two. Hysterical,

Bigelow rejects the doctor's report as madness, but a second physician confirms the original diagnosis. There can be no mistake: Bigelow has been murdered by a luminous poison slipped into his liquor glass.

Struck by terror, he races across downtown streets, mindless of passing streetcars, automobiles, and pedestrians. This sequence was apparently filmed not only on real locations but without any interference in the street life, which, captured by Laszlo's tracking camera and hard-edged, documentary-like photography, has an impressively authentic quality to it. Here anxiety and despair are brilliantly evoked by the obverse of expressionistic technique: the mise-en-scène does not "respond" to the protagonist's state of mind, is given no stimmung or mood to express. San Franciscans, going about their daily business and unaware they are being filmed, ignore the desperate man who runs in panic but to all appearances from nothing. Out of breath, Bigelow stops at a newsstand: on his left, a young couple meet, embrace, and go merrily about their business, and on his right, a display for *Life* magazine is prominently featured. Symbolism and realism combine happily here. Bigelow is caught between two levels of understanding, two ways of living: the drama of romantic fulfillment in which, until that morning, he was himself absorbingly involved; and the drama of existence, summed up by the single word *life,* whose full meaning he is just beginning to comprehend. Life is always lived in the shadow of death, experience can only end in the inability to act, and will and desire are limited by forces beyond any individual's control.

Murdered but not yet dead, Bigelow finds himself in an unusual circumstance: he can, if he chooses and proves equal to the task, discover who killed him. The doctor's remark that he has been murdered echoes in his head and makes him determined to act. From an overly amorous businessman seeking some relaxation and release in the big city, Bigelow is transformed into a hard-boiled detective, but of a special kind. Marlowe and Spade take on other people's cases; Bigelow attempts to solve his own. Like the heroes of conventional narratives, Marlowe and Spade survive to triumph, not simply by avoiding death or arrest but by learning the truth. Moreover, this truth often saves them; for example, Marlowe's story convinces the detectives to release him from any responsibility. Bigelow, in contrast, can triumph but will not survive; any truth he can discover will not avail because he is dead already, the victim of a plot that he can understand but not defeat. Yet Bigelow must solve the case because, still alive, he must do something, must choose to act, even in the awareness of rapidly approaching nothingness.

Frank begins by retracing his steps in hopes of uncovering some clue to the mystery. The jazz club is closed and the revelers across the hotel hall have returned to their everyday lives, but a chance remark from Paula puts Bigelow on what proves to be the correct track. She calls his room to tell him that a Eugene Philips, who the day before had been anxious to contact Bigelow about some business matter, is now dead. Suspecting a connection, he flies immediately to Los Angeles to interview Philips's business associate and widow in the hopes of discovering what the dead man, whom Bigelow cannot recall, wanted to discuss with him. Neither Halliday (William Ching), the company comptroller, nor Mrs. Philips (Lynn Baggett) is able (or willing) to provide any help, but Philips's brother Stanley (Henry Hart) does. He tells Bigelow that his brother leapt from his apartment window because he was despondent over not being able to prove his innocence in a criminal charge. Philips had sold some iridium, a rare metal, to a Mr. Majak, and the iridium turned out to be stolen, though Philips swore he purchased it himself from someone else, a George Reynolds.

Back at his hotel, Bigelow learns that Philips had contacted him earlier in the year to notarize a bill of sale involving some iridium provided by George Reynolds. Now realizing his connection to the Philips case, Bigelow returns to Mrs. Philips and asks why her husband did not use the bill of sale to establish his innocence. She replies that the bill of sale was mysteriously missing from his office files and Philips's attempts to locate George Reynolds proved in vain. Convinced that the company secretary, Miss Foster (Beverly Campbell), knows more than she revealed during their initial meeting, Frank returns to the office and manhandles her until she tells him that Philips had been anxious to talk to Marla Rakubian on the day he died. Bigelow finds Marla (Laurette Luez), apparently Philips's mistress, in the midst of packing her bags and in possession of a one-way ticket to Buenos Aires. Thinking that she acted with Reynolds to set up Philips, Bigelow sets out after Marla's apparent accomplice, taking her revolver along for protection. At one stop, he is shot at by a rooftop sniper, and after returning to his hotel, he is abducted by three hoods, including the obviously psychopathic Chester (Neville Brand).

They drag him off to talk to Majak (Luther Adler), the man who bought the iridium from Philips. Bigelow tells Majak that he suspects

The fatally poisoned hero of *D.O.A.* will escape from these sadistic thugs, only to die anyway. Courtesy of United Artists/Museum of Modern Art, Film Stills Archive.

Reynolds killed Philips and poisoned him, but Majak proves him wrong, pointing out that Reynolds was actually Raymond Rakubian, Marla's brother, and has been dead now for several months. In a particularly grisly scene, Majak shows Bigelow the inscribed funeral urn containing Rakubian's ashes. Majak sadly informs the dying man that he has been sidetracked but, having learned too much about the connection between Majak and Philips, must now be killed right away. Sent off on a ride with Chester from which he is not meant to return, Bigelow escapes when Chester is gunned down by a policeman as he attempts to kill his erstwhile prisoner in a drugstore.

Returning to his hotel, Bigelow finds Paula awaiting him. He despairs: "All I did was notarize one little paper, one little paper among hundreds." But he does not tell Paula that he is dying, leaving her instead with the illusion of his return. "Something," he says, "has to happen for a man to realize what he loves." Paula, however, hardly seems consoled by this admission that Frank indeed loves her. He leaves her in tears and for the last time.

At this point, Bigelow thinks, incorrectly, that Miss Foster and Stanley Philips are behind his own murder and that of Eugene Philips. (Bigelow no longer believes his leap from the balcony was suicide.) When he goes to Miss Foster's apartment to confront her, he finds Stanley sick with the same symptoms he had initially felt. It seems that Miss Foster, going through Philips's desk at the office, had discovered a love letter from Halliday to Mrs. Philips. Confronting Halliday, Stanley was surreptitiously poisoned; Bigelow warns him to get quick medical attention. Returning to the Philips apartment one last time, Bigelow threatens Mrs. Philips with the same fate her husband suffered. She quickly confesses that Halliday pushed Philips off the balcony and was forced to poison Bigelow because he could attest to Philips's innocence and thus call into question any motive for suicide. Bigelow encounters Halliday in the darkened office building, finding him dressed in the same strange costume he wore on his mission of death in San Francisco. Halliday draws a gun, but Bigelow shoots straighter and kills him. His story at an end, Bigelow himself falls dead in the homicide office, with Paula's name on his lips.

D.O.A., like many noir films, contests, even violates, some of the important norms of Hollywood narrative construction. The ordinary studio product offers a story in which the protagonist with whom the spectator identifies successfully completes the mission the script provides him with, achieves romantic fulfillment, and, as the lights fade and the music swells, goes on to live happily ever after. This conclusion is made plausible by a nearly invariable principle: the good are rewarded and the evil punished. Since the protagonist is by definition good, his successful negotiation of obstacles in his path is assured. The beginning of *D.O.A.* offers, in miniature, a standard Hollywood story of romantic attraction, difficulties in the relationship, and successful coupling. The remainder of the film, in contrast, develops a series of events that, though at first unconnected to Frank and Paula's romance, ironize and deconstruct it. Frank is not poisoned because of his excessive wanderlust and ennui, but because of an insignificant gesture he had performed unthinkingly (and safely) hundreds of times before. Thus, though the film separates the nightmare landscape of license, deception, and murder (imaged by two urban settings) from the banal everyday, this distinction is effectively undercut. Danger and death are everywhere and, ultimately, can be neither escaped nor overcome.

D.O.A. constructs, often using real locations, a darkness of unreasoning violence and terror where the innocent are victimized. Bigelow, guilty of nothing but being in the wrong place at the wrong time, is surreptitiously poisoned by a hooded figure who resembles the grim reaper. The events in which he becomes entangled, moreover, are set into motion by the double betrayal of yet another (at least somewhat) innocent party. Eugene Philips is first duped by Majak and Rakubian (disguised as George Reynolds) into selling stolen property. But then his business partner and wife, who have already deceived him with their sexual liaison, take advantage of his vulnerability and murder him. Philips himself, of course, is guilty of adultery with Marla Rakubian, who, in turn, was setting him up for her brother's intrigue with the stolen iridium. Stanley Philips, discovering the relationship between Halliday and his brother's wife, almost suffers the same fate as Bigelow but is saved when the dying man sends him off to the hospital for treatment. Majak orders Bigelow to be killed even though he was "sidetracked" into thinking Rakubian, himself already dead, was the sniper who shot at him from the roof. Bigelow may be innocent of the complicated plotting set in motion by the gangster, but he must die nonetheless.

In *Murder, My Sweet,* Velma's machinations and acts of violence are all motivated by a desire for self-preservation; in other words, they make sense. In *D.O.A.,* Halliday and Majak are such characters. But the later film offers another, quite different construction of violence, principally figured in Chester, the Majak underling who kidnaps Frank from his hotel. As Majak tells Bigelow, Chester derives great pleasure from inflicting pain and, in fact, is truly happy only when he is hurting someone. Taking an instant dislike to Bigelow, the laughing psychopath (a brilliant and intense performance by Neville Brand) taunts the dying man by poking him in the stomach, painfully tender because of the poison. In his eagerness to carry out Majak's orders (he intends to shoot Frank in the gut so that he will die more slowly), Chester allows his prisoner to escape. Then, frenzied and out of control, he incautiously starts blasting away at Bigelow in the middle of a crowded drugstore. Blinded when the shopkeeper hits him in the head with a perfume bottle, he is easily cut down by a policeman. But Chester's irrationality is hardly an inappropriate response to the world constructed in the film, where random, unexpected, and undeserved violent attack is the order of the day. Maté's vision is bleak. The only hope the film offers is the true love Bigelow finally understands he feels for Paula. But in this case, love conquers nothing and, like the desire that fuels it, proves finally irrelevant.

In the course of investigating his own murder, Frank Bigelow becomes a violent and, at times, abusive person, so single-minded in his pursuit of the criminal that the rights and sensibilities of others cease to matter. Rushing to Los Angeles, he rudely interrogates Halliday, though he has no reason to suspect the man has done him wrong. Even more unfeeling, he breaks in on Mrs. Philips and asks why her husband jumped from the balcony, a question that reduces her to tears and earns the rightful rebuke of the dead man's brother. Paula, abandoned in Banning, is left in the dark about her lover's sudden desire to track down Philips and is so upset by his behavior that she eventually flies to L.A. herself to see him. The more Bigelow discovers, the more violent and uncaring he becomes. Returning to the Philips office, he knocks Miss Foster around because he suspects she did not tell him the whole truth. Her subsequent revelation leads him to Marla Rakubian, with whom, once again, he resorts to violence to get his way. Finally, in his last encounter with Mrs. Philips, Bigelow, holding her roughly, threatens to throw the frightened, apparently defenseless woman off the balcony to her death. After getting the best of Halliday in the shoot-out, Bigelow pumps four more bullets into the body, in a paroxysm of violence emphasized by the director's isolation of the frenzied hero within the frame. Bigelow's resemblance to Chester is striking here.

Murder, My Sweet offers a deadly world in which violence is committed by the manipulative femme fatale against those who threaten her position. Velma cracks Marriott's skull with the blackjack and attempts to do the same to Marlowe. Amthor is killed by an impassioned Moose, but Velma, we learn, wished him dead and wanted Marlowe to do the deed. It is Velma who pulls the gun on Marlowe, intending to eliminate the last person able to expose her; Grayle turns the weapon on her, but this is simply a poetically just reversal. Significantly, in the final shoot-out, Marlowe is only a victim, not a participant; he is blinded, moreover, in the act of reaching toward Grayle's gun to forestall more bloodshed. While there is no denying that Dmytryk's film thematizes misogyny in a central way, the story does not feature a revengeful male violence against women. *D.O.A.*, by way of contrast, furnishes its hero with many opportunities to perpetrate (more or less righteous) violence on women who lie, act trampy, or plot with their lovers to kill. Because Bigelow's killer is another man, this violence is obviously misdirected, unless we wish to understand it as part of the protagonist's general rage against the injustice and arbitrariness of the human condition, and against a very obviously flawed human nature. Tempted by sex, the hero finds death instead, and hostility toward women is the result. Thus Bigelow's easily aroused and readily satisfied anger toward "evil" women connects to his invulnerability to women on the make, who are to him simply objects, as evidenced by the scene where he tears up the phone number given him by the beautiful blonde in the nightclub. But this anger and indifference are legitimized by the true feelings he evinces for Paula and by the evident sexual satisfaction their relationship affords—and by, perhaps, her total submission to his desires and moods.

It is interesting that sexual politics is featured so prominently in *D.O.A.* yet figures only indirectly in the way the film works through its central theme. Bigelow is doomed by chance, by the random event beyond his control; his involvement with a gallery of femme fatales and a faithful, understanding lover neither condemns nor saves him. As in *Murder, My Sweet,* the presence of a "good" woman merely lessens the harshness of the world evoked in the film, which may be terrifying because of its indifference to human destiny, but not thoroughly evil.

KISS ME DEADLY

Toward the end of the classic noir period in the mid-1950s, the generic elements whose development we have traced in this chapter found their most potent and shocking expression. As a result, the noir cityscape became even more completely corrupt. The most famous case in point is Robert Aldrich's *Kiss Me Deadly* (1955), a scandalous film based on a notorious novel by the most infamous of serie noire writers, Mickey Spillane. On the one hand, this film extends the destructiveness wrought by the ruthless pursuit of self-interest to national politics; the narrative rewrites Hammett's tale about the disputed possession of a priceless object as a nuclear apocalypse in which the end of the world is the price paid for pervasive weakness and criminality. Here the dark city becomes the nation (imaged by extensive location shooting of contemporary L.A.), whose atomic secrets, mysteriously taken from a government with no apparent power to retrieve them, are transformed into a deadly but priceless object of exchange, the possession of which brings death to all. On the other hand, *Kiss Me Deadly* represents the social apocalypse of failed sexual relations, which is here figured by a misogyny so thoroughgoing that it immunizes the powerfully masculine hero against women (and the kiss of the femme fatale here is indeed deadly). Like *D.O.A.,* Aldrich's film prominently features a hatred of women, responding like many later films noirs to an increasingly insistent theme in American popular culture.

In the immediate postwar era, Mickey Spillane took the hard-boiled detective novel further along the path earlier blazed by Raymond Chandler.[2] His first novel in the Mike Hammer series, *I, the Jury* (1947), traces the revenge exacted by the private detective on the person who caused his best friend's death; the criminal turns out to be a psychotic psychiatrist and Mike's lover as well. In the book's last scene, he forces her to strip and puts the muzzle of a .45 to her stomach. Pulling the trigger, Hammer leaves the executed woman to die in agony. Chandler's fictional universe, of course, is overpopulated by deceitful and vicious women who will stop at nothing to get what they want; again and again in the Marlowe novels, the detective finds crime rooted in a female desire gone wrong. And yet Marlowe seldom responds to this perfidy with violence. Instead, he devotes himself to saving the innocent (who are always women as well) from the machinations of the treacherous femme fatale.

Hammer is also a "knight" in the sense that he proves vulnerable to the desperation of ladies in distress, but unlike Marlowe, he has little compunction in dealing out his own brand of rough justice to wrongdoers of either sex. (The title of Spillane's first novel announces the vigilantism that defines Mike's attitude toward the corruption around him.) Hammer is not above asking women to fulfill his sexual desires—experiencing a good deal of casual sex in the course of his investigations—and has no moral qualms about using them in whatever way he must to get what he wants. We could say that Hammer is in some respects an *homme fatal*—a quality perfectly expressed by his surname, with its twin connotations of phallic power and destructive force. Hammer is more a part of the dark city than either Marlowe or Spade are, but like his fictional predecessors, he also lives by a rough moral code. The Hammer books had totaled 15 million in sales by the mid-1950s, evidencing a previously unparalleled popularity for this kind of fiction.

In transferring Spillane's antihero to the screen, Aldrich and the writer A. I. Bezzerides remained faithful to some aspects only of the Hammer character and the harsh city environment he moves in. The film version of *Kiss Me, Deadly* moves Hammer from the run-down neighborhoods and dangerous alleys of New York to the wide-open urban vistas of a sprawling Los Angeles, a territory that can be mastered only by the automobile. Here crime and criminals are hidden behind a series of outwardly respectable facades: an expensive mansion complete with swimming pool turns out to be the residence of a local mobster; a luxurious beach house provides the setting for torture, betrayal, and unimaginable destruction; the great "whatzit" that the crooks are all after is finally located in a locker at the Hollywood Athletic Club. These areas of deceptive light and affluence contrast with settings more typical of noir fiction; rented rooms in run-down sections of the city, dimly lit and unpatrolled streets that provide hiding places for assassins, a gas station that becomes a place of suffering and death. The use of real locations imparts a stylistic unity to these disparate aspects of mise-en-scène; they do not seem nightmarish or expressionistic. (Aldrich made spare use of chiaroscuro lighting, often utilizing instead framings and compositions that suggest imbalance as well as insecurity.)

Hammer himself is notably transformed. Ralph Meeker's performance emphasizes not only the brutishness and borderline sociopathy evident in the novels, but a slickness that would have seemed out of place in the original New York setting. Like all Angelenos, Hammer is worried about his image: he dresses well and drives a fancy sports car, first a Jaguar roadster, later a souped-up Corvette convertible. His self-absorption suits a developing set of social values that, thanks in part to the magazine of the same name, were to crystallize in this period around the concept of the "playboy." Mike lives in an apartment that Hugh Hefner would have approved of: it is spacious and well decorated, the place where (instead of his office) Hammer feels most comfortable. Neither Spade nor Marlowe has much of a home; unlike Hammer, they work mostly out of downtown offices; Mike spends so little time in his that a crucial letter delivered there escapes his notice until the end of the story.

This evident narcissism, objectified in the right "image," considerably modulates the outer-directedness of Spillane's character. The film's Hammer is no longer much of a detective but, apparently like everyone else in L.A., has become a hustler looking for a big score.

Rather than investigate cases, he manufactures evidence, aided by his secretary, for clients seeking uncontested divorces. In the Hammer novels, Mike falls deeply in love with Velda, his secretary, to whom, by the time of *Kiss Me, Deadly* (published in 1952, the last in the original series of seven books), Mike is quite devoted. He and Velda, in fact, are to be married. The film makes this loving relationship pathological; desperately lusting after Mike, Velda (Maxine Cooper) is teased but never satisfied by his lukewarm attentions. To keep Mike interested, Velda has to "cater" to his clients. She prostitutes herself because Mike asks her to, even as his aloofness keeps her in a perpetual state of sexual excitation. (Throughout the film, Velda unsuccessfully seeks out what might turn her self-concerned lover on.) Hammer's long-standing relationship with Pat Thompson, a police detective, is likewise transformed; these two are no longer friends, but equally selfish operators who display a callous disregard for the safety of innocents caught up in a bewildering and dangerous intrigue.

Viewers of the film familiar only with Spillane's scandalous reputation may be shocked by how Aldrich's adaptation actually deepens the cynicism and pathology evident in the original novel. Most important, the screen version plays down the principle of poetic justice that makes Mike a destructive angel who rightfully punishes the wicked. Despite the sadistic pleasure he derives from inflicting pain and devastation, Spillane's detective is capable of love and friendship; these feelings, in fact, often provide the motive for his missions of vengeance. If he distrusts the punishment that the law provides, it is only because the system is evidently corrupt and works to protect rather than eliminate evildoers. Aldrich's Hammer, in contrast, at first cares about nothing but himself and is shocked by events into only a partial and ultimately ineffectual renunciation of his desire for money. No longer an avenger figure, he is instead a fellow plotter, one of the film's gallery of schemers who, the story's apocalyptic ending suggests, have contrived to turn America's vast potential for destructiveness on the nation itself. Tellingly, the film, unlike the novel, is not about the pursuit of an ordinary object of criminal value (a misdirected shipment of heroin). Aldrich's characters, in contrast, struggle over what they do not understand and cannot finally use, destroying themselves, and perhaps our world as well, in the bargain.

Kiss Me, Deadly opens with a terrified woman (Cloris Leachman), evidently dressed only in a raincoat, fleeing down a coastal highway and looking for a ride. Because the cars will not stop, she steps out into the road and blocks the next one approaching. His Jaguar convertible goes into a spin to avoid hitting this sudden apparition, but Mike Hammer (Ralph Meeker) is unhurt. When she approaches the car sobbing hysterically, Mike offers her a ride but is hardly happy about doing so. "I should have thrown you off a cliff back there," he mutters angrily, admitting that he would not have stopped had she simply thumbed a ride. Almost immediately, Mike and his companion encounter a police roadblock; the highway patrol is looking for a woman, dressed in a raincoat, who has just escaped from a nearby mental hospital. The woman squeezes his hand, and Mike lies, passing her off as his wife.

She is Christina, named after her favorite poet, Christina Rossetti. After thanking Mike for his help, she provides a quick analysis of his character, the correctness of which subsequent events certainly confirm. As evidenced by his taste in fancy roadsters, Mike is a "self-indulgent male" who "never gives in a relationship, only takes." Sarcastically, Christina concludes that "woman, the incomplete sex," needs such a man to "complete her." She tells Mike that she was put in the hospital by "them," who removed her clothes so that she could not escape. If they are waylaid, Christina says, Mike has only to "remember me."

This initial episode offers a radical revision of its novelistic source. In Spillane's original handling, Mike is happy to pick up the frightened escapee. In fact, his dedication to her rescue motivates his subsequent desire to track down the killers and solve the case; *Kiss Me, Deadly,* like all the original Hammer novels, is a story of betrayal and revenge. In the film, Mike's self-satisfied life, imaged by a solitary ride in his expensive car, is violated by an insistently intrusive woman. He has no use for her, especially since she reads him so well (mouthing an indictment not found in the novel). The sequence at the roadblock best exemplifies the changed tone of the film. In Spillane's version, the woman takes Mike's hand and puts it under her coat to feel her nakedness as they approach the roadblock. Mike is insulted by this sexual offer, rejecting it as unnecessary; he is happy to save her from the police simply because she is a woman alone in distress. Aldrich's hero, in contrast, is quite evidently uninterested by the sexual offer. He is likewise unmoved by altruism; he acts from no higher motive. If he saves Christina, it is because at that moment he does not feel like cooperating with the police and suspects that protecting her may be profitable.

Almost immediately, the pair are stopped by criminals who have thrown a barrier across the highway and who, because of the camera angle, are faceless. Mike, beaten senseless, is held in a room where he listens to Christina being tortured (by pliers, it turns out) until her screams turn to silence and she dies without revealing the information the crooks are after. Mike can see only the leader's shoes, which the spectator of this black-and-white film learns later are blue suede. Loaded back into his car with Christina's corpse, the detective is pushed off a cliff but miraculously survives. He regains consciousness with two concerned female faces bending over him; one belongs to his partner and girlfriend, Velda, the other to a nurse. The police question him, but he says nothing. All the shots in this sequence have tilted angles, suggesting that there is indeed more wrong here than perhaps meets the eye, as Mike himself soon discovers.

Released from the hospital, he is immediately hauled in for an interrogation by both federal agents and local police. The investigator in charge completes the characterization of Mike begun by Christina. Hammer is in the business of creating evidence for the divorce courts, rather than discovering it. Depending on the client, Mike either romances wives suspected of straying (or who, for other reasons, are no longer wanted) or sets Velda up with husbands who can be enticed into compromising positions. The payoffs, either "fees" or blackmail, are good. Mike is untroubled by any imputation of immorality or illegal behavior; he obviously has no moral scruples. He tells the police nothing but is inspired by their interest. As he confesses to Pat (Wesley Addy), a cop who knows him, something big must be up. Ignoring the policeman's advice to mind his own business, Hammer instead asks a rhetorical question: "What's in it for me?"

Picking up Christina, however, seems already to have involved him inextricably in these dark doings. Mike stops by the garage owned by his Greek friend Nick (Nick Dennis) and learns that some very tough guys have been there looking for him. He discovers that his apartment is under surveillance by men parked in a car outside; he enters with great caution, only to have Velda, nervous and afraid, call him on the phone with even more news. The next scene shows Mike and Velda embracing, but the detective is obviously more interested in what his partner has to say, namely, that a certain Ray Diker (Mort Marshall) is eager to get in touch with him. Hammer knows that Diker, the science editor of the local paper, has recently disappeared. Pat arrives to tell Hammer that his detective and gun licenses are now revoked.

This rebuff encourages Mike to think even harder that something big might be in this for him.

He drives over to Diker's run-down apartment. Parking his car, Mike is shadowed by a torpedo, who pulls a knife. Mike surprises and disarms his attacker, but the man will not stay down. So Mike beats him mercilessly, and the man falls down a steep staircase, presumably to his death. Mike smiles as if nothing had happened. Diker bears the marks of a recent beating; a prisoner in his own house who is frightened of more violence, he will tell Hammer only Christina's surname and address, not what the crooks thought she knew or had. At the apartment, Mike helps a little old man with a trunk and is rewarded with the current whereabouts of Christina's former roommate, a woman named Lily Carver. Small, blonde, and apparently terrified (the character's little-girlishness is emphasized in Gaby Rodgers's convincing performance), Lily is the very picture of persecuted innocence. Like Christina, Lily is in need of a man like Mike Hammer to save her. She does not give him much to go on, only that Christina, in the last days of her life, became extremely nervous and paranoid. The police finally came and took her away. The crooks call to tell Mike to mind his own business and enjoy the reward for silence he will receive in the morning. The payoff turns out to be a shiny new Corvette convertible to replace the Jaguar wrecked in the murder attempt. The car, however, has two unwelcome and quite optional extras: a bomb attached to the starter and a trickier backup device designed to go off at high speeds. With Nick's help, Mike removes them and then asks his mechanic friend to check who might have engineered such a job. At this point, Mike is sure that he is dealing with some very powerful people and, therefore, that what they are after must be extremely valuable. He finds Velda at the ballet studio where she is working to stay in shape and tells her to forget the penny-ante divorce case he sent her on. Velda says Ray Diker phoned to give Mike two leads, men who have recently wound up dead (as Mike was supposed to do) in unusual traffic accidents. As before, this romantic encounter with Mike leads to no satisfying conclusion for Velda. Her erstwhile lover leaves to continue with his nosing around.

Investigating the first "accident" reveals that the hoods in question work for Carl Evello (Paul Stewart), a local mobster. Arriving at Evello's fancy house—complete with a pool where the boss and his underlings are enjoying the California sun—Hammer is sidetracked by a busty, apparently mindless blonde who seems to want nothing but

In *Kiss Me Deadly* Mike Hammer must compete with local hoodlums for the great "whatzit." Courtesy of United Artists/Museum of Modern Art, Film Stills Archive.

Mike's amorous interest; like the other women in the story, she fails to arouse it. Hammer puts one of Evello's hoods out of action with a judo move, and the mobster decides that he will have to deal with the detective. An attempted payoff fails, however, and Hammer leaves with Evello's pledge that he will not receive any further offers. Mike still has not located the man with the blue suede shoes.

Almost immediately, he learns from the friend of the other man killed in a traffic accident that the victim was an engineer and a scientist who apparently had something the hoods wanted. Returning to check on Lily, Mike discovers her crouching furtively in the stairwell, afraid of the men who, she says, came looking for her in the night. Meanwhile, Nick, working underneath a car, is approached by the man with the blue suede shoes, who releases the jack, crushing him to death. To keep her safe, Mike brings Lily to his apartment. She embraces him, but he pushes her away and proceeds to the garage. (In the novel, Mike falls for Lily, and she rejects his somewhat rough attempts to seduce her.) Shattered by Nick's death, Mike finds Velda unexpectedly in bed in the afternoon, and she intimates that being in bed at strange times is a result of the jobs Mike makes her do. Angry at his apparent indifference to the shame he puts her through, Velda berates Mike for wanting to find out who "they" are: "They, they're the nameless ones who kill people for the great whatzit."

Velda herself has a lead, a certain art dealer she has been "set up with" who told her about a Dr. Soberin. There seems to be some connection with Mike's case. Mindless of any danger that might threaten her (as he was in Nick's case as well), Mike tells Velda to get more information from the art dealer about this Dr. Soberin. Remorseful about Nick, he arranges to meet Velda at a local bar, where he passes out drunk—only to be told that "they've got Velda." At a dead end, Mike returns to the gas station he and Christina had briefly stopped at; he remembers that she gave the attendant a letter to mail. Mike asks him who the letter was addressed to. His answer: someone named Mike. Christina had gotten his name and, presumably, his address as well from the car registration. Mike goes to his darkened office only to find the letter sitting opened on his desk and Evello's two hoods waiting for him. The message is simply "remember me," and Hammer is kidnapped and brought to a beach house, where Blue Suede Shoes shoots him full of sodium pentothal to make him remember whatever it might be that apparently he knows.

The interrogation fails. Though his hands are bound by ropes, Mike manages to get free, knocks out Evello (who was left behind to watch him), and ties the mobster up in his place. Summoning the hood from the next room, Hammer tricks him into knifing Evello, after which Mike disposes of the inadvertent killer with some more judo trickery. He returns for Lily and talks to her about Christina's message, finally deciphering it when he reads the following lines from a book of Rossetti's poetry retrieved earlier from her apartment: "But if the darkness and corruption leave a vestige of the thoughts that we once had." The "vestige," Mike thinks, must be something Christina hid on her person before falling into the hands of the criminals. His suspicions are confirmed at the morgue where, after breaking the fingers of the elderly coroner in a drawer, he gets a key retrieved from the dead woman's stomach.

The key is for a locker at the Hollywood Athletic Club, which, after he slaps around the old and defenseless attendant, is opened for Mike.

Inside he finds a heavy, metal-lined case. Peering inside, Mike sees a blindingly bright light; his wrist is badly burned by escaping heat. Bewildered and somewhat terrified, Mike tells the attendant to lock the case in the locker until he can come back and deal with it. He goes home to find the police waiting. They ask for the key, and Mike refuses until Pat hints at the meaning of the metal case by saying, "Manhattan Project, Los Alamos, Trinity." Pat also tells him that the real Lily Carver was "fished out of the river last week." Chastened, Hammer hands over the key to the police, who refuse to help him free Velda. "I didn't know," Mike mumbles. But Pat counters with, "Do you think you'd have done any different if you had known?" Mike phones the club, but there is no answer; a shot of the locker room explains. The attendant lies dead, and the locker that contained the box is now conspicuously empty.

From Diker, Mike learns the name of the art dealer Velda had been seeing. Arriving at his gallery, Mike finds the man in the act of swallowing a whole bottle of sleeping pills. The dealer drifts off into unconsciousness before he can answer Mike's questions about Velda, but Hammer reads Dr. Soberin's name on the prescription label and remembers what Velda had previously told him. Soberin is not in his office but rather in his beach house. As it turns out, Mike is already well acquainted with the location. At this point, the film abandons its exclusive focus on Mike. At the beach house, Dr. Soberin (Albert Dekker) is revealed to be the man with the blue suede shoes. He carries in the metal case, followed by Gabrielle, the woman who had posed as Lily. Patronizingly, Soberin explains to his lover what is inside, but his wealth of mythological allusions (for example, "the Medusa's head") fails to dampen her curiosity.

As it turns out, Soberin intends to betray Gabrielle by not cutting her in on the proceeds to be realized by the sale of the "whatzit." Foolishly, he allows her to pull a gun on him, and she shoots him. Dying, Soberin warns her not to open the "Pandora's box." At this point, Mike enters the house looking for Velda. Like Soberin, he underestimates Gabrielle, and she pulls a gun on him as well. Gabrielle, however, does not shoot Mike until he moves toward her in obedience to her command to come get a kiss. Surrounded by the bodies of the men she has triumphed over, Gabrielle lifts the lid and, even though she sees the light and feels the heat, does not stop until whatever strange force inside is released, reducing her to a fiery, shrieking hulk. Mike, who has only been wounded, revives in time to witness Gabrielle's horrible demise. With the house exploding in flames, Mike finds Velda tied up in a back room and escapes to the beach. The flames intensify, and the film ends, apparently having recorded only the beginning of further nuclear destruction.

Robert Aldrich is perhaps the most political of noir directors; like *Kiss Me Deadly,* his other contributions to dark cinema use the conventional characters and settings derived from hard-boiled fiction to construct multilayered indictments of modern (usually American) culture. *The Big Knife* (also 1955), based on a Clifford Odets play, transforms its main character, the Hollywood star Charlie Castle (Jack Palance), into a typical noir protagonist whose discovery of scheming viciousness in the people around him so depresses and weakens him that he kills himself in despair. Filmmaking, Charlie discovers, is like every other American business—a ruthless racket in which those in control will do anything, even murder, to turn a profit. Similarly, *The Garment Jungle* (1957) deals with labor racketeering, centering on the frustrated efforts of a Korean War veteran to extricate his father's business from the control of a local mobster, who is not above extortion and murder to get his way. At the very end, the hero has been reduced to a revengeful maniac who has to be restrained by the police from beating the hoodlum boss to death with his fists.

In *The Maltese Falcon,* the criminals destroy themselves and each other through their greed-blinded pursuit of an object that turns out to be worthless. Aldrich's *Kiss Me Deadly* develops a similar indictment of contemporary society, but from a more political point of view. The film identifies the dark world of serie noire fiction with the everyday reality of fast-moving postwar culture. America has become a nation where maintaining the right image and looking out for number one have become the two elemental rules of conduct. The difference is that this America now possesses the power to wreak unimaginable destruction. In the allegory that Aldrich's film becomes, the nation learns only too late that the solitary and uncaring pursuit of self-interest turns that destructiveness inward. One of the last in the line of noir detectives, Aldrich's Hammer discovers that the darkness is indeed everywhere, including the natural order; it waits only to be released by the criminally minded, who are effectively unopposed. The dark world triumphs absolutely in the Manichaean apocalypse of Aldrich's noir masterpiece.

CHAPTER 4

Lost in the Dark: The Noir Thriller

The ending of *Kiss Me Deadly* develops a contradiction central to the tradition of the noir detective film: the private eye in dark cinema is characteristically as much a prisoner of the intrigue as its eventual master. Mike Hammer solves the complicated puzzle that leads him to Dr. Soberin's beach house; but, once there, he is easily overcome by Lily/Gabrielle, who is able to command a sexual favor ("Kiss me, Mike") but then shoots him before he is able to do as she orders. (This act delivers the misogynist hero to a rough feminine justice.) At the same time, Mike recovers enough from his wound to free Velda so that they can flee before the house explodes in flames. Similarly, Marlowe solves the case only to be reduced to impotence by Helen's quicker gun; he is saved not by his own resourcefulness or power but by the lucky intervention of the grasping woman's aged husband. Possessed of the truth, he is paradoxically subjected at the same time to a helpless blindness; unlike the classic detective, who delivers his solution of the crime—that is, its true narrative—to exemplify an intellectual control of a seemingly inexplicable world, the blindfolded Marlowe tells his tale to interrogators eager to blame him for the violence and death. *D.O.A.* develops this same contradiction with the greatest irony, offering us a detective who can solve the crime but cannot extricate its victim—himself—from death. Here the truth proves irrelevant, while the incredible accomplishment of the hero in discovering it satisfies only his animal compulsion to seek revenge. He escapes death (besting the villain in a shoot-out) only to succumb to it.

The films examined in this chapter illustrate a further stage in the evolution of the noir protagonist, who here finds himself much more helpless in the face of circumstances that threaten not only his power but his very identity. These films draw heavily on conventions developed within an offshoot of detective fiction: the thriller. As a critical designation, this term is notoriously inexact, ostensibly identifying a psychological effect of fiction rather than a structurally distinct form of it. By thriller, I mean here not any kind of narrative that viewers or readers find thrilling, but a specific genre of literature and film, derived from detective and adventure fiction, whose earliest significant practitioner was John Buchan, a British novelist. Buchan wrote, among other works, *The Thirty-Nine Steps*; originally published in 1914, the popular and influential film version of this book was directed by Alfred Hitchcock in 1935.

The Buchan thriller depends on the device of the double pursuit: the hero, wrongly identified as a criminal, pursues the real criminals in the hope of establishing his innocence even as he himself is hunted by the police. In its classic form, this genre became a staple of Hollywood production through the work of Hitchcock and his numerous imitators.

Hitchcock's *North by Northwest* (1959) provides a useful and masterful example. The executive Roger Thornhill (Cary Grant), enjoying an after-work cocktail with business associates, is mistakenly identified as the American agent George Kaplan by thugs who are working for an enemy spy, the sophisticated Philip Vandamm (James Mason). After being interrogated by Vandamm, Thornhill is forced to drink a huge quantity of liquor and is set loose driving a car down a hill. He survives intact, but his attempts to bring his kidnappers to justice fail; trying to get some information from a high-ranking official at the United Nations about his abduction, Thornhill finds himself holding on to a knife that has just been thrown into the man's back. His photograph is taken, and he immediately flees for his life, knowing he must locate the real killers if he is to establish his innocence in the face of such overwhelming evidence against him. Kaplan, it turns out, is really no one at all, simply a hoax perpetrated by American spies to throw off Vandamm. In a bizarre set of twists and turns, Thornhill discovers that he must become Kaplan to save himself and the beautiful American double agent Eve Kendall (Eva Marie Saint), who is posing as Vandamm's mistress. With the help of the chief American agent (Leo G. Carroll), Thornhill establishes his innocence; however, he must subsequently escape from his protector in order to rescue Kendall from Vandamm. In the process, he retrieves the microfilm that the Americans have been after from the beginning. *North by Northwest* then ends with the romantic coupling of Roger and Eve.

In the thriller, a sensational crime calls into question the effectivity of the law, making it necessary for an ordinary citizen to become a hero in order to save himself from both wrongful prosecution and the violence of the villains. Essential to this narrative movement is a misidentification or, as in *North by Northwest,* a series of misidentifications (the most important of which is Thornhill's accidental fall into the role of George Kaplan, itself a fictional slot filled in effect by no one). The thriller thus derives from a socially critical premise: if the guarantee of everyday monotony—for example, Thornhill's right to have his martini in peace—secured by the law is imperfect, then the law itself as a social force exacting discipline could be considered unnecessary and perhaps unwelcome. The thriller, moreover, initially constructs the law not only as imperfect but also as persecutory. The protagonist is forced into a dual role: he must keep the authorities at bay while he identifies and defeats the villains. An ordinary man, selected by the randomness of the event, becomes capable of feats of great strength and intellectual skill. He escapes always and against all odds, emerging as the only social force capable of preventing whatever disaster the villains have in mind. But only when he is restored to the status of citizen can the protagonist, no longer either a hero or the "wrong man," gain the heroine.

It is easy to see why this narrative genre was a popular item on the classic Hollywood menu. The thriller is, in fact, largely an adventure story that depends not only on the hero's resourcefulness and skill in escaping from constant danger but on his "license" to break the law as he sees fit in order to survive. Though permitted an excess normally allowed only to villains, the protagonist actually exercises his determination and cunning in the service of justice and the welfare of the community. The thriller hero, in other words, acts out of a licit transgressiveness that makes for exciting and suspenseful narrative but poses no problems for Production Code moralism. At the same time, the thriller develops two elements that, slightly altered, would make it into a more contestatory form: the law (or justice) is represented as both initially wrong and ultimately inadequate; and the protagonist is deprived of his identity or social standing (that is, as an obedient subject of the law) and is able to regain it only with great difficulty and after severe trial.

In the noir thriller, these two elements are given a more pessimistic inflection. On the one hand, justice and the law—including the poetic justice that usually operates metaphysically in Hollywood narrative—are shown to be ultimately flawed; either a transcendent malevolence or blind chance controls the characters. On the other hand, misidentification becomes a crisis in identity that is never resolved; the protagonists of noir thrillers discover not stability but ambiguity, even contradiction, at the core of their being. They prove unable to escape being "wrong" men or women, or they find within themselves unfamiliar, often terrifying secret sharers.

DETOUR

Edgar G. Ulmer's *Detour* (1945) did not set the pattern for this kind of narrative; the film was a Poverty Row quickie, that is, it was produced on a shoestring budget with only a few days of shooting at a small studio. *Detour,* however, is undoubtedly the finest example of a purely noir thriller. Here is a film in which the ordinary social optimism of Hollywood film is entirely overthrown in favor of a despairing view of American life that comes straight from the pulps. In fact, the original screenplay by Martin Goldsmith was very much influenced by the "black vision" of Cornell Woolrich's novels and stories. (Goldsmith also worked on another notable "B" noir film, Richard Fleischer's *The Narrow Margin* [1952], which likewise emphasizes the Woolrichian themes of entrapment and inescapable destiny.)

Detour is typical of low-budget noir filmmaking in that any kind of glamorization is excluded from the outset; well-known actors and expensive production values were simply out of the question. The use here of relatively unknown performers, minimally detailed interiors, and real locations for exteriors, however, suits the helplessness and despair of Goldsmith's story precisely. Intended as the bottom part of double bills or as main features in marginally profitable subsequent-run houses, B films were free to offer a less idealized representation of contemporary reality; their viewers in lower-class or rural theaters were drawn from the same groups that had made serie noire fiction a commercial success. *Detour*'s mise-en-scène is by turn starkly inhospitable (interiors) and grittily realistic (exteriors); in neither case does it offer the down-on-his-luck hero protection or comfort. Ulmer's fast-paced direction, moreover, makes the narrative relentless, thereby deftly masking the silliness of the outrageous coincidences upon which the plot depends. This narrational pace is a feature of the film necessitated, once again, by the limitations of B production; like most B films, *Detour* is relatively short, only 68 minutes, in fact. Ulmer uses the hero's first-person/flashback narration to cover the sketchiness of what little can be dramatized or represented given such stringent limitations on running time. Thus the narrator has much more to say than those in the other noir films we have analyzed, and the result is that this story seems a more subjective form of discourse because it is colored constantly by the disillusioned protagonist's despairing commentary.

The film opens with images of a receding highway that exemplify its obsession with the past and disregard for the present. The next sequence reveals a man wandering aimlessly on the shoulder of the same highway as cars pass him; he does not seem to care where he is going, in contrast to those who purposefully and without giving him a second thought speed on by. Finally picked up, the man sits next to the driver with a dull, glazed expression, his eyes not seeing the road ahead. Arriving later at a diner, he goes in for a cup of coffee; his hands and face are filthy, his clothes rumpled and torn, but he seems indifferent to these straitened circumstances. A trucker strikes up a conversation, hoping to find a companion for the long night haul he is about to embark upon. But the man angrily rebuffs him and is indifferent to the offer of a ride. So the trucker puts a nickel into the jukebox to play "I Can't Believe That You're in Love with Me." The ballad makes the man agitated and aggressive; he demands that the jukebox be turned off. Finally restrained by the diner owner, he sits down to finish his coffee. But the song has set loose a flood of memories that the man now, through interior monologue, narrates to himself; the noir stylization of the mise-en-scène registers this sudden inwardness. (Ambient sound is eliminated, and a harsh key light illuminates the man's eyes in close-up, throwing the rest of the image into dark shadow.) Surrendering to memory makes his isolation complete.

His story, however, is less about a lost love, as the ballad would suggest, than about the malevolent operation of fate or chance in human affairs. Though the man, who is revealed to be Al Roberts (Tom Neal), does suffer in part from domination by a selfish and manipulative woman, he is in no way the victim of a femme fatale. His flashback begins, according to the principles of associational logic, with a scene that features the song he has just heard on the jukebox. But in the past, a beautiful woman in a cheap nightclub is singing it, accompanied by the smiling protagonist on the piano. The woman, Sue (Claudia Drake), is Al's fiancée, but the happiness imaged in their joint performance is short-lived. As Sue and Al walk through the fog-enshrouded nighttime streets of a ghostly, abstract New York, she postpones their marriage. Neither of them, Sue says, has been able to make much of a career in show business, but she will go on to Hollywood and attempt to break in as a movie actress. One of them "needs to make good" before they marry; Al's hope to be a concert pianist, he confesses, is now a dream he has largely abandoned. Without the money to support Sue, Al cannot convince her to change her mind. Despite his anger and disappointment, she leaves him behind in New York.

Time passes. Back at the same club and now playing unaccompanied, Al suddenly decides to go out to California himself. He rings Sue, who, having failed to break into movies, has taken a menial job. She is obviously happy, however, at the news of his trip. With almost no money at all, Al sets out, thumbing rides on dusty, lonely highways, a huge road map of the United States serving as the ironic backdrop for his slow progress across a vast expanse of endless routes, dingy cafés, and empty spaces. The montage of grim images conjures up a dreary view of Depression-era America, populated by wandering, impoverished, out-of-work men. Al's narration emphasizes the fact of economic misery: "Money is the stuff that's caused more trouble in the world than anything else we've invented." Crushed by failure and poverty, Al, however, will soon be delivered by fate to an even crueler destiny. Miraculously, he will be chosen to acquire a fancy new roadster, plenty of spending money, and fancy clothes, all that he needs to get to California and make a fresh start. And yet this apparent good fortune, while eliminating his poverty, relieves him of his status as a law-abiding citizen as well. Al is misidentified as a criminal and then irrevocably confirmed in this new role. He never sees Sue again and is condemned instead to wander these same highways, trapped between the East Coast (his past) and the West (his future), forever fleeing a final encounter with the law he can postpone but not avoid.

Helplessness and regret inform Al's narration of these unfortunate events: "If only I'd known what I was getting into that day in Arizona." But only a miraculous foresight could have saved him from his fate because, having taken one innocent step, he was overwhelmed by circumstances that forced him to make one wrong move after another. As he is hitchhiking along a dusty, desert highway, seemingly flat out of luck, Al is picked up by a well-dressed man driving an expensive white convertible. Noticing scratches on his face, Al learns that they were made by the previous occupant of the passenger seat, a woman hitchhiker who apparently would not go along with the driver's attempt to "be friendly." The man, Charles Haskell, Jr. (Edmund MacDonald), ends his story with this observation: "The most dangerous animal in the world—woman." Haskell then shows Al an ugly scar on his arm, the mark, he says, of a sword duel with his angry father; Haskell has not been home since that fight and brags to Al about being a self-made man. The pair brought together by fate stop to share a meal, for which Haskell pays. After eating, he asks Al to drive the car. Moving quickly along the empty highway, Al feels on top of the world; his mind conjures up an eroticized image of Sue singing their song.

This moment of brief, imagined happiness is all Al is to have: this fantasy of Sue turns out to be an unrealizable goal. It starts to rain, and Al, trying in vain to rouse the sleeping Haskell, pulls off onto the shoulder of the road. As he tries to put up the convertible top, Al inadvertently opens the passenger door and Haskell, still sound asleep, spills out onto the concrete, striking his head. Al is incredulous when he discovers that the man is dead: "Until then I had done things my way, but then something else stepped in and shunted me off toward a different direction from the one I had picked for myself." Al, however, does not realize until much later that he has been detoured, for at the moment he still has the illusion of free will and self-determination. Al reasons, and perhaps correctly, that the police will never believe him if he tells the truth; instead of the possible, they will credit the probable, namely, that a penniless drifter killed Haskell for his possessions.

Misidentified by fate as a criminal, Al cannot escape from the essential paradox of his situation: to avoid detection and save his life, he must go through with what would have been the further stages of the crime, had he committed it. In other words, the only way Al can remain innocent is by becoming guilty. Al's plan depends on yet another misidentification, one he willingly accepts, though circumstances leave him little choice. He changes identities with Haskell, taking off his own clothes and putting them on the body; he then dresses in Haskell's suit, thinking that this way he will not look so suspicious driving a luxurious convertible. To make it to California he needs money, so he takes Haskell's wallet as well, including his driver's license, which will match the car's registration should he be stopped by the police for a routine check.

This process of transformation, though actually a crime, appears a wish fulfillment. Driving off, Al now has the right clothes and plenty of cash; he is more fully in possession of the good life than before the accident, when he was only a substitute behind the convertible's wheel. Meeting up with the rich and independent Haskell, Al has become him through a bizarre accident and its attendant consequences. (This essential feature of the plot was likely borrowed by Cornell Woolrich for his celebrated novel *I Married a Dead Man*, published in 1948 but based on a story that appeared only a few months after the release of *Detour*.) Like the heroine of Woolrich's novel, Al discovers that the assumption of another's identity poses two constant dangers: the threat of an exposure that would reveal the character's true self and his criminal fraud; and the unforeseen difficulties entailed in living out the life that rightfully belongs to someone else.

For Al, these two dangers become inextricably intertwined; they are also closely connected to what is the film's most unusual and striking plot twist, the sudden appearance of a female hitchhiker who is a doppelgänger of both Al and Haskell. Vera (played by the aptly named Ann Savage) is intent on both punishing Al for his usurpation of Haskell's place and profiting, like Al, from the rich man's demise. Escaping from the murder scene, Al confesses, "I kept imagining I was being followed." Actually, the danger lies ahead, not behind; it is something he rushes toward rather than flees. After crossing the California border in safety, Al feels tired and checks into a hotel, but he cannot escape who he is and what he has done.

Al's dreams are haunted by terrifying images of Haskell's death. But he awakes refreshed and formulates a plan. He will continue to pose as Haskell until he can sell the car; then he will join Sue and make a fresh start with the proceeds. But before Al can even pull out of the motel parking lot, he stops the car to pick up a bedraggled and filthy woman hitchhiker: "She looked like she'd just been thrown off the crummiest freight train in the world." It is the deepest of ironies that Al's downfall results from what appears to be his one act of charity. But Al perhaps is simply living out the implications of Haskell's identity, becoming the generous rich man who somewhat patronizingly offers rides to the less fortunate—and, of course, is doomed as a result.

Like Haskell, Al sees the woman erotically, despite her obvious social misfortune and downtrodden state; he describes her as possessing "a beauty that's almost homely it's so real." Even though she looks at him quizzically and in an unfriendly way, Al begins to fall under the spell of a romantic attachment. She tells him to "call her Vera" and then says that she will go as far as he is going. Al mutters, "I was afraid so," for he does fear that sharing the trip will afford him the opportunity to act on his feelings, something, for Sue's sake, he does not want to do. But then Vera suddenly falls asleep, assuming the same pose Haskell did before he fell out of the car. Al recalls, "I didn't like that much." This image of a Vera sleeping like Haskell proves prophetic. For when she awakes, she accuses Al of having killed the man and taking over his identity. Al's denials prove ineffective, for Vera, as she reveals, rode with Haskell in that car all the way from Shreveport to the desert; she was the "uncooperative" woman passenger who left Haskell with claw marks on his face and was then abandoned on the highway.

Initially Al had viewed Vera as someone like his former self, an impoverished drifter dependent on the kindness of strangers. Surveying her from his position of power behind the wheel, as he recalls, Al "began to feel sorry for her." Yet suddenly Vera is the one with the power, for she can easily turn him in to the police. In a sense, then, Vera is a revenger figure, an agent sent by fate to ruin Al's plans to profit from Haskell's unfortunate and unplanned death: "That Haskell guy wasn't dead yet. He was sitting next to me in the car, laughing like mad." At the same time, however, Vera represents a powerful female vengeance against male exploiters. Thrown out by Haskell after she repulsed him, Vera meets up with his surrogate, but this time she has the upper hand since she knows, and is able to prove, that the man is a criminal. Though he continues to drive, Al must now follow Vera's directions, as she quite forcefully tells him: "Just remember who's boss around here. If you shut up and don't give me any argument, you'll have nothing to worry about."

As this last speech suggests, Vera (as realized by Ann Savage's finely layered performance) is perhaps the most unusual femme fatale in classic dark cinema. The control over men exercised by these grasping and manipulative characters usually depends on naked power only in the last instance; for example, Velma in *Murder, My Sweet* pulls her gun on Marlowe only at story's end, only when her attempts to control him through the giving and withholding of sexual favors fail and he learns the truth. The noir fatal woman is normally seductive, that is, outwardly compliant, eager to please the men she wishes to use. In contrast, Vera shrilly accuses Al of murdering Haskell, bitterly rejects his pleas of innocence, and firmly reminds him of his place in their developing relationship. Vera's strength is established by her solitariness; like Al, she is on her own, pursuing a dream of the good life represented, in the mythology of the 1940s, by a new start on the West Coast. Vera has no man to support her, no one she must please except herself. In her wisecracking and brassy manner, Vera resembles the newly emancipated women of many postwar films; but her emancipation, unlike theirs, is taken to its logical conclusion, a rejection that forces Vera out on her own to find some way of "making it big."

As it turns out, both Vera and Al are doomed by the dreams they attempt to fulfill. Entrapped by the woman he attempted to help (and perhaps exploit), Al is unable to contact Sue when the pair arrives in Hollywood, intending to sell Haskell's fancy convertible: "There was now a greater distance between Sue and me that when we'd started out." It becomes increasingly evident that Vera wants more from Al than his acquiescence to the fraudulent sale of Haskell's auto. She convinces him that they should rent an apartment as Mr. and Mrs. Charles Haskell. After bathing, Vera opens her suitcase and, in a telling reversal of accepted sexual roles, offers Al a drink; her voice and manner oscillate between a seductive softness and a commanding authoritativeness. Al is obviously bewildered by Vera's double message: she wants to surrender to him but also continue to dominate his life completely. He rejects her advances, and she storms off to bed alone, reminding him that all the doors are locked and that, even if he did get out, she would only have to tell the police about his crime in order for him to be sought out and jailed. Al calls Sue but hangs up without speaking; having arrived in California, he has nothing he can tell her.

The next morning Al contemplates his relationship with Vera; if Hollywood were to tell the story, it would turn out differently: "If this were fiction, I would fall in love with Vera, marry her, and make a respectable woman of her . . . or she'd make some Class A sacrifice for me and die." The film's slice-of-life narrative, however, rejects both the social optimism and poetic justice of melodrama. *Detour* is more "realistic," less fictional because it abjures happy endings and "good" characters. Attracted and tied to Vera, Al is put off by her selfishness—perhaps because it is the precise reflex of his own—and bitter sense of deprivation. Vera, too, is angry at a system that distributes rewards unevenly. No relationship between them seems possible because she will not surrender the power that circumstances have given her. In this way, Vera is yet another version of Sue, who refused Al's offer of marriage and decided to make a journey alone to the promised land of California to seek her own fortune. Both women are strong-willed and assertive. Al, in contrast, gives up too easily—his career as a concert pianist is over before he starts it—and he becomes an unresisting victim of circumstances: Sue leaves him behind in New York, while Vera makes him a virtual prisoner of her desire. Yet Al resents being dominated and refuses to find a way of living with his fate: "Vera, unfortunately, was just as rotten in the morning as she'd been the night before."

Posing as a happily married couple (significantly, this is Vera's idea), the two impostors try to sell Haskell's car but find themselves stymied

The unlucky hero of *Detour* unwittingly murders his own companion. Courtesy of Producers Releasing Corporation/Museum of Modern Art, Film Stills Archive.

when Al cannot answer the dealer's questions about insurance. Vera, however, formulates a new plan at this very moment. As she goes through the glove compartment (something Al never bothered to do), she discovers—implausibly, from a newspaper clipping—that Haskell stood to inherit a fortune from his father, who is on his deathbed. Vera now thinks that they should keep the car so that Al can carry his imposture one more step and cash in as the eagerly sought-out heir. Al disagrees, characteristically thinking of all the difficulties involved, and the couple argue bitterly that night in the apartment. Finally, Vera, who has drunk the liquor she had hoped would put her companion in a compliant and amorous mood, lurches off into the bedroom with the phone to call the police. The cord winds around her neck as she passes out on the bed. On the other side of the locked door, Al pulls on it hoping to wrest the phone from Vera's control but strangles her instead. Once again involved in the more or less accidental death of a companion, Al knows that this time there is no escape. He cannot cover his tracks and, as Haskell, is pursued by the police. The flashback ends, and Al leaves the roadside café, only to be picked up a short distance down the road by a prowl car.

Detour's expressed theme is the ineluctability of destiny, as expressed in Al's final comment on his life: "Fate or some mysterious force can put the finger on you or me for no good reason at all." At the same time, the film powerfully represents the discontents of contemporary American life. Haskell is literally scarred by a violent and unhappy childhood whose painful memories cannot be erased by a deathbed reunion because he dies on the journey. In fact, his ostentatious wealth and power are mocked by the sudden and meaningless death he succumbs to. (We never learn if Haskell was dead before he hit the ground, but the visual evidence suggests that this is possible.) Al is the victim of a nightmarish Horatio Alger story. Impoverished, down on his luck, he travels out to California with no prospect of changing his circumstances; the chance encounter with Haskell affords him only the appearance of wealth and success, not the reality. The dream of making a fresh start ends with Al roaming, once again as a filthy bum, the roadside world between the coasts.

Victimized by at least one man, Vera desperately seeks her share of the American dream. Ironically, she discovers a pathetic and sadistic attachment to a failure—a man who only would be rich—and this pretend-husband kills her in his own weakness and lack of will. Vera, however, was dying anyway; suffering from tuberculosis, she pushed

Al to defraud Haskell's father because she had "nothing to lose." Sue, like Vera, tries to make a success of her life but finds failure at every turn; her relationship with Al is soured by his lack of ambition and pessimism, her own career in Hollywood proves a failure, and, when last we see her, she is living alone in a cheap apartment working at a menial job. It would be difficult, I think, to conceive of a narrative further removed from the glamorized wish fulfillment of the ordinary studio product. *Detour* is a unique text in which the fear and terror of the noir thriller combine with the social critique of the naturalist tradition (the film's characters would be at home in a John Steinbeck novel) to offer a powerful alternative version of contemporary American life.

THE STRANGER

Detour was written, produced, and released in 1945, the year of victory for American arms over both Germany and Japan. The film's concern with failure and powerlessness must have offered theater audiences at the time a marked contrast to official narratives of national success and irresistibility. The noir vision taking shape in Hollywood provided a fictional world that was in some important senses out of step not only with the institutionalized optimism of Hollywood storytelling but with the relieved and self-satisfied mood of a country that had weathered attack and trial only to emerge victorious in the end. And yet the themes of the dark cinema thriller could be used to suggest, in various ways, that there were still pressing items on the national agenda. Noir thrillers, in other words, could be political, if only in the limited sense that any Hollywood film, hampered by PCA restrictions, could develop and support political views.

Perhaps the most interesting case in point is Orson Welles's *The Stranger* (1946), a project completed by this normally maverick director as a testimony he could work ably and profitably within the constraints of the studio system. Thus *The Stranger,* much more than Welles's other celebrated work in dark cinema (*The Lady from Shanghai* [1948] and *Touch of Evil* [1958]), is an institutional film. At the same time, *The Stranger* is intensely personal, at least in the sense that it embodies Welles's political opinions about the immediate postwar era. The film's narrative agenda is keyed to the recent victory over Euro-

pean fascism and involves the identification and subsequent destruction of those secret horrors that might prevent a securing of victory
over problems on the home front. Here the ideological assumptions
of mainstream film are marshaled to combat a vision of American life
that had taken shape within the representational space of Hollywood
films themselves. Thus the enemy is the noir protagonist, a former
Nazi fanatic who has misidentified himself as Charles Rankin (Orson
Welles), an ordinary American working as a teacher at a Connecticut
boys' school. The narrative, by revealing that Rankin is the genocidal
Franz Kindler, works to prevent a reemergent fascism from seizing
control of America from within.

In the early postwar period, Welles took a low-paying job as an
editorialist for the *New York Post*. His writing addressed the different
problems of the post-Roosevelt era, one of which was, as he put it,
that the "phoney fear of Communism is smoke-screening the real
menace of renascent Fascism."[1] *The Stranger* deals with this political
issue in typical Hollywood fashion. On the one hand, the film offers
a wish-fulfillment reenactment of overseas victory, with the obvious
implication that domestic problems are in the final analysis really foreign ones; renascent fascism here is of the imported rather than the
native variety and can be defeated with the same moralism, self-righ-
teousness, and determination that won the war. On the other hand,
this thriller is typically noir in that it shows how misidentification
cannot be so simply resolved; the revelation that Rankin is Kindler
destroys the mental health of his young wife, who cannot bear to
think that she has given her love to such a monster. Mary Rankin
(Loretta Young) must acknowledge that evil may exist in her peaceful
small town, thus contradicting her feeling, expressed earlier in the
story, that "there's nothing to worry about" as she ventures out into
the night alone. That everyday life has a dark side is a staple theme of
those thrillers that feature spies as protagonists; this tradition, which
derives from John Buchan's novels, was further developed by the
British authors Eric Ambler and Graham Greene. The spy moves in
a world of constantly shifting identities and loyalties, a world that is
the significant underside of normal life—that is, the arena where the
struggle to preserve ordinariness actually goes on. This netherworld
cannot be exorcised, only accepted; but in *The Stranger* its horror
proves too much for the innocent housewife confronted by an evil
with unimaginable power to destroy.

The film opens with a brief sequence set in the Allied War Crimes Commission Office in which the chief investigator, an American named Wilson (Edward G. Robinson), persuades the representatives of the other nations that one of the convicted Nazis, an underling named Konrad Meineke (Konstantin Shayne), should be released so that he can be trailed to his boss, the escaped Franz Kindler, the man who planned the "final solution." This sequence is stylized in the baroque manner Welles employed in his later noir projects. A moving camera at ceiling level takes spectators into the dimly lit office, where the framing does not allow them to see all of any one figure present. The narrative then switches rapidly to a South American port where Meineke, muttering to himself, has disembarked under a phony name in order to learn Kindler's whereabouts from local Nazis. Once again, these brief scenes are complexly stylized, including the traveling shot of Meineke exiting the immigration station; here a number of moving figures at different depths and on different planes intersect, providing a visual metaphor for the story's concern with misidentification and pursuit.

Informed by his henchman that Kindler now lives in Harper, Connecticut, under the assumed name of Charles Rankin, Meineke stares at a postcard image of the small town, an image that slowly dissolves into an establishing shot of the place itself. The initial scene of traditional American life features a prominent church, tree-lined residential streets, and pedestrians going about their everyday activities. The inhabitants of this cloistered environment are unaware of how close and accessible it is to an underworld of intrigue, destruction, and death; the postcard–establishing shot dissolve eliminates any perception of distance between the noir landscape of an evil Europe and South America and the life-as-usual happiness of small-town Connecticut. The narrative continues the anti-isolationism of this stylistic figure: Meineke is shown arriving in Harper by bus, his journey there swift and apparently unproblematic. In the back of the bus is Wilson, who shadows the obviously deranged man as he makes for Rankin's house. But Meineke, realizing that he is being followed, leads Wilson into the school gymnasium, where he knocks the detective out and leaves him unconscious. Meineke finds Rankin not at home, but he meets Mary, who is excited that she and Charles are getting married later that afternoon. The narrative then picks up Rankin as he leaves his class and is approached by members of the school track team, who are starting a paper chase through the woods. After the boys leave, Meineke accosts him, and Rankin, understanding quickly that his former comrade cannot be trusted, lures him into the same woods and strangles him. As Rankin tries desperately to cover up the body and his own tracks, he realizes that the paper chase will pass close to the spot. So he frantically picks up the paper and spreads a false trail for the students, finishing just in time to get back home and marry Mary Longstreet, the daughter of a retired Supreme Court justice.

The initial scenes seem to depend on simple thematic oppositions: German/American, Nazi/democratic, insane/sane, criminal/law-abiding, murderous/humanitarian, secret/open, among others. But the film avoids the poetic justice of melodrama in a number of ways: most important perhaps, by demonstrating that justice and goodness can only be reestablished at the cost of disruption that nearly drives the female protagonist to suicide and madness; but also by focalizing the narrative, in large part, through Rankin/Kindler, with whom a certain amount of spectator sympathy is developed.

That a seeming pillar of the community could be the mastermind behind the genocidal plan to rid Europe of the Jews establishes that there is an unfathomed evil at the very center of ordinary existence. That Rankin is misidentified raises the possibility that nothing is what it seems, that everything lacks a stable, dependable identity. Rankin/Kindler is like a horrifying id whose presence and power must be acknowledged. The film, in fact, designs an explicitly Freudian project for Mary, who is forced to face up to and understand her husband's true nature. The ex-Nazi, we are told by Wilson, is a hidden threat who must be eradicated in order to protect the United States; this threat is confirmed by Rankin himself as he discusses the future of the movement with Meineke before killing him. The narrative works to expose his true identity to the whole town. The familiar becomes the strange, and the ordinary is revealed as a straightforward monstrousness in a story that recalls scapegoating rituals. This sense is strongest in the closing sequences when Rankin/Kindler, exposed at last, is fatally wounded by the moving medieval figures in the clock tower and falls off, to the delight of the assembled and enraged townspeople. *The Stranger* in this way develops a theme that is certainly relevant to the politics of postwar America: the need for constant vigilance against enemies both within and without—for Rankin/Kindler is equally the stranger who would harm an unsuspecting populace and the husband who, despite his promises and apparent kindness, really intends to murder his loving wife.

The film thus combines two different stories: it is equally a wartime drama that moves inexorably toward the victory of an aroused and irresistible America and a noir thriller that transforms the everyday world of peace and stability into an environment riddled with persecutory malevolence, thus justifying the paranoid helplessness of protagonists seemingly doomed to destruction. In *The Stranger,* victory over the forces of darkness, both foreign and domestic, can be achieved only by rejecting the false belief that all is well, that things are as they appear, that no one intends harm to anyone else. In fact, the victory of power—identified with the male urge of Wilson to see Kindler punished—can only be assured by the temporary triumph of paranoia, that is, Mary must be made to see that the man she loves and trusts is a murderer. The film's central paradox, then, is that the noir vision of the world must, if only for a time, replace the idealized insularity of Harper life if that life is to continue. Mary must accept that Rankin is Kindler if she is ever to forget him completely. (Her father tells her that marriage to a monster is no marriage at all.) Her fortunate fall into such a belief leads directly to his elimination, but the film, in the end, cannot convincingly save appearances. Noirness is disavowed, but not completely, since its forceful presence has been recognized and, in fact, leaves Mary still affected at the end.

Recovering consciousness, Wilson cannot pick up Meineke's trail, but he knows that Kindler must be one of the local townspeople. So he adopts a false identity as an antique buyer and collector who specializes in clocks; Kindler's hobby, we are informed early in the film, is clock repair, and this is the only personal fact known about a man whose official records do not even include a photograph. Extraordinarily, Harper's white-clapboard New Englandness features a church with a huge clock tower, which houses an early Renaissance clock complete with chimes and figures (even a full-size knight with a sword) meant to appear in procession on the hour. The clock is not working when Wilson arrives, but Rankin, he learns, has set about fixing it. This pursuit and Rankin's age would seem to confirm that he is Kindler, but Wilson, meeting Mary, her father (Philip Merivale), and Rankin, crosses the man off the list of suspects when he mouths anti-German statements. (Calling for the "annihilation" of an entire people, however, does have a suspiciously Nazi cast to it.) Wilson changes his mind when he recalls later that night that Rankin had said Marx was a Jew, not a German. Improbably, Wilson remains unsure of his identification and seems to command no resources other than the testimony of the townspeople. When Meineke's body is discovered, Rankin comes to fear Mary because he knows that she knows the man was looking for him. So Rankin lies to his wife: he tells her that Meineke was a blackmailer who had to be killed. Loyal to her husband and unwilling to disturb the status quo, Mary agrees to keep his secret.

This strange narrative succeeds largely because of Welles's all-too-perfect impersonation of an educated New England prep school teacher. Kindler, in other words, is too good an actor. That is, Welles does not play Kindler as a German who has difficulty—evidenced in occasional slips and uneasiness—playing the part of a legitimate American. His acting is not layered, does not reveal itself as a performance within a performance. Famous for his character roles, especially of foreigners, Welles eschews naturalist acting here. The effect is to downplay the sense of Rankin being a stranger, or an impersonator who does not truly belong to the small-town environment we discover him in. Thus Harper is not only the idealized image of communal values; it is also the locus of dangerous ambiguity, because the stranger (like Oedipus) is the one who is too well known, too familiar. It is up to Mary, then, to confirm the misidentification that makes a horror of her life.

Wilson maintains that he needs Mary's testimony about meeting with Meineke. This piece of evidence can hardly be considered conclusive, however, given the overwhelming proof already in Wilson's possession. At this point, the film signals an alteration in narrative expectations and horizons. It is no longer a question of Wilson's pursuit of Kindler—the man's eventual capture seems a foregone conclusion—but instead, of the transformation of Mary into the disoriented, persecuted, and paranoid protagonist of the noir thriller. This alteration is announced in a scene in which Rankin, who had been out locking up Mary's dog (it keeps going to the woods and disturbing Meineke's shallow grave), returns to the bedroom where Mary is fretfully sleeping. His dark shadow drifts across her prostrate form, and she awakes with a start, the distorted outline of his body totally covering hers in an ominous way. Mary tells her husband about a nightmare: it concerns the "little man" who came to visit (Meineke) and how he goes away but leaves his shadow behind to haunt her. This sequence activates a set of generic conventions that derived from the female Gothic and became prominent in noir thrillers featuring female protagonists.

In the Gothic genre, the plot is constructed around a central enigma: does the husband intend harm to his wife? The positive versions of this narrative vindicate the husband's apparent anger toward or hatred of his spouse; Hitchcock's *Rebecca* (1940) is perhaps the classic example. In the negative versions—exemplified best by *Gaslight* (George Cukor, 1944)—the husband's ultimately murderous intent is foiled by the intervention of an interested, male third party. In the noir inflection of this type, the disruption of the woman's everyday world cannot be put right; either she is killed (as in *Sorry, Wrong Number* [Anatole Litvak, 1948]) or her life is otherwise destroyed (as in *The Stranger*).

We can see this clearly in the way that *The Stranger* subverts the fundamental thematic element of the female Gothic: the saving nature of knowledge. The wife's developing awareness of her husband's true nature is ordinarily conceived as therapeutic, whether he is found to be guilty or innocent. In *Rebecca,* Maxim is cleared of all suspicions, enabling Mrs. DeWinter to surrender her feelings of persecution. *Gaslight's* heroine is deliberately being driven mad by her scheming husband, but when she discovers his plot her mental health is restored.

In *The Stranger*, the therapeutic trajectory of Mary's growing awareness of the truth is, in contrast, perversely negative: designed to bring the escaped Nazi to justice, the truth will quite probably destroy her at the same time. This "therapy" is designed by Wilson with the help of Mary's brother Noah (Richard Long) and father. Speaking to Noah, he says: "Your sister's a fine woman, but she must find out the kind of man she's married to." Such a plot direction is traditional for the Gothic, but here it makes no sense since Wilson already knows that Rankin is Kindler and that Mary's life is in jeopardy as long as she remains in Rankin's house. For obvious reasons, the discovery of the husband's true nature (and the wife's subsequent rescue or recuperation) occurs near the end of the Gothic narrative, not the beginning. But Wilson, unlike the conventional male friend of the heroine in this genre, cares little about Mary's safety. Mary, in fact, becomes a pawn in the game of cat and mouse played by Rankin and Wilson; neither one cares about her, and each sees her largely as a means to an end.

Wilson coolly predicts the various stages of Kindler's reaction to Mary's growing suspicions, intending to use her eventual realization of the truth for his own purposes. At first, he correctly foresees, Rankin will tell her a lie to gain her confidence. What he says is that Meineke was extorting money by threatening to reveal that Rankin was the guilty party in a now-finished romance with a girl from Switzerland. The finding of Meineke's body prompts a new story. Now Rankin admits to killing his blackmailer and also confesses to poisoning Mary's dog because the animal would not leave the corpse alone. This time Mary has more trouble accepting his explanation, but Rankin's offer to turn himself in convinces her of his good intentions, and she agrees to keep the secret. An evening shortly afterward at her father's house turns into a questioning session, with Wilson playing, alternately, the roles of cross-examining attorney and helpful psychiatrist.

Shown films of the concentration camp horrors that Kindler masterminded, Mary still refuses to believe that her husband could be such a man, and she runs from the house on the verge of complete emotional collapse. Wilson then calmly explains to Judge Longstreet that such an inward division will inevitably lead to a mental breakdown: "She has the facts now, but she won't accept them. They're too horrible for her to acknowledge, not so much that Rankin could be Kindler, but that she could have given her love to such a creature. But we have one ally—her subconscious. It knows what the truth is, and it's struggling to be heard. The will to truth within your daughter is much too strong to be denied."

Wilson is probably correct that Mary's hesitation to believe the evidence presented to her connects to a reluctance to own up to her own ignorance and lack of perception. But what is also intriguing here is the double value placed on the notion of truth. For the purposes of the investigation (and for those of Hollywood narrative in general), the truth, of course, must come out if the investigation is to be resolved and justice done. And yet Wilson realizes that acknowledging the truth will entail terrible consequences for Mary because the reality of Rankin's past is just too horrible, a history better left undiscussed. In the negative versions of the female Gothic, the revelation of the husband's iniquity obviously constitutes a difficulty. How to recuperate the persecuted heroine once her husband is unmasked as a victimizer? Generally speaking, Gothics of this type simply double the male/husband figure, providing a former lover or interested bystander who both aids in the identification of the husband's malevolence and negates it by coupling with the rescued heroine at the end.

In the female Gothic, the "good" male tries desperately to prevent the death or breakdown of the heroine. As a noir thriller, *The Stranger* offers a quite different character. Played by Edward G. Robinson, Wilson is ruled out from the very beginning as a romantic possibility by the iron rule of Hollywood narrative that attractive people are to be coupled only with other attractive people. (It is interesting that Agnes Moorehead was originally tapped to play the investigator.) Moreover, Mary's imminent breakdown suits his plans perfectly. As Wilson sees it, Kindler will not be able to trust a woman who is all too obviously falling to pieces. He will, as a result, have to do one of two things: flee from Harper and thus acknowledge his guilt, or see to it that Mary comes to an "accidental" end before she can tell Wilson what she knows. The victory of power can thus come only with Mary's breakdown or destruction; the urge to correct a misidentification (Kindler's masquerade as Rankin) depends for its fulfillment on violence done, in a cold-blooded way, to an innocent third party. With apparent equanimity, Wilson predicts to Mary's father that "she's headed for a breakdown" and opines that Rankin will soon try to kill her.

The plot turns out to be pathetically inept. Rankin arranges for Mary to come to the clock tower where he is working, having previously "fixed" the ladder so that it will break when she is almost at the top. But Mary is prevented from leaving the house by her maid (acting on Wilson's instructions). Rankin returns according to plan and, to his great surprise, finds her at home. At this moment, Mary finally acknowledges that he is trying to kill her and that he is Kindler. Picking up a fireplace poker, she asks to be killed, providing he does not touch her in the process: "Kill me. I couldn't face life knowing what I've been to you." Before Rankin can strike, however, Wilson arrives with Mary's brother. After he flees the house, Mary lapses into unconsciousness and is put to bed.

At this point, Gothic conventions no longer operate, for the husband has been identified as a killer and the wife has been rescued from his control. The subsequent capture and death of Rankin/Kindler, however, are presented not only in terms of the international spy thriller (the part of the story led by Wilson) but in terms of the horror film, particularly the narrative of sexual bondage and release that is the basis of the Dracula story (here Mary becomes the main character).

In other words, Mary's lost state—her mental illness, desire for death, will to vengeance—relates to the monstrosity that is her husband, a monstrosity that must be exorcised.

In *The Stranger,* monstrousness is moral, not physical; therefore it does not, for its defeat, require a specialized scientific knowledge (furnished by either science or folklore). Crucial here are clear vision and recognition, for the threat of the film's monstrousness is its paradoxical invisible visibility, the fact that it is an integral, accepted part of the everyday world that must be defamiliarized in order to be contained. From this viewpoint, Wilson becomes the man in the know who can direct and order the monster's destruction. Wilson, however, performs a task far different from that of his generic counterparts, since he does not have to lure the guessed-at presence out into the open where it will show itself (and hence, in the etymological sense, become a "monster"). On the contrary, Wilson must deconstruct the ordinary—or, perhaps better, identify the ways in which the ordinary is the same as the monstrous, thus providing a solid existential basis for what would normally be a paranoid delusion of, at least in Freud's experience, an ordinary kind, that is, the husband as homicidal maniac.

True to this vision of a nightmare world, Wilson does not rescue Mary from Kindler but rather delivers her to him. When she wakes later that night from her faint, it is because she hears the bells of the clock tower toll. The invocation of the Dracula story becomes particularly strong at this point when Mary, apparently summoned by the monster who controls her, makes her way to the church in her nightgown and with a revolver. The shot showing her traversing the older cemetery is evocative of expressionist style, with its hazy focus, chiaroscuro lighting, and deliberately artificial mise-en-scène. When she arrives at the church, it is apparent that Mary is herself now misidentified, having become a monster in response to Kindler's monstrosity.

Earlier, when discussing his plans for keeping the truth from Wilson, Rankin had told her: "Mary, in failing to speak you become part of the crime." She answered: "I'm already a part of it because I'm a part of you." If the film, at least on one level, attempts to offer a fairly straightforward series of semantic oppositions, then the transformation of Mary into a German zombie who intends to do murder works against any melodramatic resolution. Drawing her gun, Mary fires shots and apparently wounds Kindler. But before she can finish him off, he steps out onto the tower ledge by the clock face, where he is

The local schoolmaster in *The Stranger* is exposed as a diabolical ex-Nazi and then driven onto the clock face of the church tower, from which he falls to his death. Courtesy of RKO/Museum of Modern Art, Film Stills Archive.

impaled by the sword-carrying knight and then falls to his death. The Nazi who was also an American husband thus dies equally through the actions of the innocent wife determined to kill him and by means of the Germanic clock installed in the tower of a New England church.

As in all of the noir films we have thus far examined, this ending is both an obvious resolution, in that all is revealed and the villain perishes, and a failure to resolve, in that the disruption caused by Kindler's presence in Harper is not fully made right. Obviously happy, Wilson speaks about a new victory ("It's V-E day in Harper") as Mary is escorted from the church by her brother. Wilson wishes her "pleasant dreams," but she responds with a shattered, nearly blank look that reflects how tenuously she has been rescued from an ordeal that has turned her life upside down and made her wish to be dead. Mary becomes the typical protagonist of the noir thriller: like Al Roberts, she is forced to continue living in a world she will never again have cause to trust, cut off from desire and family life. Significantly, Mary cannot assent to Wilson's suggestion at story's end that all is well. Not cured by the trajectory of the narrative, she has instead been made ill, in an intriguing reversal of the way female Gothic narrative usually functions.

VERTIGO

Like most noir thrillers, *The Stranger* ironizes the power and control that male protagonists are normally able to assert in Hollywood films. Dreaming of a born-again fascism that will take over the world, Kindler finds himself murdering a helpless former subordinate, covering his tracks in the woods so that children do not discover him, and poisoning a snoopy dog. In the film's climactic finale sequence, he is hoisted by his own petard, stabbed by the same clock mechanism he had spent so much time repairing. In Alfred Hitchcock's *Vertigo* (1958), the powerless power of the noir thriller protagonist is developed more darkly, even as the issue of identity/misidentity is stated in a more hopelessly ambiguous fashion. As in the Welles films, the characters in *Vertigo* are trapped in a contest of worldviews and generic assumptions, with the result that their selves and desires are irrevocably fragmented.

The first part of the film offers a series of events derived from the woman's picture genre; here the narrative goal is solving the "woman question," the problem, usually of identity and desire, that the heroine poses for the other characters. In the woman's picture, the male protagonist often struggles desperately to cure the illness, mental or physical, that separates him from the heroine, with whom he is in love. *Vertigo*'s Scottie Ferguson (James Stewart) proves unable to save Madeleine Elster (Kim Novak), and she dies a suicide; blamed by others and himself, he retreats into a silent melancholia and is hospitalized. In the second part, Scottie, released from the hospital, discovers that his beliefs about his beloved's identity, fate, and motives must be deconstructed, revealing a plot against him. But even as he masters this plot, rewriting the identity of the heroine as that of an imposter and betrayer who only "played" at killing herself, he finds himself unable to control the course of events once again. This time her suicide is real, and the film's end leaves him shattered and in despair.

Scottie retired from the police force after discovering he suffers from vertigo, which made him powerless to prevent a colleague's death. But he is soon hired by an old friend, Gavin Elster (Tom Helmore), to follow his wife Madeleine, who, Elster believes, has fallen under the self-destructive spell of Carlotta Valdes, a long-dead relative who died a suicide after being victimized by a powerful man. Scottie trails Madeleine to a number of San Francisco locations that, he discovers, bear witness to Carlotta's presence and the reality of her influence over Madeleine; these include, most importantly, a portrait in a local gallery and the woman's marked grave. Scottie is puzzled by Madeleine's strangely obsessive behavior, but he is as yet unable to ratify or dismiss Elster's suspicions. He follows her to an old house where she goes up quickly to a rented room. Questioning the landlady, Scottie learns that the woman tenant of that room calls herself Carlotta Valdes. He mentions that a woman just entered the hotel and went to that room, but the landlady claims not to have seen her that day. The pair go upstairs and find the room empty. Looking out the window, Scottie discovers that Madeleine's car is missing as well. He leaves the hotel and drives to the Elsters' apartment, where the car is now parked.

These last sequences furnish an important clue to the structure of the first part of the film. Is Madeleine indeed possessed by a ghost and therefore able to transcend the natural laws of time and space? Scottie's experience at the hotel seems to confirm Elster's suspicions, but the

Vertigo's detective tries unsuccessfully to solve the mystery of his beloved's apparent possession by a malevolent spirit. Courtesy of Paramount/Museum of Modern Art, Film Stills Archive.

evidence is hardly conclusive. The story type here is what is usually termed "the fantastic," which involves a hesitation on the part of a central character (and the reader or spectator as well) about the interpretation of events that appear to be supernatural in origin but that might be explained naturally. Madeleine's disappearance seems to indicate that she is not human or, more precisely, no longer human, already substantially possessed by the purportedly malevolent spirit of Carlotta, who appears, as Elster suggests, to be urging her toward the permanent absence of the grave.

Scottie falls in love with Madeleine and takes on the task of solving what appears to him to be her psychological problem. Disinclined to accept any supernatural explanation for his beloved's preoccupation, Scottie attempts to discover the "key" that would show her it is "all in her mind." Thus, he assumes, Madeleine will return to "herself" and be able to continue their love affair. Her dreams about an ancient mission give Scottie the notion that a visit there will shake loose the appropriate memories from his beloved's mind. But the plan backfires. Madeleine runs away from Scottie and quickly ascends the bell tower. Disabled by a continuing attack of vertigo, Scottie lags behind in his pursuit, only to glimpse her suicidal fall from the tower through an open window. Shaken, he leaves the scene alone.

The coroner's jury rules the leap an act of self-destruction, but Ferguson and Elster continue to believe that Madeleine indeed killed herself because of Carlotta's malign influence. We see that Scottie has been convinced of this explanation in the nightmare he experiences after the trial. In this dream (the source, the film implies, of his subsequent collapse into severe melancholia), the courtroom scene is replayed, with a flesh-and-blood Carlotta (Lee Patrick) this time appearing between Ferguson and Elster in a reformulation of their final dialogue together. It is important to note that the hesitation central to the effect of fantastic narrative is left intact. Scottie's belief in Carlotta's influence leads him to retreat within his own mind, while the truth of the evidence offered in court leads to an official verdict that ignores the supernatural—a verdict that the spectator is permitted neither to endorse nor to reject.

It has been argued that fantastic narrative is a subversive genre because it refuses the normal "truth-seemingness" of realist fiction, offering a doubt about the trustworthiness of appearances and conventional forms of wisdom. In *Vertigo,* the uneasiness produced by the fantastic suits the noir thriller themes relating to identity that Hitchcock here explores. The fantastic narrative of part 1 constructs discontent as part of the represented world (the protagonist retreats into a deep and silent madness) and also dissatisfies the spectator, who must contemplate the dreadful social abyss opened up by events that elude a determining, fixing knowledge. At the end of a mainstream Hollywood film, the viewer knows everything of importance and is offered a vision of social harmony. Neither desire is satisfied here, and the expectation would be that further narration is necessary to do so. But the causal lines leading from the initial set of narrative questions are (at least apparently) closed off. Madeleine's death and Scottie's failure now make any further exploration of the supernatural largely irrelevant. The inability of love to furnish either appropriate solutions or knowledge throws doubt on the efficacy of additional effort on the part of the characters. Scottie's melancholia thus figures the state of the story, which has nothing more to "do" or "say."

Part 1 of *Vertigo*, however, is not only a fantastic narrative but a story of female development in which conventional elements of the woman's picture are presented only to be deconstructed. The two stories are joined together at an early point. Approached by Elster about the assignment, Scottie dismisses his suspicions out of hand but is persuaded to have a look at Madeleine and then decide if he will take the job. Elster arranges for Scottie to see her at a local restaurant. With an elaborate camera movement and editing patterns that literally put Madeleine on display, the narration strains to make plausible Scottie's decision to do what Elster wants. He is plainly attracted to the woman.

But the scene is a blatant non sequitur, for Madeleine's beauty has nothing to do either with the supernatural or with her supposedly deranged behavior; moreover, there is something perverse about Elster's desire to flaunt his wife's allure to another man. Later in the film, the supernatural will emerge in its traditional Gothic meaning as the influence from an exotic and aristocratic past that pulls the present toward annihilation. Moreover, the equation of Madeleine's possession with attractiveness has more to do with the film's gender politics. This is most obvious, perhaps, in the somewhat perverse aspects of Scottie's desire. When Madeleine, apparently in a trance, jumps into the bay, he rescues her and, holding her unconscious body, is finally able to express his feelings to her. Bringing her, still unconscious, to his apartment, he undresses her and lays her in his bed. Madeleine appeals to Scottie because of her weakness. The spectacle of beauty she offers him is not only unself-conscious and hence passive (she never tries to seduce him or arouse his interest); it is literally caused by an abnegation of self, by the fact that Madeleine is in the process of being swept away into another identity.

In the romance of the woman's picture, the appropriate demonstration of female surrender, when matched by the man's outpouring of tender care, furnishes the basis for succcessful coupling. *Vertigo* problematizes this development. For Madeleine's weakness is also an obsession with (or possession by) Carlotta that threatens to make her disappear completely into the fate of that broken-hearted suicide. Scottie's role becomes something of a paradox: he must formulate an alternative explanation for Madeleine's behavior and thus destroy the obsession that makes her so attractive. In so doing, he must struggle against the view that Madeleine's weakness is generated by the otherness of a vengeful female gender, by a force beyond the reach of what Elster, referring to the man who victimized Carlotta, tellingly terms male "power and freedom"—a phrase that Scottie himself uses when he discovers the truth about Madeleine.

In a film that thematizes the power of looking, it is appropriate that the struggle between Scottie and Carlotta for the possession of Madeleine is imaged rather than discussed. Following Madeleine to a local gallery, Scottie observes her fascination with a portrait of Carlotta. The editing of this sequence offers three looks: Scottie's at Madeleine, Madeleine's at Carlotta, and Carlotta's separate, implied gaze at each of them. But Scottie, looking at Madeleine, never has his gaze returned. Instead, the power of Carlotta appears to pull Madeleine away from the man who would love her toward a suicidal rejection of normal heterosexual coupling. Scottie must turn Madeleine's gaze firmly toward him, but he proves unable to do so. In the romantic scene immediately preceding her suicide, Madeleine embraces Scottie, confessing her love for him. And yet, as they embrace, her gaze is pointedly directed off-screen, toward the destructive renunciation so appropriately represented by the mission tower. (The mission is now used as a convent.) Failing to control Madeleine's desire, Scottie can only watch the woman he loves fall to her death.

Madeleine's surrender, her being swept away, is hardly passive. When the woman is "herself," she assists Scottie in his inquiry, answering the questions he poses in an attempt to devise some natural explanation for her behavior. But when Madeleine is "possessed," she resists his attentions; her strength in resisting Scottie is paradoxically offered as a weakness, as something that happens to her. Carlotta gives Madeleine a strength she would never have possessed on her own, and this strength makes a mockery of male power and freedom. The victory of this vengeful female spirit is not without its ironies: Carlotta impels Madeleine toward the same fate she was made to suffer at the hands of an exploitative man. In a sense, Madeleine becomes yet another victim of that unjust exploitation.

And so does Scottie. He incorporates the experiences of both Madeleine and Carlotta into his own repertoire of subconscious images. Standing before the tombstone in his dream (as he had watched Madeleine do), Scottie sees the grave as a dark and empty space, not as a hole in the earth. He then tumbles involuntarily into this frightening void. As he falls, the space becomes tunnel-like and vivid red. Scottie's head, separated from his body, screams silently. This image then becomes one of a male figure falling through an endless space. The castration imagery in his dream powerfully expresses the sense in which Scottie feels himself controlled, perhaps destroyed, by a malevolent female power.

In fact, he is "feminized" even earlier in the story. The sudden and terrifying advent of his vertigo means that he is helpless to prevent the fatal fall of his colleague. The experience leaves him corseted and dependent on a cane. Appropriately, the scene between Scottie and his former girlfriend, Midge (Barbara Bel Geddes), in which his experiences with vertigo are discussed, features both the prominent display of a brassiere and Scottie's pathetic attempt to conquer his fear, resulting in him fainting into Midge's arms. The coroner, of course, later indicts him for his failure to make it up the tower to save Madeleine, reminding him of the earlier episode when vertigo had paralyzed him. Appointing himself as Madeleine's therapist, Scottie is also in need of therapy. The conventions of Hollywood romance, which depend on a rigid separation of male and female roles, are thereby deconstructed. Scottie, like all noir thriller protagonists, experiences a frightening destabilization of his identity; but what is at issue in this Hitchcock film is not just the public self (for example, Roger Thornhill's misidentification as George Kaplan) but gender, that complicated and often contradictory social construct. Frightened into catatonia, Scottie becomes at the end of part 1 the very image of a stereotypically female illness. Mute and lacking any direction, he is the heroine of melodrama, awaiting the intervention of male power to effect a cure.

In a striking reversal (yet reaffirmation of traditional notions of gender), Scottie does cure himself before the end of the story. Part 2 begins with a bridge passage—reestablishing shots of San Francisco accompanied by a "hopeful" musical motif. The process of Scottie's recovery is not shown, but, while we now see him out of the hospital and back on the street, he appears to be still disturbed and ill, obsessed with recovering what he can of the Madeleine he has lost. He has become, in fact, a male version of Carlotta, wandering the streets and asking pathetic questions about a lost loved one. (Carlotta's lover had taken their child from her.) He sees a woman on the street who reminds him of Madeleine, although the resemblance seems slight; the woman's hair color, style of makeup, and clothes are very different, not to mention posture and demeanor. Only the most perceptive members of the original audience would have recognized that this new woman, whose name is Judy Barton, is also played by Kim Novak.

Following Judy to her hotel room, Ferguson quite rudely pushes himself on her, demanding to know who she is and revealing his obsession for the lost Madeleine. Feeling sorry for him, she accepts his invitation to dinner.

Having led the spectator into believing that the film's narrative will now trace Ferguson's desire to act out the obsession with the past (and perhaps, with the help of the earthier, more stable, and available Judy, find romantic happiness), Hitchcock at this point reverses, in a disorienting way, those expectations. In a subjective flashback, Judy reveals that she posed as the real Madeleine, dying her hair and otherwise altering her appearance, so that Elster, her lover and employer, could murder his wife. The flashback shows that Judy, running up the stairs ahead of a faltering Ferguson, met Elster on the tower roof, where he threw off the body of the real Madeleine, who had been previously strangled. Judy determines to leave San Francisco and reveal the truth to Ferguson in a letter whose contents she reads in voice-over narration. As she says, she hopes in this way he will be able to overcome both his guilt over and obsession with the past. But then she suddenly rips up the letter and decides to remain and make Ferguson love her for herself.

With this decision, Judy herself becomes a noir thriller protagonist, struggling to prevent a misidentification (this time an unwilling one) that would destroy the authenticity she now feels. The remainder of *Vertigo* explores the irresistible urge of Ferguson to re-create the past (and hence restore Madeleine and the self he was with her) as he confronts and overwhelms Judy's ineffectual attempts to restore the past in the present, removing the barrier of misidentity that doomed their affair even while making it possible.

Judy must resist the truth, but Ferguson must discover it if he is to regain the male prerogatives of power and freedom. As a victimized male, Ferguson can be healed only by a revengeful renunciation of the woman who used her sex to dominate and control him, exploiting the feminization effected by the onset of his vertigo. Our previous view of Madeleine as a passive subject swept into attractive weakness by forces beyond her control proves to be an illusion. Madeleine (at least the Madeleine we are allowed to know) is Judy's deliberate creation, a performance designed to lure and deceive the dupe chosen, by Elster, because of his well-publicized failure and illness. Therefore, what Ferguson does next we are allowed to understand as a form of poetic justice.

Continuing to see Judy—he has bullied her into giving up her job
to live off his money—Ferguson persuades her, first, to wear the same
clothes Madeleine did and, finally, to color and style her hair in the
same way. Before this transformation, Ferguson can feel no real desire
for Judy. When she becomes Madeleine once again, Judy reassumes
the characterization she had created; gone are the brassy manner, the
somewhat cheap appearance, the easy familiarity with the "real
world," and the defiant independence of the working girl. Judy
arouses Ferguson with the aristocratic, elegant, and mannered persona
she had first seduced him with. This part of the film endorses the
man's right to have his sexual object appear and "be" as he likes. Judy's
protests do not avail; Ferguson makes it clear that he will not, indeed
cannot, feel desire for her until and unless she becomes the other. But
this transformation is just, because it restores Judy to the self she had
once offered as her own.

And yet, in imposing his will, Ferguson is still not satisfied. The
lovers embrace, and the camera appears to pan around them in a complete 360-degree movement; as it does, the background shifts from
the hotel room to the mission stable where Ferguson kissed Madeleine
before her rush to the tower. This shifting background appears to be
Ferguson's subjective image of the scene. The implication is that this
is yet another form of vertigo, of that perceptual malady that disturbs
Ferguson's sense of where he is and, on a deeper level, what he is. (On
this symbolic level, vertigo is the malady of all those who inhabit the
unstable, threatening, and doomed landscape of the noir thriller.) Ferguson is not yet suspicious of Judy's performance. His uneasiness
must be a dissatisfaction with the remaking process itself, furthered
by his realization that the past and present cannot be joined and that
the assertion of Pygmalionesque power spoils the result, producing
the woman not as she really is.

Vertigo in this way explores, perhaps more deeply than any other
film noir, the contradiction embodied in the femme fatale: the coex-
istence of beauty and surrender with moral ugliness and unbridled
self-assertion. Madeleine indeed is a mask, and Judy is the reality. On
the one hand, Judy's Madeleine was a performance coached by Elster
to betray Ferguson. (In fact, it replicates yet another identity, the real
Mrs. Elster, who is never represented on screen.) On the other hand,
Madeleine becomes a role that Judy, if grudgingly, readopts in her
surrender to Ferguson's demands. The mask is thus both a brutal,
calculating emasculation and a loving self-abnegation. In typically

noir fashion, the ambiguity associated with the femme fatale cannot be resolved; she is both threat and lover.

This becomes clear in the scene that follows Judy's transformation and the final satisfaction of Ferguson's desire. After their lovemaking, Judy gets dressed for dinner and, apparently by mistake, puts on the necklace that once belonged to Carlotta and was given to her by Elster as part of her reward for a job well done. Ferguson recognizes the necklace and immediately understands that Judy is the "real" Madeleine. In other words, Ferguson now sees that this woman he possesses is the one he fell in love with—the past is truly restored in the present. And yet he realizes that the woman he fell in love with was not the woman he thought she was—the past is finally unmasked in the present. Ferguson, as it turns out, is a character who encounters loss in the very act of discovering power and freedom.

Knowing the truth, Ferguson now makes Judy become Madeleine in one more way. He drives her to the old mission and forces her, quite brutally at times, to climb the tower steps with him, reenacting the plot that was perpetrated against him. His anger at Judy permits him to overcome the otherwise destabilizing attack of vertigo he has; this time he makes it to the top of the tower, like many a noir protagonist uncovering the truth as he resumes the position of dominant and vengeful male. Ferguson's masculinity is restored by his successful ascent, but as he questions the woman he loves and hates (calling her, alternately, Judy and Madeleine), Ferguson cannot decide what to do. Will he deliver Judy to the police for punishment? Will he forgive and love her now that he knows all the truth the past can deliver? He never has the chance to decide as Judy, doomed by the strangest irony of her betrayal, sees a dark figure appear at the head of the tower stairs. It is, Judy thinks, Carlotta, and she backs away from Ferguson's embrace, falling this time to her death. In the film's last image, Ferguson moves forward, perhaps ready, as he had been in his nightmare, to join her in a leap into the void.

Judy believes, if just for a moment, that the Carlotta who was only a character, albeit a historical one, in an old story has come to life, perhaps to protest the victimization of another woman (the real Madeleine Elster, her distant kin) done in her name. If so, then the "story" Madeleine played out in part 1 about being urged to her death by Carlotta does come true. Nothing in *Vertigo* better illustrates the film's rejection of stock Hollywood formulas than the "return" of Carlotta, who now appears as a dea ex machina to solve the question of Judy's fate. The supernatural, as before, is only an illusion. The dark figure is, in fact, one of the convent's nuns who, as she ironically reveals, climbed to the tower because she "heard voices." Both characters, the one an imagined presence and the other flesh-and-blood, signify female renunciation or refusal. Carlotta's story is co-opted but not created by Elster. And, indeed, it imposes a set of roles and a series of patterns on the characters that they cannot reject.

Playing the role of someone possessed by Carlotta, Judy is, like Carlotta, used by a man who throws her away when she no longer suits his plans. Trying desperately to prevent the woman he loves from being swept away into self-annihilation by Carlotta's ghostly malevolence, Ferguson finds himself acting out elements of Carlotta's role and becoming, like Madeleine, someone obsessed with the dead past. Neither Ferguson nor Judy can write their own narratives. Only Elster is capable of devising and carrying out a plot that answers to his desires and interests. But it is hardly his Carlotta who writes the conclusion to the story. Judy falls and Ferguson is destroyed by yet another misidentification, by a "wrong turning" that is equally caused by the characters' failings and the fatalism of the dark world they inhabit. Like the other noir films we have examined, *Vertigo* rejects the idealization of human experience so essential to Hollywood utopianism, and yet it conforms to the notions of poetic justice enshrined in the Production Code. The evildoers (save Elster) are punished, and the truth is revealed. The film's final image, however, is one of the bleakest in the history of the American cinema. We should not be surprised that the film was not much liked by viewers expecting a more reassuring kind of entertainment at their local theaters. Like many noir productions of the mid-1950s, *Vertigo* pushes dark cinema about as far as it could go and still remain a viable commercial form.

CHAPTER 5

Trapped in the Dark:
The Noir Woman's Picture

In the noir thriller, women often appear as victims of fate or circumstance who frustrate male desire. *Detour*'s Vera is simultaneously the instrument of a poetic injustice that crushes Al and an unprotected woman, however assertively independent, whose attempt to seize power over men ironically ends in her fatal, yet accidental victimization by the man she would manipulate. Like Al, Vera is destroyed by the very course of events that initially mean her seemingly fortunate empowerment. The opportunities of the two characters, however, are differentiated by gender. Miraculously, Al appears to have found the American dream in replacing Haskell; his position is defined by an automobile and money—by, in other words, the ability to assert his independence of others within a restlessly mobile society in which money allows the unlimited satisfaction of desire. Al's downfall results from the way in which he progressively loses his independence, becoming, first, the tool of Vera's desire (driving the car where she wants to go, agreeing to her various schemes) and, finally, the prisoner of two conflicting identities, his and and the dead man's.

In contrast, Vera's empowerment is defined not by a direct and therefore independent control over Haskell's money and car, but by the leverage she is able to exert over Al. As becomes clear, in fact, she does not desire independence; instead, she wishes to claim the affections and allegiance of the man she has trapped. The ultimate irony of Vera's position is that she is unable to negotiate any passage from dominatrix to sexual object; she cannot arouse Al's desire by ordering him to want her. Appropriately, then, Vera dies as a result of her unwillingness to sever this (dis)connection to Al. Seeking a room alone to telephone the police, she is trapped and undone by the cord she unwittingly puts around her own neck; Vera's destruction spells Al's eventual doom because he is inexorably tied to her, even in death.

The Stranger and Vertigo offer similar versions of women undone by the power they come to possess over men also trapped by inescapable circumstances. At first the innocent object of Franz Kindler's desire for successful self-concealment, Mary Rankin by chance becomes the only person who can reveal that her husband is the war criminal sought by the authorities. She thus effects, if unwittingly, an ironic reversal of Kindler's plans: the very marriage he imagined would shelter him from detection becomes the relationship that most threatens his masquerade.

As in Detour, the woman discovers in the very act of being put in her sexual place (as she is either picked up or made a bride) that she possesses an unexpected power over the man who would reduce her to a simple object of his desire. But Mary's power, like Vera's, can only be asserted in ways that finally victimize her. Faced with the impossible choice between identifying her husband as a genocidal maniac and living with a man she knows is a monster, Mary retreats into a suicidal self-abandonment, asking Kindler to kill her and even offering him a weapon. Left alive, Mary is reduced temporarily to hysterical unconsciousness but awakes to become the would-be executioner of her monstrous lover. In this attempt she fails, for only with Wilson's help is Kindler driven onto the clock face and destroyed; her partial victory, however, is truly Pyrrhic, for the destruction of Kindler does not effect her return to psychological health; it appears to portend, in fact, her continuing madness.

Vertigo's Madeleine/Judy, lacking any stable identity, more complexly exemplifies the way in which the noir thriller constructs women as both victims and obstacles in the hero's path to fulfillment. As a mask, Madeleine is trapped by the way in which the irresistible force that has seized her identity empowers her to kill herself. Madeleine thus defies Scottie's attempts to control her: she climbs a tower he cannot ascend, if only to leap to her death. Fleeing from both her husband's and her lover's desire that she be healed (that is, transformed into an obedient, untroublesome woman), Madeleine is subsumed against her will into another identity. Madeleine's passive seizure of control feminizes the man she loves and destroys his object of desire even as it confirms his lack of manliness, condemning him to a mute melancholia.

As herself, Judy is victimized by one man who makes her over—furnishes her another identity that she must assume—but then asserts her own "self" in the affection she comes to feel for their intended dupe. Ironically, it is later as "herself" that Judy attempts to seduce her beloved, only to discover that it is the "other" whom he truly loves. Judy then surrenders to this otherness a second time but, like her mask, is finally destroyed by the loss of her own identity. Given a second chance, Scottie is able to understand the deception practiced upon him, yet he proves unable (just as before) to restore the object of his desire to stable selfhood. Victimized by the woman who herself is a victim, he is condemned to experience again, and more horribly, the death of his beloved.

Vertigo shows how the noir thriller can become the site for an exploration of issues related to female identity; this film interrogates how the woman's attractiveness is a construction responding to the peculiarities of male desire. Judy becomes an image *for* Elster's desire and then the image *of* Scottie's desire, and these images bear in each case the burden of restoring male power and freedom. In both *Detour* and *The Stranger*, questions of sexual politics likewise emerge when we emphasize what these two texts otherwise marginalize, the experience of the women characters in question. In all three films, male characters are featured more prominently, in the usual manner of the classic Hollywood film. The men are protagonists seeking the satisfaction of their needs and wants but whose drives toward actualization are thwarted by an unfortunate destiny (Al), inescapably hostile circumstances (Kindler), and female perfidiousness and the betrayal of a friend (Scottie). In the ordinary studio film, feminist theory has demonstrated, women can be constructed as either objects of the male gaze (and thus elements of a male fantasy that can be acted on and fulfilled) or barriers in the way of masculine self-assertion.

The two films we will consider in this chapter approach gender politics in a different way, even as they often raise the same kinds of issues as the noir thriller. During the 1930s and, especially, the 1940s, the Hollywood studios promoted and developed, as Mary Ann Doane terms them, "films that are *in some sense* the 'possession' of women, [the] terms of address [of these films] are dictated by the anticipated presence of the female spectator" (my emphasis).[1] The evolution of the woman's picture was conditioned by a number of factors, the most important of which contributed to both films analyzed in this chapter: perhaps more than in previous decades, there was a group of female stars in the late 1940s with strong box-office appeal. It was therefore natural that Hollywood sought out vehicles for the exhibition of these attractive personae, of whom Loretta Young and Joan Crawford are prominent examples. At the same time, the 1930s had witnessed the increasing popularity of the woman's novel—books written by a woman, featuring a female protagonist, and constructing a female reader. The woman's novels that found popularity during this period revealed the existence of an eager readership. With its close ties to popular literature, Hollywood quickly attempted to capitalize on adaptations of these books (or to produce scripts modeled on them) and to devise strategies for converting their readers into spectators.

Molly Haskell, for one, has found much to admire in the 1940s woman's picture, especially the fact that it occasionally presents "a woman who begins as a victim of discriminatory circumstances and rises, through pain, obsessions, or defiance, to become mistress of her fate." Though expressed through the "suds of soap opera," the rise of such a heroine is given "stature and conviction not through a discreet contempt for the female sensibility but through an all-out belief in it."[2] The famous *Now, Voyager* (Irving Rapper, 1942) usefully exemplifies this tradition. It is certainly in some ways a story of education that traces the upward movement of its female protagonist. Bette Davis first appears as the fat, heavy-browed, and hysterical spinster Charlotte Vale, but she eventually achieves both sleek attractiveness and a healthy independence from her Victorian-minded, domineering mother (Gladys Cooper).

And yet it is the very failure of Charlotte Vale that allows her eventually to "succeed." Cured of her melancholia at an asylum by a helpful psychiatrist (Claude Rains), Charlotte simultaneously becomes attractive; she loses weight, begins to dress fashionably, has her hair done in a modern style, shaves her eyebrows, and gives up wearing eyeglasses. Her doctor launches her on a voyage of female self-assertion—a cruise to South America—with the instruction that she try to meet people, presumably men. Though shy, Charlotte manages to attract a handsome foreigner, Jerry (played by the dashing Paul Henreid), who is, unfortunately, married to an invalid wife he does not have the heart to leave. When she returns home, Charlotte attempts to get over her disappointment by beginning a relationship with Elliot

(John Loder), an old family friend, but when she sees Jerry again, she breaks it off. At this point, she is thrown into despair by her mother's sudden death after a particularly bitter battle in her continuing war for independence. A trip back to the asylum results in her encounter with Jerry's adolescent daughter (Janis Wilson), herself a victim of depression and a lack of positive thinking. Charlotte abandons her own concerns and becomes a "doctor" in treating the girl; this experience convinces her to adopt a new vocation. She reopens the family home as a shelter for disturbed or neglected children, with Jerry's daughter the most important resident. Meeting with him again, she is not bitter that life has denied her the fulfillment of her sexual needs and desire for a family; instead, she convinces Jerry that she is happy with her lot.

On the film's own terms, this finale constitutes a happy ending that ratifies Charlotte's development into a functioning and useful adult— the goal, of course, of the neo-Freudian therapy practiced by her psychiatrist. Charlotte has indeed "sought" and "found," though not exactly what he had in mind. Blocked from marriage by the force of true love, Charlotte has discovered a socially acceptable way to be Jerry's wife and the mother of his child. The price of this accommodation is the renunciation of sexual and social fulfillment. In Charlotte's platonizing metaphor, the couple thus constituted can have the "stars" but not the "moon." On a deeper level, the ending is perhaps not so positive. The film demonstrates that female desire may truly be satisfied only as part of a social fantasy (the exotic cruise) but must inevitably be frustrated in the real world of social pressures and roles.

For the role of assertive and desiring woman, *Now, Voyager* substitutes that of the self-sacrificing mother who is confined to the family home from which she had previously escaped only with the greatest difficulty. In this role, Charlotte can attain the power of independent action because she has renounced sexuality, hoping instead for the normal development of Jerry's daughter. And yet this compromise represents a gender victory of sorts. The transformed Vale mansion, with its liberated and loving attitude toward child-rearing, opposes itself to the male-dominated sanitarium. The ancient system of family, symbolized by the home, contrasts favorably with modern forms of surveillance and control, exemplified by the progressive, if paternalistic, science of psychiatry. Charlotte finally rejects the voyage out, with its cures that send the patient beyond the comforting web of family relationships on a journey of desire that must end in failure. She instead

embarks on a voyage within, in the process rediscovering a landscape—the home where she was born, raised, and made miserable—
that better corresponds to her unique powers and personal history.

Noir versions of the woman's picture, in contrast, destroy the equi-
librium of the mainstream type, in which, as I have shown, the female
protagonist is simultaneously made subject to a patriarchal society but
allowed a certain independence, a "room of her own." A number of
feminist critics have suggested that the noir film in general resembles
the male-dominated ordinary studio product; in the films discussed so
far in this study, we have seen that this is certainly true, for women
characters figure only marginally in them. But this characterization of
dark cinema must be altered to make room for the films noirs we
discuss here. Like the mainstream woman's picture, these films focus
on the experiences of a female protagonist, particularly her struggles
with a male-dominated sexual economy. Such a focus obviously dif-
ferentiates them from other types of noir film, which they otherwise
closely resemble. Noir women's pictures are particularly interesting
since, in keeping with the pessimism of dark cinema in general, they
represent more starkly the discontents and disabilities that are conventionally the protagonist's lot in postwar melodrama.

CAUSE FOR ALARM

Cause for Alarm (1951) opens with what appears to be a more positive
version of the Vale family home: images of a cheery and sunlit suburban house, evidently the residence of a prosperous family, play over
the credits, accompanied by a rich romantic theme. (The film's subtle
and nuanced scoring was done by André Previn.) The detailed realism
practiced here by the director of photography, Joseph Ruttenberg,
bears little resemblance to his earlier, more expressionistic work on
The Bribe (1949); in fact, both the upscale, suburban mise-en-scène
and the "standard" cinematographic style initially promise a mainstream domestic melodrama. But the director, Tay Garnett, immediately undermines this expectation. A sudden cut to the house's
interior, accompanied by a transition to "ominous" music, shows us
an unsmiling young woman (Loretta Young) vacuuming the rug. In
her voice-over, she confesses that "this is where I live; I'm a housewife." But it is not the daily drudgery, the work to maintain the ap-

pearance of respectability, that displeases Ellen Jones, or so she goes on to admit. Things are not right in the Jones household; her husband George (Barry Sullivan) is upstairs, confined to bed with a serious heart ailment. And Ellen, feeling strongly the pressure to attune her mood to his needs, says that there seems no point to going on about the household routine with George lying ill. Guiltily, she describes her state of mind as "dangerous," because "I was beginning to feel sorry for myself."

As they unravel according to a relentless logic, the events of this day punish Ellen for her unhappiness, which seems a volatile mixture of dissatisfaction with her role as childless housewife and frustration at George's confinement, perhaps at his lack of leadership and sexual power as well. The narrative, in fact, corresponds precisely to the paradox of Ellen's distorted view of her own importance and her feelings of oppression. She accepts responsibility for holding the family together, but, completely at George's beck and call, Ellen cannot control even her own destiny. The film, however, thematizes not only the powerlessness of the American housewife—thereby reframing as an issue of gender politics the noir protagonist's subjection to an ineluctable fate—but also explores one of the principal discontents of heterosexual coupling. A man sometimes "wins" a woman away from the affection she feels for another man. But this victory is never final, for the rejected suitor is a continual reminder of the woman's fickleness, of the possibility that she can be "won" back. In the course of this film, the family home, which seems happy when viewed from without, is revealed both as a prison for the wife who cannot control her own fate and as the apocalyptic site where the male power that has formed the couple destroys it.

In *Cause for Alarm,* noirness is thus not an alternative world of temptation, illicitness, or irresponsibility; it is simply the repressed underside of an otherwise ordinary domestic life, which, under the proper circumstances, can become a terror for the woman subject to a patriarchal sexual economy. Coupled with a man who, because of his unreasonable jealousy, intends to kill her, Ellen becomes a protagonist by default, her mission one of self-preservation. She must extricate herself from the fatal ties of this marriage gone wrong, even as she discovers her inability to complete even the smallest of seemingly unproblematic domestic tasks. Though her safety hangs upon it, she cannot retrieve a letter from the postman. Like Charlotte Vale, Ellen finds that the family home is a desperate landscape from which she cannot escape. But unlike Charlotte, she discovers that domestic life holds out no promise of happiness, however compromised; the bright image of respectable bourgeois existence with which the film begins becomes an ironic icon, a deceptive surface that hardly conforms to the much darker reality within.

Though she hopes that "things would be different when he was well and strong again," Ellen quickly learns that the heart condition George suffers from is the correlative of a deeper psychological imbalance. While Ellen asks after his welfare, the camera shows George in bed hiding a letter he is writing. A close-up reveals that this letter, addressed to the district attorney, charges Ellen with trying to murder her husband because she is in love with another man, Dr. Ranney Grahame (Bruce Cowling), George's physician and erstwhile best friend. Meanwhile, Ellen, trying to understand what has gone wrong with her life, flashes back to happier days when she met George in a military hospital. At the time, she was dating Grahame; while waiting for him to finish his rounds, she strolled inside a ward to comfort the wounded airmen there. Unbeknownst to her, George, suffering only from a hangover, had crawled into a bed there while also waiting for Grahame. Playing the pitiful invalid, he enticed Ellen into massaging his brow. Her gesture of compassion afforded him the opportunity to grab and kiss her, but she fought him off. Grahame then entered the room and uncovered George's masquerade, but Ellen was obviously intrigued by the man's crude attentions, by the male power and confidence he exuded.

Later the three go to the beach. When Grahame is called away on a hospital emergency, George takes full advantage of his friend's absence to pursue her aggressively, something that Grahame, though obviously in love with Ellen, had evidently never done. By the time George must return overseas, he and Ellen have become lovers; at the airport, Grahame stands by without protest as George tells her that he will "never let her go." But George's brashness and confidence have another side, and it is briefly hinted at in these sequences. Watching a nurse wheel a patient through the ward at the hospital, George remarks that there is "nothing a woman likes better than shoving a man around," showing that his male ego is more fragile than it otherwise appears to be (and revealing a misogynistic cast of mind). Not surprisingly, then, George's relationship with Ellen is based on the power he can wield over her, on the fact that he took her away from Grahame, the man to whom she was originally attracted. This power, however, seems to depend more on weakness, and the opportunity it offers for manipulation, than on outright assertion; after all, George does pretend to be wounded in order to seduce Ellen. Perhaps George's misogyny and passive aggressiveness make Grahame uneasy about the man's relations with Ellen. He asks, "Are you sure he's right for you?" Obviously charmed by George's male magnetism and unwilling to evaluate him dispassionately, Ellen responds, "I don't know . . . it's something you feel."

The flashback returns us to a present where George continues to plot against Ellen, though she is not yet aware of it. Faking an attack, he sends her out to fetch another doctor, but when she cannot find one and brings Grahame to his side, George accuses them of conspiring against him. He declares sarcastically that she has taken his power from him: "You always know best nowadays." When Grahame counters that George has a wonderful wife, he quips, "I don't think I'll be tying up her exclusive services." Leaving George alone, Grahame and Ellen confer downstairs about the man's mental state, obviously worried by his barely contained jealous rage. According to Grahame, when a man lacks physical power, he can become subject to all kinds of "imaginary fears."

George's jealousy, then, is cast as the result of his illness, although, in a larger sense, it seems more an unavoidable discontent associated with the socially sanctioned scheme of heterosexual coupling whereby the woman becomes the prize in the competition between two men. If the woman is conceived as responding only to the power of the man who wants her, then he will feel his possession of her threatened by any display of weakness on his part. This scene between Grahame and Ellen, it must be noted, intimates that her husband's fears, though obviously exaggerated, may not be unfounded. Not only is his former friend now in a position of control over him as his physician, but Ellen also depends greatly on the doctor's concern and help. George has been displaced as the sole and unquestioned male authority in her life. In response to Grahame's offer of assistance at any time, day or night, Ellen murmurs, "I don't know what I'd do sometimes if I didn't remember that." That this conversation is staged in whispers beyond George's earshot, with the two characters framed tightly together, offers the very image (if not quite the fact) of a conspiracy against the invalid husband. The narrative, in any case, depends on this establishment of a continuing close relationship between the former lovers. At the end, with George discredited and dead, Grahame becomes Ellen's male support, and the implication is that someday soon the pair will be a romantic couple again.

The next scene adds a further dimension to Ellen's unhappiness, the fact that she and George are childless, a condition that is attributable not only to his present impotence but to his selfish refusal to share Ellen's love, even with a child. The man whose powerful desire captures her affections makes a poor husband: he wants neither a wife nor a family, only Ellen as a possession. And yet Ellen yearns for motherhood. Billy (Bradley Mora), the little boy from next door, wanders into her kitchen, where he is apparently a frequent and welcome visitor. But Ellen, once again subordinating her own needs to those of her husband, shoos Billy away because she is afraid he might disturb George's rest. Returning upstairs, however, Ellen does confront George with her dissatisfaction: "Everything in our lives, every breath, every thought has been for ourselves. . . . I don't think people can do that and be happy."

If what Ellen says is true, then George's illness, a condition that turns her into a slave attendant upon his every whim, is hardly an unfortunate accident, but rather the reductio ad absurdum of a demanding narcissism. Implying that it might be time to grow up, she says that they could "change all that now," but George dismisses this suggestion with a jealous sneer, fuming that as soon as he went back to work she would take up with Grahame. Ellen, however, quite softly replies that she would then have time to "compare notes with every other woman on the block," at last assuming her rightful place as a proper wife and perhaps mother. But these hopes are quickly dashed when she leaves the room and George goes back to his letter writing.

Having finished, George summons Ellen back to the bedroom and entrusts her with mailing the letter. She delivers it to the postman, another self-concerned male unhappy with his life; because his feet are tired and his back aches, he wishes he could "lie down for a while," thus surrendering the responsibility for supporting his family in much the same way George has. In fact, the postman (Irving Bacon), with his crankiness and inclination to feel put upon, becomes another version of George; when she must approach him later to get the letter back, Ellen can no more cope with his complaints and uncertainties, his overemotionality and unfounded accusations, than she can with George's.

Returning to the bedroom, Ellen mentions her encounter with little Billy, and George responds with a chilling tale from his childhood, one that Ellen evidently has not heard before. As a young boy, George's hobby was building ships in a bottle. After finishing a particularly difficult project, he returned to his room to find the boy from next door handling it without permission. George became so enraged that he attacked his friend with a rake: "Where his face had been so white it was all blood. . . . I felt safe." Horrified at her son, George's mother made him give the ship to the beaten child as a punishment, but George let it fall to the ground and break, feeling a pride of possession in this act of destruction: "It was mine more than it had ever been before." The boy, George confesses, looked like Grahame. Ellen reads the obvious lesson of this autobiographical revelation: she will play the role of the smashed ship in the competition between the two former friends.

This scene is significant because it provides another order of explanation for George's illness and psychopathology. George, we are asked to believe, has always been violently possessive, always willing to deprive or hurt himself in order to inflict harm on those he sees as his enemies. The effect is to deepen the critique of his cockiness and self-confidence, of the untroubled ease with which he seduced his best friend's girl. George's illness, then, can be seen as a fitting punishment for his asocial exercise of sexual power, for his drive to take what he wants even by deception; that is, because he is not a real man emotionally, he must endure being helpless as a child. The scene in the hospital, in which George plays at being wounded to attract Ellen, thus rhymes ironically with this sequence in the bedroom, when George again uses his illness to control and manipulate. And Ellen, seduced by his initial deception and show of force, suffers in turn the consequences of her surrender of self, her dependence on feelings rather than reason. In other words, because she did not stay with the man who truly cares for her, she must endure an incomplete and dissatisfying marriage. Resenting his accusations of infidelity and conspiracy, she tells her husband, "I can't let you talk that way anymore." But George pays no attention to this empty show of force and immediately locks the door. He then tells Ellen about the letter to the district attorney and his plot to incriminate her, a plot that includes his taking overdoses of the heart medicine he had asked her to refill. Apparently too impatient to let his plan take effect and eager to see

Ellen suffer, George pulls a gun, but he collapses dead of an attack before he can shoot her with it. His dying words are, "There are just too many things against you." And he is not wrong.

Like Al Roberts in *Detour*, Ellen does not call the police because she is afraid circumstances are indeed against her, even though, with Grahame's testimony, it is difficult to imagine how she could be considered in any way responsible for George's death. Instead, feeling guilty, she acts guilty and attempts to cover up the traces of what might appear to be a crime. For the rest of the afternoon, Ellen does her best to appear innocent but ironically only arouses suspicion. Her life has become a nightmare, just like, as she says, "one of those awful dreams, the kind I used to have when George was overseas." The repressed underside of Ellen's marriage reveals a new kind of terror, not the more expected form of tragic loss—a husband killed or wounded in the war—but the unimaginable: a husband transformed from a lover into a suicidal killer.

As she descends the stairs, Ellen is faced with her first test. The druggist is on the phone about the prescription refill she had ordered for George; in near-hysterics, Ellen protests that the only reason she wants more pills is that George dropped the others down the sink. After hanging up, she asks, "Why didn't I tell him about George?" Though rhetorical, this question is answered by the narrative. Ellen's dissatisfaction with a childless marriage, her lack of grief at her husband's death, her evident deep connection to Grahame, all contribute to her sense of guilt, a feeling heightened by the fact that, as the opening sequence demonstrates, she counts herself solely responsible for the welfare of her household. George's plot even makes her feel guilt at not being a proper wife or woman. She is tormented by paranoid thoughts about the woman next door, with whom she has never established friendly relations, worrying excessively about how she appears to others exiting the house in a frantic attempt to extricate herself from George's plot.

Getting back the letter will prevent her misidentification as a murderer and adulteress. The camera tracks Ellen as she runs hysterically through the sunny streets of her neighborhood looking for the postman. Explaining the regulation—he can give the letter back only to the person who mailed it, something Ellen obviously cannot allow to happen—the man becomes increasingly agitated at her lack of sympathy for his position. Frustrated, Ellen grabs unsuccessfully for the letter, and the postman stalks off in disgust, even though she pleads with him to help her avoid George's pretended wrath: "It was my fault. . . . I mailed it by mistake." It is ironic that Ellen must play the part of a wife on an errand for a demanding, invalid husband in order to save herself; in imitating this character, Ellen, of course, is able to give a method performance, "using" the emotions and gestures that were a genuine element of her own self before George's death. In fact, it might even be poetically just that Ellen, acting for herself, ostensibly acts for George. Perhaps she never loved him—the film offers no real evidence of her affection. Perhaps she only took joy in his possession of her.

Meanwhile, George's Aunt Clara (Georgia Backus) has arrived at the house and gets in with the help of an increasingly suspicious neighbor. Ellen must be friendly to the woman, who insists on seeing her nephew, but she barely holds herself back from hysterics. At her wit's end, Ellen manages to make Aunt Clara leave only by saying that George found her last visit disagreeable. Well aware of George's selfishness, his aunt fumes: "A man wrapped up in himself makes a very small package." She may be right about George, perhaps about men in general, but however small they may be, men are shown in this film to have a nearly irresistible power over women.

In *Cause for Alarm,* the war between the sexes is fought on several fronts. Knowing that she must face another man in charge, Ellen goes to the post office to retrieve the letter, determined that she must "look like every other housewife making a simple request." Much like Walter and Phyllis in *Double Indemnity,* Ellen is forced to cover her secret life with a mask of normality; in fact, she becomes an actress who in some ways plays the role she had always wanted, that of a simple housewife taking care of family business. Before she can get out the door, yet another man, a notary public apparently summoned earlier by George, blocks her way. Only with great difficulty, and at the cost of arousing his suspicions, does Ellen get rid of the man, who could easily be, as she says to herself, "another witness." Desperate to control herself at the post office, Ellen again becomes hysterical when the official there will not return the letter without first examining its contents. Though she rather convincingly imitates a housewife frightened of arousing her husband's wrath ("I must have the letter for him when I go home"), Ellen's tears and pleading get her nowhere. The letter is sent on to its destination: the district attorney.

She returns home dejected. Her neighbor Mrs. Edwards (Margalo Gillmore), sees her distress and makes an offer of friendship that Ellen, feeling her fate is now sealed, can view only ironically. She has no answer for the woman. Inside her house, now filled with threatening shadows, she calls Grahame to prevent him from coming over to see George. But once again, her efforts prove in vain as the doctor pulls up in his car at that very moment. Trying to stop him from finding the body, she lies that George has gotten another doctor, but Grahame sees through her deception. Ellen tells him the truth, but he can think of nothing to do. Normally, in the female Gothic, the woman's friend saves her from the husband's homicidal intentions; but in this noir version of that generic element, Grahame stands by mute and helpless, in acknowledgment perhaps of his own complicity. The female Gothic stages a competition between two men in which the rejected suitor or "old friend" who truly loves the woman, not the husband who for selfish reasons seeks her destruction, wins out in the end, often after a physical struggle, as in the archetypal *Gaslight*. But Grahame is given no such heroic part to play; he can do nothing to defeat George or his plan. In this dark inflection of romantic conventions, the faithful and loyal lover can neither rescue Ellen from the deranged husband nor help establish her innocence.

As events prove, Ellen is powerless to escape from George's insane plot. (Is this because in a way she is responsible for his jealousy? Do not her guilty actions after the fact cast significant doubt on her claim to be innocent? Does she not, in fact, become guiltier the more she struggles to appear innocent, even lying to Grahame at the end?) But in the noir world, chance, not poetic justice, is the ruling principle. At the brink of total despair, Ellen and Grahame are startled by yet another visitor. It is her postman returning with George's letter, which, it seems, was mailed without sufficient postage. Grahame burns the incriminating evidence, thus becoming a full partner in Ellen's attempt to keep George's plot from the police, who will, presumably, never be informed of the dead man's criminal conspiracy. The story ends with Ellen's ambiguous declaration that "I knew what people meant when they said their heart was broken." Does Ellen feel sorrow at last for the man who, however sick, was her lover and husband? Or does she rather feel disappointment about her lost chance at the American dream? The film's deus ex machina resolution certainly does not offer what the Hollywood happy ending usually does: the fulfillment of the protagonist's desire. All Ellen wanted was life as an ordinary housewife with a happy husband and children; though it evokes a pleasant neighborhood where such family life might go

In *Cause for Alarm* the heroine is saved from a false murder charge by the return of a letter, but she may not find happiness in the arms of the man who has always loved her. Courtesy of RKO/Museum of Modern Art, Film Stills Archive.

on, the film finally offers no evidence of such domestic bliss. Its only representations are of a parentless child, a solitary old woman, a postman miserable in his marriage and job, a professional man frustrated in love, a couple torn apart by jealousy and mistrust, a husband driven mad by illness and impotence, and a wife nearly destroyed by her eager acceptance of a sexual economy that cannot afford her happiness.

POSSESSED

In *Cause for Alarm,* the woman's sexual desire is represented as unproblematically fulfilled in the most conventional terms: courted by two men, Ellen is swept off her feet by the one who wants her more—or who at least appears to want her more. Desired, she can desire in turn, especially since her sexual display cannot in any sense be construed as a lure. Ellen walks in on George "by accident," and she innocently assumes a position that makes possible his physical advances only under the mistaken impression that he needs motherly comfort. Any pleasure she subsequently takes in possessing George derives from his possession of her; in the terms of romance fiction, she is appropriately "swept away" into sexual normality. The film's narrative depends very much on Ellen's willingness to be the typical married woman; she worries about her husband, desires children, and without complaint goes about the work that "makes" a home. Loretta Young's all-American prettiness, her evident vulnerability, and her performance history as a dutiful wife in other films (*The Stranger* exemplifies the kind of roles in which she was usually cast) all further this characterization; there is no hint in her screen persona of the self-assertion, the aggressive sexuality, the manipulative power associated with the typical femme fatale of many films noirs.

And yet the narrative is motored by the uncertainty and passive power of Ellen's desire, by doubts about her loyalty that are generated by her unthinking acquiescence to both romantic and sexual "common sense." If the woman's desire is aroused by the man's, and if she responds with surrender to his power to possess, then it appears that she can be "kept" only by the forceful and continual assertion of his will. But George, as Aunt Clara would say, is a very "small package."

His power derives from the narcissistic urge to be catered to, to be treated like a child; it is significant that his initial sexual approach to Ellen follows a request to be mothered. As George's "possession," Ellen is denied a full adult life; as his caretaker, she is dominated by his neediness but controls him in a way that he demands but also resents. It is hardly any wonder that their coupling is barren and that he imagines himself a victim.

Sensing her unhappiness, George decides to destroy the woman he no longer has the power to keep. Ironically, his plan fails because of a foolish oversight: not putting enough postage on the letter to the district attorney. The result is that the very scenario he had hoped to avoid—Ellen and Grahame together again, with him dead—comes true. In a further irony, George's failure endorses the very principle of heterosexual coupling that had enabled him to take Ellen in the first place: the woman will belong to the man who desires her most, who can do the most to keep her. Grahame gets Ellen in the end because of his unwavering desire. In fact, this cultural value is so deeply ingrained and difficult to challenge that it works to produce the effect of a somewhat happy ending for an otherwise quite dark story. Ellen, we may choose to believe, is finally with "the right man." But such an outcome, to be thought happy, must repress the woman's previous sexual history, the fact that she was someone else's at one time; for what is to prevent Grahame in turn from feeling uncertainty and jealousy, since Ellen had previously thrown him over for George? *Cause for Alarm* tries to marginalize and dismiss George by showing him to be sociopathic and violent, even when still a child; he was therefore never a proper husband, and their marriage was no marriage. And yet the force of George's discontent disrupts, perhaps permanently, Ellen's acceptance of things as they are. The film's title hints that there are difficulties in the conventional system of heterosexual exchange more threatening than this one man's pathology.

Curtis Bernhardt's *Possessed* (1947) examines issues of desire and power from a different but related perspective. In this film, Louise Howell Graham (Joan Crawford) is rejected by the man she loves, the *homme fatal* David Sutton (Van Heflin), but agrees to marry her rich and older employer, Dean Graham (Raymond Massey). Frustrated by unfulfilled desire and haunted by thoughts about her complicity in the death of Graham's first wife, Louise eventually becomes schizophrenic, or such is the diagnosis of the film's medical experts. Feeling persecuted and betrayed, she kills Sutton in a jealous rage and lapses into a profound melancholia from which, at film's end, doctors are only beginning to rouse her.

This narrative, written for the screen by Sylvia Richards and Ranald McDougall from a *Comospolitan* novelette penned by Rita Weiman, adopts a more feminine point of view than *Cause for Alarm*, written in its entirety by men. On one level, *Cause for Alarm* stages, and takes no little delight in, a scenario of revenge against a wife suspected, with some reason, of secretly harboring affection for a former beau and, perhaps more seriously, of being a witness to her husband's weaknesses, both physical and mental. The misogyny evident in this film is substantially different from that which, as we found in chapter 3, is so prevalent in the noir detective film; yet it is undeniably present, if only to confer "entertainment value" on the terror that the more or less innocent woman must suffer. In contrast, *Possessed* offers a critique, though somewhat compromised, of heterosexual coupling motored—or not, as the case may be—by a male desire that is selfish, weak, and unstable.

The issue of female assertiveness is raised, though obliquely, in *Now, Voyager*. Charlotte arouses Jerry's desire because the spectacle of attractiveness she presents is unconscious and defective, not a lure designed to trap him. When he meets her, Charlotte is still painfully shy, cannot stand being looked at, and is as yet incapable of stage-managing her appearance as a woman; the very clothes she wears are borrowed, as revealed by a note Jerry finds pinned to her dress. Being desired by Jerry not only allows Charlotte to desire him in turn; it also affords her the self-confidence and poise, the sense of being a proper woman, that her psychiatrist hoped a shipboard amour might provide. Back in Boston, Charlotte begins to present herself quite deliberately as an attractive and available woman. Meeting Elliot, the old family friend, she dazzles him with her display of sex appeal and charm. But Charlotte has now become too self-confident to accept the passive role expected of a woman in a romantic relationship; she pushes Elliot toward sexual involvement, suggesting a wild night on the town to warm them up, and he rejects her, shocked at her brazenness. The narrative eventually restores Charlotte to her proper place, that is, the family home, which signifies repression and self-abnegation.

Possessed offers a darker version of the discontents associated with the overly forward or active expression of female desire. The film opens with a romantic piano theme playing over images of a dark, deserted city. The camera locates a woman framed often only in fragments, wandering aimlessly down these nighttime streets. A close-up shows that her face is blank, devoid of all emotion, the psychological correlative to her apparently random behavior. Then a streetcar stops, and she starts to get on but halts at the open door to tell the conductor, "I'm looking for David." He closes the door and coldly goes on without her. This sequence develops in miniature the film's overall narrative. The woman is lost because she cannot find the man to whom she is attached, and the failure of her desire is ignored—the driver moves on without a thought for her safety or pain. Walking in front of a church as the parishioners stream out, she thinks one of them is David, and she can barely be dissuaded from following the man. Finally she enters a diner and discovers that she can no longer speak. An ambulance is summoned to wheel her away at high speed to a hospital.

As in *Now, Voyager,* the medical gaze is now turned on this catatonic figure in order to solve the enigma of her illness, which, as in the other film, appears closely connected to frustrated desire. Charlotte's doctor, however, treats her with respect and kindness, gradually bringing her to an awareness of her thwarted development. In *Possessed,* the experience of surveillance and diagnosis is much more impersonal and frightening. Louise's entrance into the hospital is shot with a subjective camera. A long tracking shot from her viewpoint on the stretcher reveals a ceiling festooned with vaguely menacing lights and machinery, as well as a gallery of unconcerned faces that bend down to examine the mute patient (with whom the viewer, of course, is forced to identify). Hustled off to "Psycho" because nothing organic seems to be the matter, she is then looked over by two male psychiatrists: Dr. Willard (Stanley Ridges) and his intern (Clifton Young). Dr. Willard suggests that her problem is a common one: "Beautiful woman, intelligent, frustrated . . . frustrated just like all the others we've seen." This instant diagnosis of blocked desire turns out to be correct, of course, but the doctor is hardly sympathetic. Instead, he is an archly patriarchal figure who sees women as prisoners of their own nature. Patronizingly, he observes that his new patient must have encountered "trouble of some kind, simple perhaps, but she was unable to cope with it."

These sequences are complexly focalized, first offering the woman as a subject whose trials demand sympathy and then constructing her as the object of a professional and patriarchal discourse about female nature. This discourse is made readily available to the spectator (who thereby identifies with the physicians approaching Louise as a "problem" of diagnosis and treament). But throughout the flashback that constitutes the bulk of the film, the viewer is positioned to identify with the protagonist, who is almost always present on screen, often alone. At the same time, this narrative is not generated freely by Louise, who, lacking treatment, would have remained mute. Her story is an answer to the psychiatrists seeking a solution to her mental problem; they furnish her with a rhetorical motive even as they elicit and control the flow of her memory through their questions. Because she is at the mercy of a maladjustment, Louise thus becomes a "question" as well as a figure of identification; she is an enigma that can be resolved only by discourses over which she wields no direct control, discourses surveilled and articulated by men. Such a female protagonist cannot function in the same way as her customary male counterpart in the classic Hollywood cinema. Becoming a mute and motionless recumbent figure whose presence generates a calculating analysis that she cannot even hear, much less answer or controvert, she attains an objectness inconceivable for a male character. Louise is unable to lead the action, unless action can be conceived as a series of missteps that deliver her to inactivity. The more "active" Louise is, the "sicker" she becomes; in fact, her most assertive act, shooting David, is her most transgressive, and it brings on a complete breakdown. Like Ellen Jones, Louise discovers that the more she does, the less she is able to alter her destiny.

The only power Louise truly possesses is self-knowledge; her mute body can only in the vaguest way be "read" for symptoms and history. It is the subjective self that holds the key to the puzzle of her withdrawal. Louise's mute body, then, must be made to yield its secrets to a male interrogator. As in *Cause for Alarm,* in which only Ellen knows the whole truth necessary for relating her experiences, Louise is in a position of epistemological superiority. But a confession is coerced, if in a benevolent way. At first unable to say a word, except when Dr. Willard mentions David's name, Louise is given back her voice by his treatment. An injection of narcotics relieves her anxiety and transforms her into a more willing subject; no longer troubled and pained, thanks to the intervention of male-directed therapy, Louise can now speak to herself, and to her doctors, in a way that would not have been possible even before her breakdown. She gives the doctors her name but balks at the idea of a thoroughgoing self-revelation: "I'm not going to tell you everything." In response, however, to the doctor's command to "tell me about David," she does begin to speak, as if to indicate the powerlessness of her position in this romantic relationship. A haunting Schumann theme becomes audible on the sound track, and the image of Louise's face fades to reveal her lover's hands on the piano.

This stock image of romantic harmony is at once undermined by the scene that unfolds. The pair are alone in a luxurious cabin where David plays expertly as Louise finishes dressing, with the door open, in the adjacent bedroom. The scene is thus as explicitly postcoital as the PCA would at that time allow. For Louise, these moments of psychological intimacy that follow making love are precious. She declares, "We never seem to have enough time together." But David seems unaffected by her avowal of affection and interest; he is, as he says, "making love to the piano," an act dedicated to her. Schumann is the music he has picked for Louise, because of its "tenderness," yet David is the self-confessed master of many tunes; each of his lovers has elicited a different musical response, even as each could be characterized by a single dominant emotional quality. The image of David's hands at the piano, initially, for Louise, a metonymy of her fulfilled desire (with the instrument a displacing metaphor for her own body), becomes the symbol of her lover's unstable, polymorphous sexuality: the instrument and the pianist remain the same, but David can play an infinity of melodies, each of which stands for, indeed replaces, a woman who has aroused his sexual interest. David's women are thus reduced to the amusement and entertainment he derives from his smooth, expert handling of the piano. In fact, this "playing" is so self-absorbed and self-contained that the man prefers it, at least in this scene, to the willing flesh-and-blood companion seated next to him.

Louise feels threatened by David's evident narcissism. She confesses: "Before I met you I never felt very keenly about one thing or another. . . . I just existed." On one level, this admission conforms to the norms of heterosexual coupling we have already seen functioning in *Cause for Alarm*. The woman must wait until the man desires her; she feels nothing, literally *is* nothing, until given meaning and purpose by his attentions. Her emptiness, her lack of self, are then filled by him and his needs. On another level, however, such a confession of surrender is problematic. Rhetorically, Louise is making a plea for David's continued attention, for his reciprocation of her love; in other words, she has not been truly swept away into the identity of the other who desires. Louise has the audacity to express what she wants, even if, in so doing, she conceives it as simply a function of David's presence, for she was nothing before he came into her life. In this way, she transgresses the patriarchal rule that women are not to demand anything from the men they love. In conventional Hollywood romance, the woman is chosen by male desire and given an identity (if only a sense of belonging and purpose) by the man's continued affection and needs. The problem is that David lacks this stability. Having once played a melody, he has the appetite to play another; having gotten all that he wants (the temporary possession of the woman's body), David desires to move on. Louise, however, wants to control her lover, to transform David into the willing object of her desire: "I want a monopoly on you." But he will not countenance such a transformation of conventional sexual economy. David rejects Louise. He is going away to continue enjoying his independence. On the brink of hysterics, she demands that he take her home in his speedboat.

The sumptuous house Louise enters, however, does not belong to her. She is only an employee, the nurse for Mrs. Graham (Jane Harker), who is bedridden. The next sequences provide a telling contrast to the life that David leads and will lead. He has freedom of movement, lacks attachments, can go wherever his fancy leads him; the speedboat indexes his affluence as well as a desire for the tools and symbols of self-indulgent leisure. Louise, in contrast, is a servant whose first gesture upon returning to the Graham house is to put on her nurse's uniform and answer the bell her mistress is insistently ringing. Dean Graham reprimands her for not being present earlier but apologizes when Louise reminds him it is her night off. Pauline Graham then berates her for flirting with her husband and turning him against her. She is the very type of a neglected, abandoned woman, an example of what Louise herself might and, in fact, does become: "I lie here all alone with no one to take care of me. . . . It's his fault I'm like this, all his fault." Just as in *Cause for Alarm,* the wrongly accused man and woman disavow any affection for one another, but once the accuser is out of the way, they indeed get married. This suggests that Mrs. Graham's suspicions are not entirely unfounded.

The next morning reveals that David and Graham are business associates. David comes to the house to ask for an engineering job, a request that the wealthy and more reserved entrepreneur readily grants. As he leaves the house, David meets up with Louise, who replays her hysterical possessiveness from the night before. At first,

Even in the company of the two men in her life, the heroine of *Possessed* is alone and feeling the effects of the mental disturbance that will destroy her life. Courtesy of Warner Brothers/Museum of Modern Art, Film Stills Archive.

she apologizes for her aggressiveness, but when this has no effect on the coldhearted man, she threatens, "You can't go away without me. . . . I won't let you." David turns away in silence and gets into his boat as Louise angrily screams his name.

At this point, the flashback is interrupted by a cut-back to the present. Louise evaluates her painful experience: "He did it deliberately to hurt me." The two doctors do not correct this interpretation but understand it as a sign of Louise's paranoia, her "inappropriate" feeling that she was wronged. In short, Louise's story must be evaluated—and if necessary, corrected—by the scientific discourse over which the doctors alone exercise control. The younger one asks, "Do you see the beginning of a persecution complex?" But, as the older one points out, Louise's problem is less psychological than ideological. She is simply not being a good woman in her persistent desire to desire;

Louise, he says, made "no attempt to evaluate the situation or see the man's viewpoint." Louise's feelings of abandonment and betrayal are dismissed by yet another element of their developing diagnosis. Her problems, the two suggest, did not begin with David's rejection of her love: "The seeds were there . . . her obsession for this man made them grow." Interpreting Louise's love for David as an "obsession" transforms into an illness what is in origin a social problem—that the woman has no right to her object of desire, that she must be rational and assume the "man's viewpoint" about the collapse of her romance. As *Now, Voyager* suggests, however, mental illness and the transgression of social norms are simply different aspects of the same maladjustment.

The cut-back ends, and the next image we see indicates the final punishment for being an improper woman. A limp female body, the face hidden by a mass of wet hair, is pulled by a policeman out of the lake at the back of Graham's house. It is his possessive and jealous wife, who has committed suicide in despair over her failure to keep her restlessly busy entrepreneur of a husband interested. The brief initial scene at the Graham house, in fact, suggests that her constant demands for attention and affection, in addition to becoming an "illness," destroyed any love he had for her. Coming back from town, Louise confesses to Graham, "I feel it was all my fault." Though her employer assures her that she was not to blame, Louise's guilt is the reflex of her perhaps unacknowledged wish to take the rich woman's place, to acquire the power available to an influential man's spouse. Later, in fact, Louise confesses to David that she married Graham only to make herself more attractive to her first lover, in the hopes of winning back his interest with newfound wealth. Even if Louise did not want Mrs. Graham dead, she suffers the consequences of such a wish, gaining both the love of the widower and the hatred of Carol (Geraldine Brooks), his college-age daughter, who believes her mother's fears about the nurse's enmity and jealousy.

A cut-back to the present offers Louise's comment that something then happened that "made me ill, as I am now." And yet the sequence of events as she narrates them seems to hold out the promise of some solution to the problem of her desire. David has departed for Canada, while the Graham household, with Louise now acting as a surrogate mother for the widower's young son, has moved to Washington. Months pass uneventfully until one day Louise returns to the house, where she is now much more at home (no more uniform and on much friendlier terms with her employer), to find David sitting in the living room. A close-up reveals her barely contained horror and joy at this surprise. Left alone with Louise by Graham's sudden departure for a business conference, David confesses to a continuing interest in other women. He was not lonely in Canada, even though the country is sparsely populated, because "man does not live by bread alone."

David's flippancy, his lack of commitment, his unconcern for others, his swaggering attitude toward sexual conquest and satisfaction, become increasingly evident in this part of the film; the result is to make him a much more unsympathetic character, the source of the trouble that Louise is experiencing with the system of heterosexual exchange. His ex-lover now knows him better. She asks sarcastically, "Are you sure you can get along without someone to help you admire yourself?" Understanding that he is incapable of love, she nonetheless cannot break her connection with him. Eager to leave her employer to avoid seeing David, she is persuaded by Graham to marry him. Louise is psychologically vulnerable, as she confesses: "Something happens when a woman isn't wanted, something terrible." Now desired, she may desire in turn, but her love for David still puts a barrier in the way of a happy marriage. A quite drunk and very sarcastic David shows up uninvited at the wedding reception. Obviously hurt that she would actually choose another man even though he no longer wants her, David flirts with Graham's daughter. Outraged and angered, Louise throws him out of the house.

And yet fate seems against her. Louise and Carol attend a local symphony concert and run into David, whom Carol invites to sit with them. The orchestra then plays the Schumann piece that was "her" song, and Louise becomes too agitated to remain. Back home in a darkened house filled with swirling shadows, Louise begins to show the signs of mental distress. She is awakened by the clock ticking and the rain falling gently outside her window; obviously distraught, she then hallucinates that David and Carol return together and embrace passionately at the door. The hallucination continues with a heated argument between Louise and Carol, who bitterly accuses the jealous woman of murdering her mother. Finally, Louise pushes Carol down a long flight of stairs to her death. At this moment, Carol's actual return home brings Louise back to her senses. Her imagined scenario does not come to pass as Carol quite tenderly asks after her and proceeds quietly to bed.

Recognizing that she is troubled, Louise seeks out a doctor, using an alias. His diagnosis is a "neurasthenia" that is manifesting itself in extreme suggestibility; this accounts for the hallucinations she has experienced. The doctor's explanation is finally unsatisfactory, however, for it addresses only the passive aspects of Louise's disturbance, not her barely contained jealous rage. Thinking his new patient may become hysterical, the doctor underestimates the violent content of her fantasies; he pays no attention, in other words, to her hallucination as a wish fulfillment. He is surprised when Louise forcefully rejects his advice to see a psychiatrist and storms out of his office.

Once again, Louise tries to escape from the circumstances that trouble her. She asks Graham for a divorce but reveals only part of the reason for her continuing distress: she tells him that she cannot forget his first wife. Graham will not let her go, however, and insists that they spend some time alone in the lake house. Upon their arrival, Louise goes in alone and immediately hears voices and thinks she sees Pauline Graham in the master bedroom. But Graham quite tenderly convinces her that his first wife is indeed dead and allays any fears that Louise may have been responsible for her suicide; he reminds her that, in fact, she was in town enjoying her day off when Pauline jumped into the lake. Louise believes her husband, and an immense weight appears to have been lifted from her mind. The couple return home happy and playful; it seems that Louise has begun to feel true affection for Graham and will be able to forget David.

But it is not to be. Louise and Graham go to a local nightclub to celebrate and there find a very drunk David with Carol. It seems they are planning to get married. Louise does her best to break up this relationship, revealing the truth about David's selfishness to Carol. She also lies, however, saying that David has always been in love with her and was friendly with Carol only in the hope that Louise would see him again. Carol angrily counters that David told her Louise was a former girlfriend who simply would not let go. The next day David comes over to accuse Louise of lying to Carol. She admits he is right but reminds him that she told him of her vow to do anything to keep him from leaving her. David, in turn, confesses to being interested in Carol only for her money. He leaves angry, and Graham returns to tell Louise he has made arrangements for a psychiatrist to see her. Frightened, she agrees, but then sneaks out and goes over to David's apartment, where she finds him packing for a wedding trip with Carol. She wants him to persuade Graham not to make her see a doctor, but David agrees with her husband's diagnosis. Yelling "you're all against me," Louise pulls out a gun and points it at him. He dares her to shoot, but, to his surprise, she does, emptying the gun into his fallen body.

The film then closes with a scene between Graham and Dr. Willard (Louise is now mute after having been sedated). Willard says that she is "completely unbalanced" and therefore not truly responsible for killing David, but he holds out little hope that the courts will see it this way. Louise's present condition, however, is purely temporary: "There's every reason to believe that someday she will be herself again." But when she is Louise once again, she will suffer unimaginable pain, not only guilt for what she has done but the loss of the one man she truly loved. *Possessed* ends with Graham's statement of support: he will stand by her no matter what happens. Like Charlotte Vale, Louise does get a "room of her own," but not a social space she in some sense controls: Louise remains under the surveilling gaze of her physicians and husband, her recovery only foreseen, not yet effected.

Louise's illness is overdetermined, not generated by the kind of simple problem that Hollywood narrative is designed to resolve. Louise does not lose touch with reality simply because of her irrational guilt over the death of Mrs. Graham (Dr. Willard's conclusion); yet her hallucinations show that she feels illicitly linked to her former employer. In typical Hollywood fashion, the narrative demonstrates that, with the proper male assistance, Louise can recover from feeling responsible for Pauline's suicide. Yet the stability she experiences after Graham's patient and tender treatment is immediately undermined by the unexpected appearance of David. Louise cannot escape from this disastrous relationship despite her best efforts. Twice she attempts to abandon the Graham household where he is a visitor, but she is prevented each time by Graham, who can offer her respect and affection, if not passion.

Her lack of true independence keeps David in her life, while the man is eager in turn to keep Louise in bondage, feeding his ego with the thought that she can never get over him. The narrative shows that David's death is hardly tragic but rather poetically just: he is properly made to suffer not only for hurting Louise but for his gold-digging plans to run away with Carol. And yet poetic justice in this film does not deliver the protagonist from punishment; instead, she is condemned by her one act of aggression, which is presented as "improper." Louise seeks David out for help and kills him by mistake out of "irrational" anger and fear. But irrationality is hardly convincing as an explanation for Louise's breakdown. It is not really the case, as Dr. Willard opines, that Louise has always been "possessed" by inner demons and has unreasonably latched on to David as a consequence.

Louise, instead, has been "possessed" once by David and cannot deal with the sadistic way he continues to toy with her now-frustrated desire. The film, however, offers no answer for this ideological problem. Unlike the mainstream woman's picture, *Possessed* cannot imagine a proper "place" for the transgressive woman. Though now controlled, Louise is not cured in any sense, despite the fact that the film achieves closure by offering a series of explanations for her aberrancy. As with all films noirs, we are far here from the Hollywood tradition of a happy ending.

CHAPTER 6

Conclusion

During the height of dark cinema's popularity on American screens, fundamental changes were occurring in the industry that would spell the demise of Hollywood production based on popular genres. In the late 1940s, the five major studios—MGM, Paramount, RKO, Fox, and Warner Brothers—were forced by legal setbacks to divest themselves of their theatrical holdings. As a result, they no longer had a guaranteed market for their product and had to abandon the assembly-line approach to filmmaking that catered to the weekly desire of the population to "go to the movies." The 1950s and 1960s witnessed the dismantling of complex studio infrastructures: payrolls were trimmed, production was cut back, and, eventually, studio lots were sold to developers. While genre filmmaking never disappeared, it was displaced in importance by one-off and blockbuster modes of production as Hollywood tried to compete with the generic fare now being supplied for free on television. American filmmakers became more interested in creating the unique or spectacular than in mining an area of popular taste by producing series of similar films. One of the casualties of this revisionism was the film noir.

Films noirs were usually low-budget ventures, even the "A" productions. In fact, that such films did not require expensive forms of spectacle was an important reason the studios were eager to make them. But unlike other studio types, such as the western and the musical, noir stories could not be turned into blockbusters to suit the commercial requirements of a new age; their claustrophobic depiction of urban malaise was simply not suited to the glamorizing afforded by the wide-screen processes that came into vogue at this time. Moreover, the demise of the double bill and the closing of many subse-

quent-run urban theaters—a response to dwindling ticket sales—
deprived film noir of many of its primary consumers. We cannot say,
however, that the American taste for this kind of story had disappeared by the late 1950s, even though histories of dark cinema generally suggest 1958 as the end of the era. The continuing enthusiasm
for noir narrative is evidenced by a number of highly successful early
television shows obviously modeled on dark cinema, including
"Dragnet," "Peter Gunn," "77 Sunset Strip," and "Perry Mason"; in
fact, these programs often revived the careers of performers formerly
active in noir films, such as Jack Webb and Raymond Burr. It is in-
disputable that popular taste for noir narrative has never waned since
its advent in the 1940s; perhaps the most popular genre in the 1990s,
the so-called erotic thriller (of which more below), is a direct descen-
dant of the classic film noir.

As Hollywood was forced to restructure its institutions and rethink
the kinds of entertainment it would offer the American people, a different kind of film began to achieve a significant, if limited, popularity
on U.S. screens. In the late 1940s and early 1950s, the number of art
houses that specialized in exhibiting European films with a high-culture appeal increased dramatically, particularly in major cities. Two of
the effects of this development are important to the subsequent history
of film noir. First, the presence of art houses on the cultural landscape
was both a symptom of and a contributing cause to a dramatic change
in American film culture: the ever more widely shared notion that
films could be art, not just pleasant diversion. Second, the American
acceptance of European art film encouraged the national cinemas concerned to continue producing films that offered an alternative to Hollywood. As we saw in chapter 1, the critical concept of film noir
became an important element of this "alternativeness" in French film
culture; here were Hollywood films, it was thought, that subverted
the socially conservative narrative that the American industry usually
offered. Because this alternative cinema came to define itself by a rejection of Hollywood entertainment values, the film noir, somewhat
ironically, became an important instrument of this different vision.
The French directors of the early 1960s most prominent in the development of an exportable alternative cinema—Jean Luc Godard, François Truffaut, Jean Pierre Melville, and Claude Chabrol—explored
fully the capacity of noir conventions to offer a new film-viewing
experience, one more in line with the developing principles of a cinematic modernism.

After its classic period, then, film noir exerted two separate influences on subsequent developments in the American cinema. On the one hand, noir remained a popular narrative type, never completely dying out—directors such as Don Siegel kept the cinematic tradition alive—but enjoying a different form of cultural life on the small screen. On the other hand, film noir became an important influence on the constitution of an alternative cinema that, at first, offered a different film-viewing experience, though eventually its style and themes were co-opted by mainstream American cinema. Art films, including those of the neo-noir variety, proved to have entertainment potential. And so by the late 1970s, many of the techniques and themes associated with the art cinema of an earlier period became a more or less standard part of mainstream productions. This development has been favorable to the revival of film noir as a popular form, especially because an enthusiasm for dark cinema has never disappeared. Film noir, then, continues today to be popular among the two main groups of filmgoers: the average viewer and those eager for art rather than simple entertainment. American filmmakers, who must address an audience divided to some degree along the lines of cultural politics, have found the neo-noir thriller both an artistically and commercially viable form. Today, neo-noir narrative enjoys almost as much popularity as classic dark cinema did during the 1940s and 1950s.

In closing, I will discuss briefly three neo-noir films of the post-studio era that reflect, in very different ways, the institutional and formal changes outlined above. But first, we must analyze in more detail the alternative textual qualities of the European art cinema.

As we have seen, the classic Hollywood film was characterized by a particular form of realism. The studios were not interested in constructing fictional worlds that were palpably similar to those of its consumers; such realism would not have proved attractive enough to moviegoers eager for escapism, for the enjoyment of various kinds of fantasy. If escapist and obviously characterized by wish fulfillment, commercial entertainment films are still realist, although in another sense. Pleasure in an alternative, fictional world depends on the spectator's limited investment of belief and interest. In other words, to enjoy a narrative film, spectators must endow that flickering play of light and dark on the screen with a certain reality; paradoxically, the film images must be considered a plausible, alternative world if they are to be engaged with as fiction. In short, the Hollywood film was constructed on the principle of verisimilitude: seeming to be true, if always in a limited fashion, to its spectators. As a medium, of course, film does not require this kind of engagement. Various forms of countercinema (the later films of Godard are useful examples) dispute even this partial surrender to fictionality and to the psychological motors, primarily identification, that increase such pleasure with the text. The countercinema film distances the viewer with a textual performance that constantly announces its own constructedness and arbitrariness. But this has never been the modus operandi of the American commercial cinema.

To make engagement easy for its consumers, the classic Hollywood film depended on coherence of different kinds.

1. Time relationships were clearly constructed; even if it presented the events of the story out of chronological order, the narration always enabled viewers to identify the beginning, middle, and end.
2. The succession of images constructed unambiguous spatial relations for viewers, creating an implied world in which the various settings were related readily to one another.
3. Endings strongly emphasized closure, not only in the sense of a socially desirable conclusion (the hero completes his mission and gets the girl), but also through the elimination of significant gaps or enigmas (everything ultimately "makes sense").
4. The narrative was driven by distinct, individual characters whose easily defined qualities motivated the events in question.
5. These events related causally to one another, producing a story line of interlocked incidents.
6. Finally, stylistic or thematic expressivity was always subordinated to the demands that the story make simple sense; the studio film was not the place for the artist to devise a personal style or themes that would be emphasized more than the story he had been contracted to tell.

The noir films analyzed in this book exemplify how dark cinema challenged but did not subvert these different kinds of coherence. In the noir detective film, the rapid succession of events appears random and often meaningless, making it quite difficult, if not impossible, for the average spectator to follow the story; yet a final explanation of the "case" makes clear how everything connects in the prescribed Aristotelian fashion. The noir thriller offers conventional forms of closure, with the fates of the different characters dependent on poetic justice and the reestablishment of the social order; yet such endings are extraordinary in that they often defeat the viewer's desire for the main character to succeed and be happy. In addition, the noir thriller offers misidentified or fragmented identities whose complexities and contradictions are not always resolved at the end of the final reel. Unlike its mainstream counterpart, the noir woman's picture does not provide compromised yet satisfying wish fulfillment—that is, the heroine put back in her place but offered a different, rewarding life. Nevertheless, such films otherwise produce a strong sense of closure: the heroine always comes to the "end of the line," however unhappy such a conclusion might be.

Art cinema poses a stronger challenge to mainstream practice. But these films largely remain within the orbit of traditional narrative and construct a coherent fictional world, however much the viewer may be denied easy access to that coherence. For example, many art films do not consistently construct unambiguous temporal and spatial relations, nor do they build up plots from causally related incidents. But this departure from mainstream practice is often motivated in a thoroughly traditional fashion. The succession of cinematic images and sounds may be generated not by an authoritative, objective narrator (the classic Hollywood film depends on the implied presence of such an agent), but by the subjective consciousness of a character (as in Federico Fellini's *8½* [1963]). Similarly, a rejection of Aristotelian plotting may be explained by the film's realist concern with a world of characters and their relationships rather than with any intrigue in which they are involved (as in Truffaut's noir effort *Shoot the Piano Player* [1962]). Because both these approaches to filmic construction play down narrative lines driven from incident to incident, they open up—and motivate—greater stylistic expressiveness and display. Furthermore, because the art cinema has always marketed itself as a cinema of auteurs, greater freedom for thematic expressivity has characteristically been allowed the directors involved; Bergman's obsession with sin, guilt, and death and Truffaut's with the mysteriousness of the female spirit are transtextual themes one expects to see developed in the oeuvres of these two cineastes. The more obvious presence of an author makes it possible for art films to advance significant ideas—even through various digressions—and yet not undermine the creation of an enjoyable fictional world. The art film, in other words, can be reflexive, self-conscious, and rhetorical, but it is less so than countercinema productions in which the contestation of mainstream conventions of representation and storytelling is politically motivated.

As a cinematic form, classic film noir has much to offer the art cinema director: a fascination with subjectivity, exemplified by first-person narration and the representation of inner consciousness; the subversion of middle-class values regarding law and order, family, sexual expression, material success, and poetic justice; a critical perspective on the discontents of modern urban life; a tradition of stylistic expressivity; and the thematizing of alienation and the limits of human freedom, ideas very resonant with the existentialist ethos of many 1960s intellectuals, especially in France.

For about 20 years, from the immediate postwar era until the mid-1960s, the majority of art films exhibited in this country were foreign-made; if film noir had an effect on this alternative cinema, it did not have much influence on U.S. production. Until 1968, American film-makers operated mainly under the old rule that their business was providing wholesome entertainment for a general, undifferentiated audience. The art cinema by this time had become associated with sophisticated, urban adult spectators who would be pleased, not offended, by the erotic and the naughty. In fact, the term "art film" enjoyed a secondary development in the 1950s: it became a euphemism for soft-core pornography, much of it imported from Europe (for example, the Swedish *I Am Curious Yellow* [Vilgot Sjöman, 1967]). A significant number of the few American films produced during this period for art cinema distribution, such as Sidney Lumet's independently produced 1966 project, *The Pawnbroker,* did achieve unexpected financial and critical success. The message to the Hollywood establishment was clear: there was profit to be made in films that were both "adult" (that is, featuring increased amounts of sex, violence, and profanity) and "arty." The result was the abolition of the PCA and the installation of a ratings system designed to identify films intended for "mature" audiences; this system paved the way for the production of films that never could have been made during Hollywood's classic period because they violated the letter and spirit of the Production Code and, in addition, did not conform to lowest-common-denominator marketing principles.

The developing American art cinema of this period echoed the enthusiasm of French New Wave filmmakers for film noir. John Boorman's 1967 film *Point Blank* (based on *The Hunter* [1963], a potboiler serie noire novel by Donald Westlake, published under his pseudonym Richard Stark) usefully exemplifies the way in which classic noir themes and characters could be given a new inflection by techniques imported from alternative filmmaking—the most obvious influence on Boorman being the French director Alain Resnais. Westlake's *The Hunter* is a revenge story fully in the tradition of Mickey Spillane's *I, the Jury* (1947). The protagonist, Walker, is betrayed by his partner in crime and lives to exact a terrible vengeance, not only on his traitorous friend but on the friend's "organization," which, Walker believes, has appropriated his share of the loot. Like Spillane, Westlake glorifies the phallic power of his hero (who becomes the archetypal "hunter" of the title) and the more or less righteous violence he perpetrates on those who have done him wrong.

These noir elements, however, figure largely as a pretext for a very different kind of production (though the film still does offer some of the visceral pleasures of Westlake's original narrative). Like Resnais's famous *Hiroshima, Mon Amour* (1960), Boorman's film uses its narrative framework as a point of departure for a complex and finally pessimistic meditation on memory, time, identity, and desire. The opening sequence is composed of a succession of shots (none of them easily readable) that depict the apparent murder of Walker (Lee Marvin) by his partner. A close-up on the dying man's face then motivates a flashback with whispered voice-over narration. The flashback has a double structure or "reach," tracing not only the events of the immediate past that have led to Walker's murder but those of the more distant moment when Walker was reunited with his old army buddy Mal (John Vernon), who would later betray and murder him. From a juxtaposition of images with three different time values (for the flashback continually returns to the present), it gradually becomes clear that Mal approached Walker with a plan for robbing syndicate couriers, seduced his wife Lynne (Sharon Acker), and then conspired with her to rob Walker of his share once the job was done. Here the narration is entirely subjective, replicating the stressed and disordered associational workings of a dying man's consciousness.

Walker's story appears to have reached an end when the flashback recapitulates his shooting by Mal. But then these subjectively marked images give way to apparently objective ones detailing Walker's ascent from the jail cell in a deserted Alcatraz prison where he is lying wounded. Though obviously distraught, the Walker we now see shows no evidence of the bloody attack; he enters the choppy waters on the shore and, with the slow-motion movements of a dreamer, begins making his way toward San Francisco across the bay. These sequences are, of course, impossible in the sense that a man shot point-blank does not recover enough to get to his feet, much less attempt a swim in dangerous waters. Although not obviously marked as such, this narrative present thus must also be subjective, not the actual record of Walker's miraculous defiance of death, but a dying wish to wreak vengeance on his betrayers. Such an interpretation is clinched by the following sequence, which shows a hale and hearty Walker aboard a harbor tour boat; the guide recounts how no one has ever been able to escape from Alcatraz to the mainland because of the shifting tides and currents of the surrounding water. Walker stands expressionless, his presence a controversion of both history and natural law, his continued existence an impossibility acknowledged by his own visionary consciousness—that is, Walker's own imagination conjures up the tour guide's statement that the narrative of escape that is the content of his wish fulfillment could never take place.

The revenge narrative thus echoes in the subjunctive mood Walker's frustrating experience in the indicative: the inevitability of betrayal, the death of expectation, the discovery of inescapable dead ends. In short, even the world as Walker wishes it to be cannot fit his desire. The phallic narcissism of Westlake's narrative is given a new inflection: it is not a factual record of experience that traces the impressive achievement of a hero unstoppable in the attempt to get his own back, but the ironic projection of impotence and failure. The traditional noir hero often dreams of a better world. Boorman's refiguration of this theme dismisses the possibility of comforting illusion, offering a darker vision of the noir nightmare. This protagonist cannot even wish himself successfully out of the trap he falls into.

The subjectivity of this narrative then motivates and explains the implausibilities of Walker's actions. Warned of his former partner's angry presence, Mal takes refuge in an apartment building bristling with hoodlum guards, but Walker simply walks straight and undetected to the elevator after manufacturing the flimsiest of diversions to occupy them. Mal, meanwhile, does not sense that anything is up even though Walker has sent his former sister-in-law to entertain him. Snatched from what he hoped to be a bed of pleasure, Mal is wrapped like a corpse in a sheet and then hurled from the penthouse roof. Attacked by the guards and pursued by the police, Walker easily gets clear of the building, calmly joining the crowd of rubberneckers gawking at Mal's bloody corpse.

Walker's earlier confrontation with Lynne, however, develops another aspect of this subjective flash-forward: we see how wish fulfillment hopelessly fragments the experience of Walker's hypothetical self, trapping him between imagined space and time on the one hand and reminiscence on the other. Breaking through the door of her apartment, Walker grabs the unresisting Lynne and rushes to the bedroom. Mal is not in the bed, but Walker empties his gun into the mattress anyway, then collapses beside Lynne as she remembers their courtship. Walker, of course, imagines Lynne remembering as he would have liked her to do, and the tone of her account is at first idyllic. Yet this dream is not all that Walker would wish. Lynne recalls meeting Walker as a group of his coworkers circled around her like marauding predators. Thus the special privacy of their beginning is spoiled by Walker's present knowledge of his wife's faithlessness, producing a recollection that in effect contradicts itself. Like Resnais, Boorman shows that memory can never be pure, making the Proustian point that it is always shaped by either the psychological or rhetorical pressures that impinge upon the experience of reminiscence. Remembering her life with Walker, Lynne conjures up images of Mal as well, and these images, as Lynne comments on them, displace Walker from her thoughts. The act of remembering in this way recapitulates her betrayal even as it attempts to locate a past moment of unalloyed happiness with Walker. Like Walker, Lynne reaches a dead end. The guilt she suffers (which is inflamed, not soothed, by memory) is too intense, and she proceeds to take an overdose on her bed while Walker remains immobilized on the couch. He later discovers her body, tenderly putting his wedding ring next to hers. But then Walker's narrative becomes "stuck" as his mind searches for an escape from this dead end. A cut reveals Walker entering Lynne's bedroom again, but this time there are no bullet holes in the bed and no body on it, only an enigmatically symbolic cat. Puzzled, Walker meanders into the bathroom, where he finds whole a decorative decanter he had previously smashed. And yet "putting together" what had been both conjured up and fractured by the imagination leads to nothing more than the hero's mesmerized and empty contemplation of the glass object he holds. This sequence crystallizes *Point Blank*'s construction of empty spectacle as well as of a spectator who finally can only contemplate that emptiness.

At this point, the film undergoes a formal transformation: the flash-forward becomes more objective, less marked by the fault lines of Walker's imaginative rhetoric, his search to locate a happier ending than reality has given him. *Point Blank,* in other words, becomes more a mainstream film. Its "blankness" becomes less a feature of its structure and more a theme. The hero's imagined revenge encounters no insurmountable obstacles, and yet it cannot locate any final object or "point." Walker is amazingly successful not only in disposing of Mal but in confronting, one by one, the various executives of the organization that has stolen his money; he eludes their various traps, always staying one step ahead of their attempts to assassinate him. And yet this modern corporation does not—in fact, cannot—easily disgorge its treasure. The final scene returns Walker to Alcatraz, a return that acknowledges not only the unsatisfying circularity of his desire but the appropriateness of the abandoned prison as an objective correlative for his developing view of existence. There yet another betrayal takes place, and Walker's experience repeats itself, but only in part. The

Out for revenge, the tortured hero of *Point Blank* struggles to survive in the surreal nightscape of San Francisco. Courtesy of MGM/Museum of Modern Art, Film Stills Archive.

police detective who had been helping him in his hunt turns out to be the top executive of the "firm"; Walker has simply been a handy tool in his plan to get rid of troublesome subordinates. Walker is thus displaced from his own narrative of desire, which turns out to have another (if only imagined) author. But Walker never surrenders to the man's plot. He refuses to come out of the shadows; he will neither claim his money nor wreak final vengeance. The film concludes with his (in)decision to merge with the darkness, to forgo identity and purpose, to be, in fact, dead.

Point Blank was a commercial success because it permitted two kinds of readings. On the one hand, Boorman follows classic narrative conventions closely enough to produce a familiar kind of story: the hero is an alienated but self-sufficient character whose extraordinary cunning and abilities make him an effective object of spectator iden-

Point Blank's avenger is never fooled by his enemies, but neither does he get the money he's after. Courtesy of MGM/Museum of Modern Art, Film Stills Archive.

tification. On the other hand, the film problematizes our enjoyment of this traditional narrative by revealing its impossibility and by withholding the pleasure of the hero's triumph at the end. Regarding *Point Blank* as an art film, we might point out how it dismantles storytelling conventions in the very act of furthering them, how it constructs a story that is ultimately no story at all, simply a blank point of consciousness. With its obvious borrowings from Resnais and often obtrusive stylization, Boorman's film is about as close to European art cinema as any American film of this period. Yet *Point Blank* still appeals to spectators uninterested in meditations on the role of memory in the constitution of the self and eager only for an exciting action film.

The films of the Hollywood Renaissance, which flourished in the 1960s and early 1970s, the decade following the demise of the PCA, manifest a similar strategy, one perfectly suited to the revival of film noir, the story type that could be given both "popular" and "art" inflections by filmmakers and spectators alike. The most famous of Hollywood Renaissance films heavily indebted to classic dark cinema is undoubtedly Martin Scorsese's *Taxi Driver* (1976), a work that, because of its graphic representation of violence, developed a reputation at the time for unremitting realism. *Taxi Driver,* indeed, is largely styled in the manner of art cinema realism: dialogue is made to appear unplanned or extempore, location settings predominate, method-acting techniques are used, and a minimal, deglamorized stylization—especially characterized by unbalanced compositions—predominates. These elements are perhaps best associated with Scorsese, whose earlier work about life among the disenfranchised and deprived in New York—*Mean Streets* (1973)—has a similar art cinema realism look and feel. But *Taxi Driver* has two authors. The script by Paul Schrader, a film historian and theorist noted for his critical work on noir, manifests a reverent nostalgia for classic dark cinema, including an extended homage to its expressionistic stylizations.

The collaboration between Schrader and Scorsese produced a rich and complex, if often somewhat contradictory film. The narrative reflects not only the psychotic alienation of the noir thriller but also the contemporary discontents associated with life in the most impersonal of American cities. Travis Bickle (Robert De Niro) is a revenger figure like Boorman's Walker. But traumatized by the sordidness he finds himself in, Travis does not seek to right a personal wrong. He understands neither his feelings of revulsion nor his attendant fantasies of apocalyptic destruction. Travis's alienation is at first too complete for him even to identify an enemy. He is presented as the individual locus of a certain contemporary social ill: a fast-moving urban world makes no room for, takes little notice of, those on its fringes. And yet he is also an extended cinematic reference. Schrader and Scorsese suggest that we understand New York as the site of an urban malaise first represented by the original cycle of noir films. Noir stylizations in the film develop a complex connection between the social reality and its different artistic embodiments; *Taxi Driver* is in this way metageneric, a commentary on the very generic elements of which it makes use. Visually, the film suggests a continuity between the cinematic past and present.

For example, the New York evoked by the film's famous slow-motion shots (with no natural sound) of a yellow cab moving over steam-swept pavements evidences Schrader's fascination with the unreal landscape of classic dark cinema, the aestheticized correlative of the main character's viewpoint and desire. Images such as these construct a strangely beautiful underworld whose stimmung is the perfect backdrop for Travis's darkly obsessive experiences with a night gallery of the dispossessed, the criminal, the psychotic, the abandoned. But this stylization is supplied by the filmmakers' vision, not the character's. Travis does not imagine himself as a protagonist from a noir film; he has few points of cultural reference. It is the aestheticization of Travis that evokes the expressionistic cityscape of classic film noir. And yet Travis, like the filmmakers who created him, also manifests, if in a different way, the urge to transform, even glamorize, the sordidness he lives in. Just as *Taxi Driver* is defined by two different approaches to representation—a detailed realism as well as an expressive stylization—so Travis acknowledges the ugliness of his world even as he sets about transcending it through the discovery of a beauty and innocence from which he can draw strength.

Unlike the traditional noir protagonist, Travis figures initially in no narrative of his own; his life is directionless, his isolation complete. Arriving in New York (from where, we never learn), he takes a job driving a hack because he cannot sleep; some inner demon, some inchoate dissatisfaction whose origin is never traced, keeps him awake. A desire for connections and an urge toward self-destruction are both evident in this decision to become a taxi driver; he takes all fares, does not restrict himself to the safer areas of Manhattan. At first, Travis is simply an observer of the human condition, a witness to violence and

Taxi Driver's deranged hero listens to the violent revenge scenarios imagined by his fare (director Martin Scorsese). Courtesy of Columbia/Museum of Modern Art, Film Stills Archive.

lust but never a participant; the closest he comes to experience is wiping the blood off his backseat after every night shift. One fare is a desperate husband (played by director Scorsese) who makes Travis park outside the apartment where his wife is conducting an affair; as the distraught man rehearses bloody and violent scenarios of revenge, Travis sits expressionless, neither condemning nor agreeing, a character who has not yet made the choice to act and attain selfhood.

But this does not mean Travis is not thinking, that he has surrendered to the anomie of those around him. His voice-over narration—ostensibly a diary—details reactions to sleeplessness and loneliness even as it evidences his desire that experience become meaningful. Travis's life becomes a story when he encounters an upscale and angelic-looking young woman, Betsy (Cybill Shepherd). Betsy, he thinks, is different from the depraved and self-destructive individuals who are usually his temporary companions; interestingly, she first appears in full sunlight, boldly crossing a street, not hiding at night in the shadows like the other women he sees, hookers who crowd the dirty sidewalks he drives by. He boldly and charmingly makes her acquaintance. Travis's naturalness and apparent innocence initially attract Betsy. But when he takes her to a porno film–his usual diversion—she is shocked and disgusted; he is quite genuinely abashed at her reaction, not knowing that such films are in poor taste. She refuses to see him again, despite his unrelenting attentions. He begins to stalk her but is finally chased by a policeman from the office where she works.

Betsy helps runs the campaign of Senator Palantine (Leonard Harris), a slick, John Lindsay–esque presidential candidate, who now becomes the object of Travis's developing obsession. Meeting an arms dealer, he buys a huge arsenal of handguns. He goes into training and becomes convinced that his life does indeed have a purpose: to assassinate this candidate. Travis never reveals why he chooses to become an assassin or why he decides on this particular target. The implication is that he feels not only rejected by Betsy but disenfranchised and ignored; this gesture will make him "somebody." While readying himself for his "mission," he meets a 12-year-old prostitute named Iris (Jodie Foster), who seems hopelessly under the control of her pimp, Sport (Harvey Keitel). Travis becomes obsessed with saving the child from her captor and arranges to leave her enough money to pay for a bus ticket home before making what he thinks will be a suicidal attempt on the candidate's life.

In a bizarre turn of events, Travis, fully armed, is frustrated by the Secret Service as he moves closer to his target. Though he flees in confusion, the fatal energy of violent protest, once shaped, must express itself in action. Travis proceeds to the brothel where Iris is kept. In one of the bloodiest sequences ever seen in an American film at the time, he kills Sport and his mafiosi employers. Iris screams hysterically, uncertain whether Travis means to kill her as well. Surrounded by bodies, he tries to shoot himself, but all the guns are empty. Travis passes out from loss of blood before the police arrive and awakes to find himself a hero for rescuing Iris. No criminal charges are pressed, and he recovers from his wounds enough to resume work as a taxi driver. A final encounter with Betsy suggests his detachment from her but also continuing madness. Travis is still the dispossessed loner he was at the film's beginning.

Taxi Driver is richly stylized, and not only in the sense that it conjures up images and sounds expressive of its main character's malaise and discontent. As in all art cinema, the film's excessive style also announces the presence of the director (who, in a bravura turn, plays a madman within it). For example, a complicated overhead shot, with natural sound suspended, moves the spectator up and away from the gory display of Travis's "heroism"; in a series of close-ups, the camera tracks across the scene of Travis's violence, lingering on the bloody bodies as Scorsese makes sure that the viewer has every opportunity either to enjoy the violent tableau or to discover its moral meaning. The thematic development in *Taxi Driver* is also reminiscent of the European art film. The lack of closure at film's end violates Hollywood norms; that Travis is still on the loose is intellectually provocative, a comment on the way America glories in and rewards the perpetrators of a pervasive, malignant violence. Furthermore, *Taxi Driver* thematizes the complex connections between a political machine that addresses dissatisfactions and disenfranchisement (this candidate vows to "let the people rule") and the violent protest generated by an alienation so profound it cannot be controlled by the smooth machinery of the electoral process and becomes, in fact, directed against such slickly packaged and hypocritical populism. Travis is not just a madman, Scorsese says, but the index of a deepening social crisis: the film was made at the end of a period in American life that was scarred by the assassination of political leaders. (Ironically, the obsession of a "Travis" among the film's viewers, John Hinckley, with the actress Jodie Foster led to yet another assassination attempt; like its prototype in the film, the shooting of President Reagan was also a failure.) In *Taxi Driver,* noir themes and narrative are marshaled toward both political and artistic statement in a fashion typical of the Hollywood Renaissance.

With the advent of the videocassette recorder, which made classic Hollywood and foreign films increasingly available during the 1980s, many "cineliterate" adult spectators who had patronized art and revival houses began to spend more time in front of the television, using the apparatus as a home cinema. This is the audience whose theatrical patronage made possible the commercial success of films such as *The Godfather, Part II* (Francis Ford Coppola, 1974); the structural and stylistic intricacies, not to mention the thematic ambiguities, of such films held little appeal for the lowest-common-denominator market. Art cinema thus became less of a commercial proposition at the very moment when Americans shifted away from oppositional cultural politics with the election of Ronald Reagan. A former studio actor claiming the highest office in the land was a strangely appropriate political event for Hollywood; the film business at this moment took a right turn back toward the representation of consensus values, its hallmark before 1968—the very period in which Reagan had been active in the industry. Following the principle that what had worked before would work again, American producers recycled updated versions of its classic film types, including dark cinema. Hoping to please customers who wanted entertainment more than intellectual stimulation, filmmakers especially turned to the action/adventure genres; these easy-to-understand narratives were readily transformed into elaborate visual forms. Rather than drama, spectacle was what most theatrical customers (the majority of whom were now under 30) were eager to see. Thrilling car chases, complexly orchestrated representations of bloody violence (aided by the invention of the exploding blood bag), soft-core sex, and unlimited profanity became the most commercial appeals of nonstop-action blockbusters such as *Die Hard* (John McTiernan, 1988) and *The Terminator* (James Cameron, 1984).

A handy vehicle for such "attractions," the thriller, especially in its dark inflection, has become perhaps the most popular genre of the last decade. What was for various reasons (including censorship prohibitions) a dramatic form during the studio period has now become increasingly spectacular, the site for mesmerizing displays of violent action and permissibly naughty sex. The current designation "erotic thriller" aptly captures the sense in which these narratives are designed both to excite and arouse. Films such as *Deceived* (Damian Harris, 1991) and *Dead Again* (Kenneth Branagh, 1992) not only are oriented toward crowd-pleasing spectacle but recycle many of the evidently still popular noir themes we have examined in this book: fractured identities, conscienceless psychopathology, self-destructive dissatisfaction with middle-class values and ordinary living, the dark underside of domestic life, and the dangerous lure of the illicit or forbidden.

Perhaps the most interesting example of this neo-noir type is Paul Verhoeven's *Basic Instinct* (1992), a film notorious for its graphic sexual sequences. (To capitalize on this interest, the producers released a "director's cut" version for the videocassette market that includes even steamier encounters between stars Michael Douglas and Sharon Stone.) *Basic Instinct,* however, does not offer simple soft-core pornography; its engagement with issues of gender and sexual pleasure is much more complex, very much in the tradition of Hitchcock's *Vertigo*. A superficial reading of *Basic Instinct* might emphasize only the misogyny undeniably present in these story materials. The villain, Catherine Tramell (Stone), is a highly intelligent, well-educated, rich, and beautiful young woman who also happens to be a sociopath. Here is a character who exemplifies many of the often contradictory qualities associated with the postfeminist woman, qualities that have crystallized around popular culture icons—particularly Madonna, the celebrity who obviously served as the model for Stone's performance. She is good-looking (enjoying the spectacle of her own body) but also exceptionally intelligent and talented, hard-working but self-indulgent, attracted to men but unrestrained by heterosexual protocols, concerned about her well-being but reckless (with a yen for cocaine and very unsafe sex), economically independent but needing a network of friendships, especially with the men required to satisfy her not inconsiderable sexual appetite.

And yet this paragon of achievement and self-possession is without question a compulsive and conscienceless killer, especially of any man who might wish to control her. The postfeminist woman in *Basic Instinct* is thus alluring but deadly. She is less an ideal than a fascinating aberration of social and personal development whose compulsions are never explained by psychoanalytical discourse—a discourse that this well-educated character has in any case mastered and now uses to full advantage. The response of the detective protagonist to Catherine, while contradictory, is thus entirely appropriate: he falls in love with her but intends, until the end, to see her punished for her crimes. And according to ordinary moral standards, Catherine deserves punishment. By the end of the film, we realize that she has been responsible for killing a widening circle of friends and acquaintances, including her parents, her college adviser, a lover's husband, and the rock star with whom she enjoyed zipless sex.

With the exception of her parents—whose "accidental" demise has made Catherine rich with insurance money—these victims are not murdered for gain, but for pleasure. Like most serial killers, Catherine discovers an intimate connection between sexual satisfaction and murder, even though she is not presented as under the control of an irresistible compulsion. Her intellectualizations and lack of moral feeling make her instead a female version of the Marquis de Sade, whom she otherwise closely resembles in authoring "fictional" narratives of depravity and murder. Unlike the femme fatale of classic serie noire and

In *Basic Instinct* self-absorbed and violent sex preoccupies the protagonists.
Courtesy of TriStar/Museum of Modern Art, Film Stills Archive.

film noir, Catherine, however, is presented sympathetically, at least in large measure. She becomes the love object of Nick Curran (Michael Douglas), the detective who is convinced of her guilt. At film's end, Catherine has freed herself of suspicion (though Nick knows the truth) and has perhaps abandoned murder for love. There is no doubt, in fact, that she comes to feel genuine affection for Nick. The detective, it turns out, is something of a fellow traveler (he has a reputation for being a "shooter"), and the couple, who enjoy an obvious sexual compatibility based on shared sadomasochistic tastes, seem made for each other. Unlike the contemporary mainstream thriller, in which melodramatic notions of poetic justice and conventional morality still operate, *Basic Instinct* ends by endorsing a true love based on shared psychopathology. Nick knows that Catherine may kill him at any moment (the camera locates an ice pick hidden under her side of the bed as it shows them making love at the very end), but he has surrendered to his "basic instinct," disregarding reason and thoughts of self-preservation.

In the corrupt world of the story, this decision hardly seems misguided. Sex, as well as the drugs that can enhance its pleasures, is offered as the supreme, perhaps only true value. Though she is rich and talented, Catherine seems the victim of a Nietzschean ennui. Her novels are records of her own experiences with murder and manipulation; she tries to write Nick into the narrative of her current writing project, but he fails to come to the end she envisions for him: death at her hands. A member of the monied leisure class, Catherine finds degrading self-indulgence more appealing than the traditional pursuits of the rich and famous. Looking for Catherine at a local discotheque, Nick finds her sitting unabashed on a toilet in the men's room, sniffing cocaine and enjoying the joint embraces of a black lover and her lesbian friend Roxy (Leilani Sarelle).

The police are hardly better than the crooks. It is clear not only that Nick suffers from the same homicidal impulses as Catherine but that he is equally conscienceless, having "beaten" a lie detector test in the same way Catherine beats one. At the film's beginning, he is trying to be good. Reprimanded by the department for his drinking, drug problems, and violence, he has given up all forms of indulgence, including smoking; furthermore, he has taken up with the department psychologist, Dr. Beth Garner (Jeanne Tripplehorn). Meeting Catherine, however, he begins drinking and smoking again. She seems to have released his sadomasochistic drives as well: a lovemaking session with Beth turns into a brutal attack. We can hardly say, however, that Nick alone has gone "bad." Beth, it turns out, is a former lover of Catherine's who may herself have homicidal tendencies, while the internal affairs officers who are monitoring Nick also seem to have illegal connections to the woman Nick is investigating. Like the classic noir detective story, *Basic Instinct* limns an environment of universal venality and degradation. The only operative principle of this world is the pursuit of self-interest. And so Nick understandably surrenders to the corruption around him, trying to find something of value in it. What he and Catherine share is, in his words, "the fuck of the century." Sexual compatibility emerges as the only good worth pursuing, even if the wages of this pursuit is death. Such a linkage of sexual surrender and self-destructiveness is undoubtedly appropriate in a world haunted by the medical fact that sex can and does kill. The pessimistic view of hard work and self-restraint that first attracted a film audience in the 1940s has been successfully updated for 1990s filmgoers, who are similarly pleased by a sympathetic portrayal of the dark underside of the American dream. Like other erotic thrillers, *Basic Instinct* demonstrates that the film noir is still an important part of our national cinema.

NOTES AND REFERENCES

Chapter One

1. My brief account here is based largely on Thomas Schatz, *Hollywood Genres: Formulas, Filmmaking, and the Studio System* (New York: Random House, 1981).

2. See David Bordwell, Janet Staiger, and Kristin Thompson, *The Classical Hollywood Cinema: Film Style and Mode of Production to 1960* (New York: Columbia University Press, 1985); hereafter cited in the text.

3. See Larry May, *Screening out the Past: The Birth of Mass Culture and the Motion Picture Industry* (Chicago: University of Chicago Press, 1980), esp. 167–236.

4. For full details, see Leonard J. Leff and Jerold L. Simmons, *The Dame in the Kimono: Hollywood, Censorship, and the Production Code from the 1920s to the 1960s* (New York: Grove Weidenfeld, 1990); hereafter cited in the text.

5. Wartime production conditions are detailed in Clayton R. Koppes and Gregory D. Black, *Hollywood Goes to War* (Berkeley: University of California Press, 1987).

6. The code is printed as an appendix in Leff and Simmons.

7. Nino Frank, "Un Nouveau genre policier: L'aventure criminelle," *L'Ecran Française* 61 (28 August 1946): 8–9, 14 (my translation); hereafter cited in the text. A full translation of this article and the other early French materials discussed in this chapter will appear in R. Barton Palmer, ed., *Perspectives on Film Noir* (New York: G. K. Hall, forthcoming).

8. Jean Pierre Chartier, "Les Américains aussi font des films noirs," *Revue du Cinéma*, no. 2 (1946): 67–70 (my translation); hereafter cited in the text.

9. Pierre Kast, "Court traité d'optimistique," *Positif*, no. 6 (1953): 3–9 (my translation); hereafter cited in the text.

10. For details, see James Monaco, *The New Wave* (New York: Oxford University Press, 1976).

11. Roger Tailleur, "Le Cheval rose ou les velleités humaines," *Positif*, no. 9 (1954): 32–33.

12. "The Star as Director," *New Republic* (3 November 1947): 30.

13. *New Yorker* (18 October 1947): 113.

14. "Montgomery on Horseback," *Newsweek* (20 October 1947): 97.

15. Manny Farber, "B-Plus," *New Republic* (4 December 1944): 746; hereafter cited in the text.

16. My account here is based on Pam Cook, ed., *The Cinema Book* (New York: Pantheon Books, 1985), 119–46.

17. Jacques Doniol-Valcroze, "Dmytryk ou les arêtes vives," *Cahiers du Cinéma*, no. 1 (1951): 13–14 (my translation).

18. Gilles Jacob, "Du Côté de chez Huston," *Cahiers du Cinéma*, no. 12 (1952): 8 (my translation).

19. Raymond Borde and Etienne Chaumeton, *Panorama du film noir américain* (Paris: Editions de Minuit, 1955) (my translations); hereafter cited in the text.

20. My account here is based on Cook, 147–54.

21. Colin Wilson, *Underworld U.S.A.* (London: BFI, 1971).

22. Raymond Durgnat, "Paint It Black," *Cinema* 6/7 (1970), 49; hereafter cited in the text.

23. Paul Schrader, "Notes on Film Noir," *Film Comment* 8, no. 1 (1972): 8–13; hereafter cited in the text.

24. J. A. Place and L. S. Peterson, "Some Visual Motifs of Film Noir," *Film Comment* 10, no. 1 (1974): 30–32; hereafter cited in the text.

25. Alain Silver and Elizabeth Ward, eds., *Film Noir: An Encyclopedic Reference to the American Style* (Woodstock, N.Y.: Overlook Press, 1979), 1; hereafter cited in the text.

26. J. P. Telotte, *Voices in the Dark: The Narrative Patterns of Film Noir* (Urbana: University of Illinois Press, 1991), 20.

27. Tony Bennett and Janet Woollacott, *Bond and Beyond: The Political Career of a Popular Hero* (New York: Methuen, 1987).

28. Robert Ottoson, *A Reference Guide to the American Film Noir: 1940–1958* (Metuchen, N.J.: Scarecrow Press, 1981).

Chapter Two

1. For an interesting account of these literary developments, see Geoffrey O'Brien, *Hardboiled America: The Lurid Years of the Paperbacks* (New York: Van Nostrand Reinhold, 1981).

2. His career is traced in Francis Nevins, "Cornell Woolrich on the Silver Screen," *Armchair Detective* 20 (Spring 1987): 39–51; 160–75.

3. Robert Warshow, "The Gangster as Tragic Hero," in *The Immediate Experience* (New York: Doubleday & Co., 1962), 131.

4. Place and Peterson offer the best analysis of noir visual features; the account that follows is based on their work ("Some Visual Motifs").

5. Two accounts of the film's production history are Richard Schickel, *Double Indemnity* (London: BFI, 1992) and William Luhr, *Raymond Chandler and Film* (New York: Frederick Ungar, 1982); the latter hereafter cited in the text.

6. See Tzvetan Todorov, *The Poetics of Prose,* trans. Richard Howard (Ithaca, N.Y.: Cornell University Press, 1977), 42–52.

Chapter Three

1. See Luhr, *Raymond Chandler*, for a detailed discussion of these connections.

2. My account of these developments is based on Max Allan Collins and James L. Traylor, *One Lonely Knight: Mickey Spillane's Mike Hammer* (Bowling Green, Ohio: Bowling Green State Popular Press, 1984).

Chapter Four

1. Quoted in James Naremore, *The Magic World of Orson Welles* (New York: Oxford University Press, 1978), 141.

Chapter Five

1. Mary Ann Doane, "The 'Woman's Film': Possession and Address," in Mary Ann Doane, Patricia Mellencamp, and Linda Williams, eds. *Re-Vision: Essays in Feminist Film Criticism* (Frederick, Md.: University Publications of America, 1984), 68.

2. Molly Haskell, *From Reverence to Rape: The Treatment of Women in the Movies* (New York: Holt, Rinehart and Winston, 1974), 161.

FILMOGRAPHY

Basic Instinct (TriStar, 1992)
Director: Paul Verhoeven
Executive Producer: Mario Kassar
Associate Producers: William S. Beasley, Louis D'Esposito
Assistant Directors: Louis D'Esposito, Nina Kostroff
Screenplay: Joe Eszterhas
Production Designer: Terence Marsh
Director of Photography: Jan De Bont
Music: Jerry Goldsmith
Cast: Michael Douglas (Nick Curran), Sharon Stone (Catherine Tramell), George Dzundza (Gus), Jeanne Tripplehorn (Dr. Beth Garner), Denis Arndt (Lieutenant Walker), Leilani Sarelle (Roxy), Dorothy Malone (Hazel Dobkins)
Running Time: 128 minutes
Premier: 19 March 1992
16mm rental: not available

Cause for Alarm (MGM, 1951)
Director: Tay Garnett
Producer: Tom Lewis
Assistant Director: Jack Greenwood
Screenplay: Mel Dinelli and Tom Lewis, from an unpublished story of the same title by Larry Marcus
Art Directors: Cedric Gibbons, Arthur Lonergan
Director of Photography: Joseph Ruttenberg
Music: André Previn
Cast: Loretta Young (Ellen Jones), Barry Sullivan (George Jones), Bruce Cowling (Dr. Ranney Grahame), Margalo Gillmore (Mrs. Edwards), Bradley Mora (Billy), Irving Bacon (postman), Georgia Backus (Aunt Clara)
Running Time: 74 minutes
Premier: 29 January 1951
16mm rental: MGM United

Criss Cross (Universal-International, 1949)

Director: Robert Siodmak
Producer: Michel Kraike
Assistant Director: Fred Frank
Screenplay: Daniel Fuchs, from the novel *Criss-Cross* (1935) by Don Tracy
Art Directors: Bernard Herzbrun, Boris Leven
Director of Photography: Franz Planer
Music: Miklos Rozsa
Cast: Burt Lancaster (Steve Thompson), Yvonne De Carlo (Anna Dundee), Dan Duryea (Slim Dundee), Stephen McNally (Pete Ramirez), Griff Barnett (Pop), Richard Long (Slade Thompson), Edna N. Holland (Mrs. Thompson)
Running Time: 88 minutes
Premier: 12 January 1949
16mm rental: Swank Motion

Detour (Producers Releasing Corporation, 1945)

Director: Edgar G. Ulmer
Producer: Leon Fromkess
Assistant Director: William A. Calihan, Jr.
Screenplay: Martin Goldsmith
Art Director: Edward C. Jewell
Director of Photography: Benjamin H. Kline
Music: Leo Erdody
Cast: Tom Neal (Al Roberts), Ann Savage (Vera), Claudia Drake (Sue), Edmund MacDonald (Charles Haskell, Jr.)
Running Time: 68 minutes
Premier: 30 November 1945
16mm rental: Budget Films

D.O.A. (United Artists, 1950)

Director: Rudolph Maté
Executive Producer: Harry M. Popkin
Producer: Leo C. Popkin
Assistant Director: Marty Moss
Screenplay: Russell Rouse and Clarence Green
Art Director: Duncan Cramer
Director of Photography: Ernest Laszlo
Music: Dimitri Tiomkin
Cast: Edmond O'Brien (Frank Bigelow), Pamela Britton (Paula Gibson), Luther Adler (Majak), Beverly Campbell (Miss Foster), Lynn Baggett (Mrs. Eugene Philips), William Ching (Halliday), Henry Hart (Stanley Philips), Neville Brand (Chester), Laurette Luez (Marla Rakubian)

Running Time: 83 minutes
Premier: 30 April 1950
16mm rental: Budget Films

Double Indemnity (Paramount, 1944)

Director: Billy Wilder
Executive Producer: B. G. DeSylva
Producer: Joseph Sistrom
Assistant Director: C. C. Coleman, Jr.
Screenplay: Raymond Chandler and Billy Wilder, from the novel (1936) by
    James M. Cain
Art Director: Hal Pereira
Director of Photography: John F. Seitz
Music: Miklos Rozsa
Cast: Fred MacMurray (Walter Neff), Barbara Stanwyck (Phyllis Dietrich-
    son), Edward G. Robinson (Barton Keyes), Porter Hall (Mr. Jackson),
    Jean Heather (Lola Dietrichson), Tom Powers (Mr. Dietrichson), Byron
    Barr (Nino Zachette)
Running Time: 106 minutes
Premier: 7 September 1944
16mm rental: Swank Motion

Kiss Me Deadly (United Artists, 1955)

Director and Producer: Robert Aldrich
Executive Producer: Victor Saville
Assistant Director: Robert Justman
Screenplay: A. I. Bezzerides, from the novel *Kiss Me, Deadly* (1952) by
    Mickey Spillane
Art Director: William Glasgow
Director of Photography: Ernest Laszlo
Music: Frank DeVol
Cast: Ralph Meeker (Mike Hammer), Albert Dekker (Dr. Soberin), Paul
    Stewart (Carl Evello), Maxine Cooper (Velda), Gaby Rodgers (Gabrielle/
    Lily Carver), Nick Dennis (Nick), Cloris Leachman (Christina), Wesley
    Addy (Pat Thompson), Mort Marshall (Ray Diker)
Running Time: 105 minutes
Premier: 18 May 1955
16mm rental: MGM United

Murder, My Sweet (RKO, 1944)

Director: Edward Dmytryk
Executive Producer: Sid Rogell
Producer: Adrian Scott

Assistant Director: William Dorfman
Screenplay: John Paxton, from the novel *Farewell, My Lovely* (1940) by Raymond Chandler
Art Directors: Albert S. D'Agostino, Carroll Clark
Director of Photography: Harry J. Wild
Music: Constantin Bakaleinikoff
Cast: Dick Powell (Philip Marlowe), Claire Trevor (Velma/Helen Grayle), Ann Shirley (Ann Grayle), Otto Kruger (Jules Amthor), Mike Mazurki (Moose Malloy), Miles Mander (Mr. Grayle), Douglas Walton (Marriott), Esther Howard (Jessie Florian)
Running Time: 95 minutes
Premier: 18 December 1944
16mm rental: RKO General Pictures

The Pitfall (United Artists, 1948)

Director: André de Toth
Producer: Samuel Bischoff
Assistant Director: Joe Depew
Screenplay: Karl Kamb, from the unpublished novel by Jay Dratler
Art Director: Arthur Lonergan
Director of Photography: Harry J. Wild
Music: Louis Forbes
Cast: Dick Powell (John Forbes), Lizabeth Scott (Mona Stevens), Jane Wyatt (Sue Forbes), Raymond Burr (MacDonald), Byron Barr (Bill Smiley), Jimmy Hunt (Tommy Forbes)
Running Time: 86 minutes
Premier: 24 August 1948
16mm rental: Ivy Films

Point Blank (MGM, 1967)

Director: John Boorman
Producers: Judd Bernard, Robert Chartoff
Assistant Director: Al Jennings
Screenplay: Alexander Jacobs, David Newhouse, and Rafe Newhouse, from the novel *The Hunter* (1963) by Richard Stark (Donald Westlake)
Art Directors: George W. Davis, Albert Brenner
Director of Photography: Philip H. Lathrop (Metrocolor; Panavision)
Music: Johnny Mandel
Cast: Lee Marvin (Walker), Angie Dickinson (Chris), Keenan Wynn (Yost), Carroll O'Connor (Brewster), Lloyd Bochner (Frederick Carter), Michael Strong (Stegman), John Vernon (Mal Reese), Sharon Acker (Lynne)
Running Time: 92 minutes
Premier: 18 September 1967
16mm rental: MGM United

Possessed (Warner Brothers, 1947)

Director: Curtis Bernhardt
Producer: Jerry Wald
Assistant Director: Sherry Shourds
Screenplay: Sylvia Richards and Ranald MacDougall, from the *Cosmopolitan* magazine novelette "One Man's Secret" by Rita Weiman
Art Director: Anton Grot
Director of Photography: Joseph Valentine
Music: Franz Waxman, Leo Forbstein, Leonid Raab
Cast: Joan Crawford (Louise Howell Graham), Van Heflin (David Sutton), Raymond Massey (Dean Graham), Geraldine Brooks (Carol Graham), Stanley Ridges (Dr. Harvey Willard), Dr. Willard's intern (Clifton Young), Erskine Sanford (Dr. Max Sherman), Don McGuire (Dr. Craig), Jane Harker (Pauline Graham)
Running Time: 108 minutes
Premier: 29 May 1947
16mm rental: MGM United

The Stranger (RKO, 1946)

Director: Orson Welles
Executive Producer: William Goetz
Producer: S. P. Eagle
Assistant Director: Jack Voglin
Screenplay: Anthony Veiller, with uncredited contributions from John Huston and Orson Welles, from an unpublished story by Victor Trivas and Decia Dunning
Art Director: Perry Ferguson
Director of Photography: Russell Metty
Music: Bronislav Kaper
Cast: Edward G. Robinson (Wilson), Loretta Young (Mary Longstreet Rankin), Orson Welles (Franz Kindler/Charles Rankin), Philip Merivale (Judge Longstreet), Richard Long (Noah Longstreet), Konstantin Shayne (Konrad Meineke)
Running Time: 95 minutes
Premier: 21 July 1946
16mm rental: Arcus Film

Taxi Driver (Columbia, 1976)

Director: Martin Scorsese
Producers: Michael and Julia Phillips
Associate Producer: Phillip M. Goldfarb
Assistant Director: Peter R. Scoppa
Screenplay: Paul Schrader

Art Director: Charles Rosen
Director of Photography: Michael Chapman
Music: Bernard Herrmann
Cast: Robert De Niro (Travis Bickle), Jodie Foster (Iris), Albert Brooks (Tom), Peter Boyle (wizard), Cybill Shepherd (Betsy), Leonard Harris (Senator Palantine), Harvey Keitel (Sport), Martin Scorsese (distraught husband)
Running Time: 113 minutes
Premier: 11 February 1976
16mm rental: Swank Motion

Vertigo (Paramount, 1958)
Director and Producer: Alfred Hitchcock
Associate Producer: Herbert Coleman
Assistant Director: Daniel McCauley
Screenplay: Alec Coppel and Samuel Taylor, from the novel *D'Entre les morts* (1954) by Pierre Boileau and Thomas Narcejac
Art Director: Hal Pereira
Director of Photography: Robert Burks (VistaVision)
Music: Bernard Herrmann
Cast: James Stewart (Scottie Ferguson), Kim Novak (Madeleine Elster/Judy Barton), Barbara Bel Geddes (Midge), Tom Helmore (Gavin Elster), Lee Patrick (Carlotta)
Running Time: 120 minutes
Premier: 12 May 1958
16mm rental: Swank Motion

SELECTED BIBLIOGRAPHY

BOOKS

Alloway, Lawrence. *Violent America: The Movies 1946–1964.* New York: Museum of Modern Art, 1971. Excellent stills. Useful discussion of film noir.

Borde, Raymonde, and Etienne Chaumeton. *Panorama du film noir américain.* Paris: Editions de Minuit, 1955. The most important book ever written on dark cinema. Excellent discussions of notable individual films.

Deming, Barbara. *Running away from Myself: A Dream Portrait of America Drawn from the Films of the Forties.* New York: Grossman, 1969. Fascinating account of one viewer's experience with the film noir *avant la lettre.*

Hirsch, Foster. *The Dark Side of the Screen: Film Noir.* San Diego: A. S. Barnes, 1981. The best of the several popular, fan-oriented books on dark cinema. Excellent stills.

Kaminsky, Stuart. *American Film Genres.* Dayton, Ohio: Pflaum Publishing, 1974. Contains the best analysis of 1960s neo-noir film.

Kaplan, E. Ann, ed. *Women in Film Noir.* London: BFI, 1978. Contains essays by divers feminist critics. Important.

McArthur, Colin. *Underworld U.S.A.* London: BFI, 1972. Interesting though dated genre approach to film noir.

O'Brien, Geoffrey. *Hardboiled America: The Lurid Years of the Paperbacks.* New York: Van Nostrand Reinhold, 1981. Important history of popular literature developments behind the film noir.

Ottoson, Robert. *A Reference Guide to the American Film Noir, 1940–1958.* Metuchen, N.J.: Scarecrow Press, 1981. Important guide to the noir canon. Good synopses of individual films.

Shadoian, Jack. *Dreams and Dead Ends: The American Gangster/Crime Film.* Cambridge: MIT Press, 1977. Useful analysis of the crime genres and the advent of film noir.

Silver, Alain, and Elizabeth Ward, eds. *Film Noir: An Encyclopedic Reference to the American Style.* Woodstock, N.Y.: Overlook Press, 1979. Indispensable guide. Excellent stills and filmographies.

ARTICLES

Damico, James. "Film Noir: A Modest Proposal." *Film Reader* (1978): 48–57. Important contribution to the debate over whether film noir constitutes a separate genre.

Durgnat, Raymond. "Paint It Black: The Family Tree of Film Noir." *Cinema* (U.K.) 6/7 (1970): 49–56. The first full-length discussion of film noir in English.

Gross, Larry. "Film Apres Noir." *Film Comment* (July/August 1976): 44–49. Best analysis of relationship between New Wave filmmakers, especially Godard, and noir narrative.

Maltby, Richard. "Film Noir: The Politics of the Maladjusted Text." *Journal of American Studies* (April 1984): 59–71. Excellent historically oriented analysis of film noir's moment in American culture.

Porfirio, Robert G. "No Way out: Existential Motifs in the Film Noir." *Sight and Sound* (Autumn 1976): 212–17. Discusses the relationship between the themes of film noir and philosophical ideas of the existentialist movement.

Telotte, J. P. "Film Noir and the Dangers of Discourse." *Quarterly Review of Film Studies* (Spring 1984): 101–12. Discusses oppositional and modernist elements in the film noir.

INDEX

THE AUTHOR

R. Barton Palmer holds undergraduate degrees from Dartmouth College and the University of Durham (England), which he attended as a James Reynolds Fellow. In 1973 he received his Ph.D. in medieval studies from Yale University, where he held a Wilmarth S. Lewis fellowship. He became interested in film in 1982 and enrolled at New York University, receiving an M.A. in cinema studies in 1984 and a Ph.D. in 1989. Currently he holds a joint appointment as professor of English and communication at Georgia State University, where he has taught since 1973.

As a medievalist, he has been involved in a long-term project: editing and translating the narrative poetry of Guillaume de Machaut, Chaucer's contemporary and the most renowned author of fourteenth-century France. Four volumes have appeared in the Garland Library of Medieval Literature thus far, including, most recently, *The Fountain of Love (La Fonteinne amoureuse) and Two Other Love Visions* (1993). The first book in the series was declared an "outstanding academic book" by *Choice* magazine. Palmer is the editor of a collection of essays on the subject, *Chaucer's French Contemporaries: The Poetry/Poetics of Self and Tradition* (1994), and has also published extensively on modern literature and literary theory.

As a film scholar, Palmer is interested in American film history as well as critical theory and practice. He is the author of a number of articles on the American cinema and Hollywood genres in such journals as *Film Criticism, Journal of Popular Film and Video, Wide Angle, Cinema Journal, Mosaic, Quarterly Review of Film and Video,* and *Persistence of Vision.* He has edited a book of essays on film criticism method, *The Cinematic Text: Methods and Approaches* (1989). Forthcoming is another edited volume: *Perspectives on Film Noir.*